EAMONN BREDIN

246.41B

Disturbing the Peace

the way of disciples

D1081013

the columba press

the columba press

55A Spruce Avenue, Stillorgan Industrial Park,
Blackrock, Co Dublin

First edition 1985
Third edition 1991
Reprinted 1993, 2006

Cover by Bill Bolger
Origination by The Columba Press
Printed in Ireland by
ColourBooks Ltd, Dublin

ISBN 0 948183 00 4

Nihil Obstat:
Philip Leo O'Reilly STD
Imprimatur:
✠ Francis McKiernan
Bishop of Kilmore

CONTENTS

*to the memory of
my mother and father*

PREFACE

The Acts of the Apostles tell us, 'In Antioch the disciples were for the first time called Christians' (11:26). These followers of 'the way' of Jesus now bore the new name that had been conferred on him. Later in the Acts, disciples are described as people 'who have turned the world upside down ... and they are all acting against the decrees of Caesar, saying that there is another king, Jesus.' And it continues: 'The people and the city authorities were disturbed when they heard this' (17:6-8). The gospels tell us why all this happened; they proclaim the good news of the life, ministry, death, and resurrection of Jesus of Nazareth. It was in his name and in his power that disciples had gone forth into the world to challenge and disturb its deceptive peace.

Those for whom the gospels were first written already confessed Jesus to be Lord and Saviour. Nevertheless, they were constantly being called to renew and deepen their discipleship of him. They were invited again and again to identify with the poor, the sick, the tax collectors, the sinners who first responded to him, so that they might appreciate ever more deeply what discipleship should mean. The gospels offer the same invitation to us today.

This is the theme I have attempted to follow in this book. In my efforts to highlight the question of discipleship I have drawn on some of the writings about the mystery of Jesus Christ that have been published during the past fifteen years or so. I have tried to rediscover the basis for the renewal of discipleship today by following the path taken by the early disciples. The concentration on such a specific area imposes obvious limitations on the aim and scope of this book. It is, therefore, not intended to offer a comprehensive approach to the mystery of Jesus Christ and it leaves aside many of the questions usually dealt with in christology. While its concern is with discipleship, the application to the world of today of what is rediscovered about this theme must be left to the reader. However, suggestions for further reading are indicated in the footnotes, which I have tried to keep to a minimum, and in the bibliography. Scriptural quotations are taken from the RSV translation of the Bible.

Because of the nature of this book, echoes of a hundred voices will be heard in its pages. I gratefully acknowledge their influence on me at the level of both language and ideas. I would like to mention two of these influences: David Power and Herman Lombaerts whose lectures and writings on symbols and symbolisation have influenced parts of this presentation.

Finally, I would like to thank Kay Murphy for typing the manuscript, and Fiona Biggs and Cecilia West for their generous help with the final preparations for publication.

Eamonn Bredin

INTRODUCTION

Small protective sanities.
Brendan Kennelly

Women and men who follow the way of Jesus Christ are called Christians. They derive their name from him (Acts 11:26) and accept the invitation to become his disciples. In so doing they are attempting to follow his way, do his truth, and live his life. 'If you continue in my word, you are truly my disciples, and you will know the truth, and the truth will make you free' an 8:31-32). Such is the way of life demanded of all who would call themselves Christians. And all are invited! Discipleship must never become the prerogative of the few or the lifestyle of an elite.

Yet we know in our hearts that true discipleship will always be difficult, constantly challenging, and its fullness perhaps quite rare. Discipleship is something far more challenging and demanding than the mere adherence to a system of ideas or obedience to a collection of rules. Discipleship is a living personal fellowship with Jesus Christ. But, we ask, who is Jesus Christ and what does this fellowship imply?

Much has been written about what it means to be a disciple of Jesus Christ. The very volume of output on this subject indicates that it has always been an area of both interest and difficulty. That interest, and indeed the fascination with Jesus Christ, persists today despite the growth in religious indifference. The difficulties also persist but their causes are complex and undoubtedly call for further analysis.

In the twenty years since Vatican II, the Roman Catholic Church has been engaged in a massive program of renewal in Christian life. Much of the writing on the mystery of Jesus Christ which emerged during those years offered a fresh, exciting foundation for just such a renewal. Yet when we look around us or into our hearts, we are forced to ask why so little has changed, why so little of what is available has impinged upon us. The books, the scholarship, the insights exist yet their desired effect has somehow been neutralised. We begin to wonder whether we might not have a certain resistance to even hearing what is new and challenging. Is this in turn a symptom of a deeper reluctance to engage in the hard craft of renewing our lives, of allowing new insights to transform our lives? Are we unable or even unwilling to see the source for structures? Do we allow the drag coefficient of the given and the familiar to impede development?

We know from experience how tempting it is to rest satisfied with 'the way things have always been' and, consequently, to give up the quest for the vision which should inform and shape our discipleship in today's world. In our day-to-day life it is easy to sink into a rut of inevitability, to unquestioningly repeat the patterns of the past, to feel at home in their protective security. Even when we genuinely struggle to live as disciples of Jesus Christ it is all too easy to become side-tracked from the goal, to become preoccupied with non-essentials, to try to escape into the familiar, to use excuses to delay progress.

If this is the level at which we encounter our most serious problems with discipleship it seems futile to begin by trading new definitions for old. Instead we should try once again to appreciate the demands of discipleship. This would then provide us with a criterion against which to assess the difficulties we experience in living discipleship today.

The Challenge of Discipleship

We all have our own stories of how we became and why we remain Christians. Yet we would all agree that we are followers of Jesus Christ because in him we have glimpsed something of the mystery of our human involvement with God. We continue in his way because we believe that the final truth about God and ourselves is found in Christ.

We feel impelled to respond to the invitation offered to every would-be disciple: 'Come and see,' a simple, yet radical call. Accepting it means moving out of the familiar and being prepared to follow the path of discipleship wherever it may lead. Answering it means being willing to set out and continue on a journey that leads us onward, upward, and inward. It involves being constantly coaxed and lured forward by the newness of what God and his Christ wish to achieve in us and through us. Ultimately, it means entering into closer union and deeper communion with the beckoning, ingathering God and Father of Jesus Christ who desires to make all things new.

10

We are called to follow him who is 'the way, the truth, and the life' (Jn 14:6); (but note how frequently 'the way' is mentioned in the New Testament). However, if we are really convinced that this is God's work, that it is about his future impinging on our present, then it necessarily involves both the radically new and the not-yet. Discipleship must always involve us in a profound but usually unacknowledged not-knowing. It means that we who choose and daily re-choose the path of discipleship must always move beyond what has been achieved, to acknowledge that there is much that we do not know, to try constantly to discern the way forward. It means admitting that each achievement can only be a new beginning, that each stage is a further impulse .into the unknown, each struggle to 'come and see' is marked by radical newness and profound not-knowing. Discipleship cannot be otherwise, for we are not simply called to be *different* but to be *new* men and women.

The Christian tradition has always spoken of contrast, challenge, opposition, contradiction and above all the symbol of the cross to disclose what is involved in this call. We become aware of the cost and the contradiction of discipleship when we meditate, for example, on the experiences that brought St. Paul out of a crucifying Saul.

> I believe that nothing will happen that will outweigh the supreme advantage of knowing Christ Jesus my Lord. For him I have accepted the loss of everything, and I look on everything as so much rubbish if only I can have Christ and be given a place in him. I am no longer trying for perfection by my own efforts, the perfection that comes from the Law, but I want only the perfection that comes through faith in Christ, is from God and based on faith. All I want is to know Christ and the power of his resurrection and to share his sufferings by reproducing the pattern of his death.
> (Phil 3:8-11JB)

If this is a description of discipleship, then obviously we cannot plot or plan or map out the details of such a life journey in advance. To do so would mean running the risk of literally following our own way.

Such a risk is real, not because we are wilfully wrongheaded, but because we muddle along with only vague and unquestioned ideas about discipleship to guide us. Because of this we may indeed suffer from a self-imposed unclarity and impoverishment in our following of Christ. In such a case it would make sense to admit our clouded vision and proceed to take stock of the situation in order to make progress. But we tend to shy away from the unpleasantness of such an undertaking, ultimately because we are simply afraid of the new, the unfamiliar, the untried. We do not want to launch out into the deep, we are afraid of being left with 'nothing, neither a past for precedent nor a future foreseeable.'[1] Practical people like us always need sure ground underfoot. We like to know exactly where we are and where the next step will lead us even long before we get around to taking it. In fact very few of us, if we are honest, like being disturbed, or being made to feel uncomfortable. We dislike being asked to give up the familiar*y of old routines, or to move beyond the tried and tested. We want the familiar 'comfort zones' that we are used to. We hold on tightly to our snug familiarities and we resist everything that might dispossess us. Deep down we know the cost of accepting an alternative and living it, of waking up and being alive. Indeed, we find a coma preferable to a challenge.

Familiarity

The temptation on our Godward journey, the constant threat to our discipleship, is familiarity. There is frequently a contradiction between the familiar image of discipleship with which we claim to be working and the actual daily grind of enfleshing that image. The shortfall between the impressive ideal and the actual lived levels may be very serious indeed. But familiarity ensnares us more seriously when we begin to justify things as they are and ourselves as we are. For example, while we may indeed introduce or at least tolerate changes, we do so precisely to ensure that no real change can take place, that the familiar remains untouched.

At a different level, we may be enthusiastic about many things and yet be deluding ourselves into thinking that just because we have the right words, are familiar with them and know how to use them, we are truly being disciples. We may develop a very impressive 'spiritual' vocabulary-but what is its real meaning? What is the relationship between this faith vocabulary and the raw, unedited experiences of daily life? The verbal formulae take over and we begin to think that we know Christ, that we even know what it means to have in us 'the mind that was in Christ Jesus,' that we know how 'to reproduce the pattern of his death.'

Such a style of discipleship will seem clear and not too painful, quite cozy and familiar, but it has obviously claimed to know too much and ignored the not-knowing that must of its nature characterise discipleship. Could anything about Jesus Christ be neat or cozy or settled? Can a disciple lay down limits, calculate or dictate the terms in advance? The answer must be no. The demands of discipleship must constantly disturb and dis-ease us.

Images and Idols

Sometimes we try a different approach, protesting that we have little knowledge of the theology of Jesus Christ. Yet, we cannot even say who we are without giving voice to a christology. Our daily lives are sustained by a theology and a spirituality that are simply the articulation of our dominant image of Jesus Christ. This image in turn determines our understanding of discipleship and its implications for our Christian living. It has been derived from many sources: family, church, school, legend, folklore, art, personal experience, prayer, and the practice of Christian living. While retaining its basic characteristics, it has been substantially modified over the years.

We must constantly question its validity: How appropriate is this image? How realistic is it? How adequate is it? How is it related to what actually happens in our lives? To what extent is our image of Jesus Christ true to Jesus Christ himself? More bluntly, to what extent has our vision of Christ been re-created in our own image and likeness so that it now bears far more resemblance to us than it does to Christ? If we feel at ease with our image of Christ or of discipleship, if we feel at home with our spirituality, is it because in the process of their creation we have in fact ruled out or at least diminished the pain and the cost of true discipleship? Has our image of Christ been made to fit us like a second skin? If this is the case it can only be because we have rid ourselves of the strangeness, the otherness, the scandal of Jesus Christ and the contrast between him and us? Are we in danger of idolising Christ, domesticating him, turning him into just another household god?

Jesus Christ left no writings or personal memoirs so we must rely on what others tell us about him. Access to him is always mediated through disciples. We wonder about the adequacy of their mediation. We wonder too about the whole-heartedness of our own response to it.

This question becomes more acute when we remember that many of those who came in contact with the historical Jesus of Nazareth seem to have constantly misunderstood him. On occasion Jesus had to escape from the crowds who wanted to take him by force and make him king, make him play the role they wanted him to play. Can he now escape from the roles we force him to play? How do we misunderstand him? If we heap titles on him, pray to him, use all the correct formulae about him, we may simply be keeping him at a distance. Yet he desires to work from within our lives. He seeks to lay claim to our hearts, to eternally disturb us, to whisper to us about perfection. He asks us to believe that he is still passionately involved in our lives, that he is still healing us, making us whole by troubling us and challenging us to be different.[2]

We are challenged to love, to repent, to forgive, and to celebrate, confident that he is involved in the heart of our struggle, involved in the interaction between God, self, and neighbour. He is not asking for new titles or slogan shouts, nor cries of 'Lord, Lord,' but rather a 'new heaven and a new earth in which justice dwells' (2 Pet 3:13). Because this is so demanding we engage in subtle tactics of avoidance. When we say we look to Christ or when we search for the origins of Christianity, are we conditioned to see only a projection of ourselves? Would Jesus Christ recognise himself in the image we have of him? How much of what we strive to achieve would be subsumed into *his* struggle for a new heaven and a new earth?

1. THE PATH OF DISCIPLESHIP

Let him Easter in us,
be a dayspring to the dimness of us.
G. M. Hopkins

All is not well with our following of Jesus Christ today. This becomes clear when we contrast the demands of the call to discipleship, 'come and see,' with our undemanding and tamed version of that call. Can we overcome some of these difficulties? We are already aware of the powerful influence our image of Christ exerts on us at all levels, and we recognise that a whole theology and spirituality are compressed into that image. But perhaps it would help if we examined in more detail some of the influences that mould our image of Jesus Christ and discipleship. Obviously, classical christology will be among the more powerful and formative of these. Should such theology prove to be a less than adequate foundation for discipleship, we will have to search for a new starting point.

Classical Christology

It seems fair to say that, for most Roman Catholics, the dominant model of Jesus Christ is the incarnation of the eternal, only-begotten son, the second person of the Blessed Trinity.[1] The theology that elaborates this model is often referred to as 'classical christology.' Much has been written in recent years about this christology, frequently in a critical vein.[2] Here we will simply note how it has influenced the way we think of Jesus and some of the problems it has raised for our discipleship.

At the origin of Christianity stands an historical individual, Jesus of Nazareth, whom Christians confess to be the Christ of God, the saviour of the world. Here we have a historical person who is given various titles in order to proclaim his universal saving significance. It would indeed be strange if Christians did not have a profound interest in this Jesus of Nazareth who is the subject of their confession of faith. Who Jesus is tells us who the Christ is and what salvation means. However, classical christology had little time for the historical life of this person, Jesus of Nazareth. It took the approach that Jesus Christ was God, that he made this claim for himself in many ways, especially by giving himself titles that obviously implied divinity, and he proved this claim many times by working miracles during his lifetime and finally and definitively by raising himself from the dead. This basically, was the approach presented in apologetics and handed on in religion classes.

The emphases of classical christology become more understandable when we recall a little of the history of the church. From the time of Arius (condemned at the Council of Nicaea, AD 325) when the divinity of the son was denied, there was a certain reluctance to speak of the full integral humanity of Jesus Christ. This reluctance was intensified after the Council of Chalcedon (AD 451), which declared that Jesus Christ must be 'acknowledged in two natures united in one person and one *hypostasis.*' The theology that developed this statement declared that Jesus Christ was only one person, a divine person, and although he had a human nature he was not a human person.

It is extremely difficult to speak about the full integral humanity of Jesus Christ if we use this model and this language as a starting point. The same difficulty lurked in the minds of priests and teachers of that time when they preached or taught about Jesus. Above all, it created a tension in the lives and prayers of the people of God. They experienced the profoundly Christian desire to be united with all aspects of Christ's life, but they were aware of the difficulty that this presented for them because of the emphasis on Christ's divinity in the theology of that time.

Despite this, they retained a vivid interest in the humanity and suffering of Jesus Christ. Their intuitive grasp of the crucial significance of his humanity found expression especially in meditating on the sorrowful mysteries of the rosary, reflecting on the 'mysteries of Christ's flesh,' doing the stations of the cross, devotion to the Sacred Heart. Thus they were enabled to identify with him and to relate their own experience of life and suffering to the memory of his life, his suffering, and his victory over death through resurrection in a transforming way. Yet, the tension remained.

The starting point for classical christology was the definition of the universal significance of Jesus Christ given by the Councils of Nicaea, Constantinople (AD 381), Ephesus (AD 431), and especially Chalcedon. These theologians began not with

Scripture but with the Trinity and asked how, since he was already God, did one of the Trinity become human? Presupposing Christ's divinity, they then went back to Scripture to find a basis for this presupposition. They stated very clearly that Jesus Christ was God and although they did not deny he was man, they certainly did not emphasise this truth. What passed as a christology based on the decree of Chalcedon had smuggled in its own presuppositions and so gradually came to adopt positions that were difficult to reconcile with the real teaching of that council.

The tragic irony of the situation was that while these theologians regarded themselves as staunch defenders of the faith of Chalcedon, they sometimes came dangerously close to espousing the heresy of monophysitism (only one divine nature in Christ) opposed by Chalcedon. When other theologians pointed to the monophysite strain that lies near the surface in classical christology, they encountered fierce opposition. They were doing no more than restating what was proclaimed in the Council of Chalcedon itself, yet they were sometimes accused of heresy by people who regarded themselves as defenders of Chalcedon.

At the level of popular piety, despite the desire to identify with the humanity of Jesus, this monophysite strain is still to be found. 'Jesus is God' is thought to be the complete confession of Christian faith. Attempts to speak about the real humanity of Jesus Christ, to speak about his solidarity with us, about human limitations in him, may be countered by the response, 'But he was God.' Such a response based as it is on a partial and incomplete christology has disastrous consequences for Christian religion and morality. How can we seriously maintain the demands of discipleship if they can be neutralised by saying 'it was easy for Jesus because he was God?' That kind of 'theology' saps the authenticity of Christian life.

Classical christology still exerts so much influence that some people may be confused to learn that the full Christian confession of faith about Jesus Christ as Chalcedon put it is, 'that he is truly God and he is truly man, composed of body and rational soul, that he is consubstantial with the Father in his divinity, consubstantial with us in his humanity, like us in every respect but without sinning.'[3] That quotation from the decree of the Council itself speaks of the solidarity between Jesus Christ and us. He is bone of our bone and flesh of our flesh. But was this emphasis clear within classical christology or within the religious education programs derived from it?

The question facing us now is, 'Can we do credit to the fullness of the message of the tradition? Can we speak of Jesus Christ as "consubstantial with us in his humanity," as being, "like us in every respect but without sinning," while confessing his true divinity and knowing that we must hold both truths if we are to remain Christian at all?'

Pope Leo I, who sent a famous letter to the Council of Chalcedon, said in a sermon, 'It is as dangerous an evil to deny the truth of the human nature in Christ as to refuse to believe that his glory is equal to that of the Father.'[4] Some Christians may find it difficult to accept the full truth of that statement. We have been conditioned to use only God-talk of Jesus Christ. But we must do more. We must use God-talk and human-talk of him. To refuse to do so is to deny the truth of the Incarnation. God did not become God in Jesus Christ; God became human.

How then are we to cope with these difficulties which seem to beset any approach to discipleship which bases itself upon 'classical' christology? Can we once again make our own Chalcedon's confession of faith in 'Jesus Christ, true God and true man' and give equal weight to each word? How can we realign our discipleship with the true faith of the church of Christ?

Another Starting Point

We have become aware of the limitations of classical christology. It is partial and incomplete and does not do justice even to the Council of Chalcedon which it claims to represent. It clearly does not provide the kind of basis for the renewal of discipleship needed today. However extensive its field of force, it is only one of the formative factors that shape our image of Jesus Christ. The source of all those other influences is the church which claims to incarnate the word, the work, the spirit and tradition of Jesus Christ in its whole way of life, in its proclamation, its pursuit of justice, and its liturgy. If the church's claim to be the community that seeks to "hear the word of God and do it' (Lk 8:21), to keep alive the memory of Jesus Christ and to live by his spirit, is true, then it offers the possibility of living contact with him today. For it was in this church that our faith in Jesus Christ had its origin. It was only through coming into contact with believing Christians that we began to believe. It was this web of relationships which enabled us to understand what lived discipleship could mean.

While we may begin with the church as we know it, we must also inquire about the validity of its claim. We must continue asking: Who is this Jesus Christ whom the church always points to as both its origin and its meaning, its starting point and its unique centre? Why do church people sum up what is of supreme importance to them as Christians by saying 'Jesus Christ is Lord,' 'Jesus Christ is Saviour,' or most simply, 'I believe in Jesus Christ'? When we listen to the church's answers to these questions, we find ourselves involved with language in the sense of the thought and talk and discourse about Jesus as the Christ that we call christology. Above all we are in touch with the total language of tradition, with the flesh-and-blood language of the witness of the countless Christians who have peopled these centuries.

Here we are being drawn back to the ultimate origins of all Christian language, the well-spring of all our professions of faith and forms of Christian life. We are led back behind creed and council to the source for which they claim to be summary and clarification. We find the real genesis of our language, our church life, our worship, our discipleship in the communities that gave us the New Testament.

These groupings of Christians existed (so their writings tell us) because their lives had been totally changed by knowing Jesus of Nazareth whom they confessed to be the Messiah or the Christ. They came together in a new way because they wished to embody, proclaim, and celebrate the good news that he is. They wished to live a life of witness that would be consistent with their faith in Jesus Christ. They wished to remember and be challenged by his whole way of life, to celebrate his saving presence among them so that they might respond to it more adequately. Together they struggled to hear ever more faithfully the implications of the good news that brought them to birth so as to incarnate it in lives of dedicated service. It is these communities then that are 'an (open) letter from Christ ... written not with ink but with the spirit of the living God ... on tablets of human hearts' (2 Cor 3:2-3).

We must turn to these communities and to their writings if we wish to learn more about the identity of Jesus Christ and the meaning of discipleship. What we find on the pages of the New Testament is the end-product of the struggle by these Christians to find a language that would be commensurate with their experience of the mystery of Jesus as the Christ. When we look more closely we recognise something of the shape of our own struggle as members of a church and as disciples within a given cultural setting. We realise that, like us, they too were wrestling with presuppositions, familiarities, and ingrained certainties (see chaps. 10 & 11). The social, cultural, mental, religious, and political climate that had eased them into the Jewish religion was also what made it difficult for them to believe anything different. So we are put in touch with their struggle to bring to expression their transforming experience of coming to faith in Jesus as the Anointed of Yahweh, in whom alone is salvation found. They are insisting on the continuity between faith in Jesus as Messiah and their Jewish faith, and they are trying to understand and proclaim him in that light. But they are also stressing the discontinuity between that faith and their cultural Jewish faith and are searching for ever more adequate ways to live their new faith and express it in lang-uage. We are struck by their awareness of the problem; the liveliness of their discipleship compared to the dullness of our own, the richness of their language contrasted with the fatigue of our statements and formulas.

We obviously need to return to these origins, this source, if our following of the way of Jesus Christ is to be in any way adequate. Instead of assuming that we understand and appreciate the language we use about Jesus Christ and about ourselves as disciples, we should begin by enquiring about the origin of this language (word and witness) in order to understand it. This approach should give us an opportunity to correlate what we find in the Scriptures with our present-day grasp of things.

From the vantage point of contact with these communities we begin to see other aspects of our present difficulties more clearly. These communities were searching painstakingly for the interpretation that would be most adequately commensurate with their transforming experience of coming to acknowledge Jesus as the Christ. The multiplicity of approaches to this mystery in the New Testament testifies to their care for language and meaning. We find both a profound experience and a corresponding, deepening interpretation of that experience. Yet there was a real danger that when this interpretation reached a 'final stage,' when it ceased to be revised, some people might separate the interpretation from the genetic experience which gave rise to it and the contemporary experience of which it was supposed to be an interpretation. (The interpretation is 'built into' the experience but must be articulated.) It would no longer be a vibrant and transforming interpretation of the raw experiences of people because of its own innate truth. Instead it could become like some kind of slogan or ideology imposed on people by other means.

If any group of Christians no longer struggles to truly hear the person and the revelation that brought them together initially there is a grave danger that they will smuggle their own presuppositions into what they do and say. Their statements, their profession of faith, their interpretation of life may still sound orthodox (they are still using the community's language) but something very serious has occurred. What is now being spoken of and lived as discipleship of Christ may have only a very tenuous link with the concrete historical realities of the message and ministry of Jesus. Instead of being grounded in these realities and founded in this history, this 'faith' floats free and becomes unhistorical or mythological. This 'discipleship' becomes a disguised expression of the groups' own dominant concerns and 'Jesus Christ' becomes one more mythological 'Lord,' made in his creators' image and likeness. The contact with the foundational Easter and pre-Easter experiences of the first followers of Jesus, and with the real life and death experiences of his present followers, is lost.

So those who still protest their allegiance to Jesus Christ might in fact be tending toward being gnostic (salvation comes through special knowledge) or docetic (God does not make genuine contact with humanity but only appears to do so) in their approach. 'Discipleship' might mean little more than assenting to these set formulae and being marginally involved in ritual activity. That this could happen is evident from Paul's account of the Corinthian church and from other explicit and implicit references in the New Testament. It is further documented in the history of the heresies that plagued the early church. But the danger was and is real for everyone.

Today, even if our verbal formulae are orthodox and accurate, even if we can quote chapter and verse of conciliar statements, this does not mean that we have avoided this danger or overcome the difficulty. No formula as formula, no doctrinal statement even, *is* the mystery of Jesus Christ. It is language about that mystery and as such can never measure up to the fullness of the mystery. Language does not deliver up the mystery to us and using language about the mystery can never be a substitute for living it. Words must not be allowed to substitute for deeds. As church we cannot simply repeat formulae – we must constantly and actively listen to the word to which these formulas claim to give insight. Only in this way can we 'continue in my word' (Jn 8:31) so that we may live it now.

Some people today wonder whether we take all this seriously. They point out that on the question of discipleship we usually tend to work with the conclusions arrived at by others. We often seem to be unaware of the influence of historical developments so we take for granted what are in fact dense theological summaries. Because we 'do not know history we are at the mercy of recent history' and so we end up believing that what exists today is to be maintained vigorously, for we are convinced that it is in true harmony with 'what was from the beginning.' This can lead us to depreciate our Christian faith and to be insensitive to the genuine questions that others may have about what we regard as immutable.

These people feel that we may in fact be somewhat gnostic in our approach. They believe that our christology has tended to become a theoretical theological system or, worse still, a set of propositions which has lost living contact with both the genetic and present-day experience of Christianity. Consequently, they believe that this christology and the discipleship that it informs do not enable us to interpret and shape our living and dying in the most transforming way possible. Yet this is precisely what we need to be able to do – to read our life stories in an integral and hopeful way in terms of the fullness of what took place in Jesus Christ.

To help us to do this we need to remain in contact with christian witness, with the movement started by Jesus of Nazareth and with the Scriptures as our privileged mode of access to this movement. However, it is not a simple matter to decide to begin with Scripture. We must be prepared to admit that we will also tend to read the Scriptures in terms of our dominant image of Christ. What the New Testament is saying will be filtered through to us in terms of the current models of Jesus Christ and christology. This becomes a problem only when we do not acknowledge it to be the case, for then we cannot set about introducing any corrective measures. We will try, therefore, to be aware of this difficulty in our approach and attempt to remedy some of its shortcomings.

Biblical Scholarship

In choosing this approach, we will rely heavily on the work of Scripture scholars to open up the complex riches of the Scriptures for us. Some people may feel that this prospect is rather daunting or that it will make us unsure of our ground. They may remember that these scholars were the first to raise questions about the approach to Scripture which sustained and was sustained by classical christology. Many of us can remember our own reaction when we heard it said that the gospels are not biographies but confessional, kerygmatic documents from beginning to end; that they interpret and proclaim Jesus as Lord and Christ after Easter and in the light of Easter; that they speak 'from faith to faith.' It may have been disconcerting for some of us to hear that the gospels are not primarily concerned with giving us historical facts about Jesus or that not everything attributed to Jesus in the gospels was necessarily spoken by him in the form in which we now have it. We may remember trying to incorporate into our understanding of the divine inspiration of the evangelists, the announcement that a long period of oral tradition, liturgical development, and catechetical adaptation lies behind the gospels.

Yet, far from de-stabilising our approach, the findings of these scholars have given us a new and much stronger basis for it. Those using the methodology of critical biblical scholarship have given us new insights into Jesus' extraordinarily warm and attractive but enigmatic personality. These insights can help us greatly in speaking and teaching about him in a vibrant way. He stands out clearly as someone with whom we could genuinely identify and yet he remains so utterly mysterious in our attempts to know him or follow him that he forever draws us beyond everything we might achieve. He becomes someone whose way of life forever challenges, questions, and sustains us. We could credibly pray to him and feel called to celebrate his presence to us.

The Quest for the Historical Jesus

What has emerged from these studies is both exciting and challenging, yet the reactions to the foregoing statements about the gospels are readily understandable – Roman Catholics were unfamiliar with the Bible itself and unaware of the developments in biblical research. Indeed, until about two hundred years ago such statements would have been unthinkable for any Christian. The church quite simply did not accept that any development took place between the ministry of Jesus and the christology of the New Testament – such a distinction would have been meaningless. It was agreed that the gospels were literal accounts of the words and actions of Jesus who really spoke as he does in both the synoptics and John. The year 1778, when certain *Fragments* of H.S. Reimarus were published posthumously, marks the beginning of the modern era of biblical studies. Reimarus, in a very provocative way, made a radical distinction between the 'Jesus of history' and the 'Christ of faith' preached by the churches. Reaction to what he said launched generations of Protestant scholars on what was later called 'The quest for the historical Jesus.' The details of that 'quest' need not concern us here.[5] We simply note that despite the conflict, the scepticism, and the overweening confidence that characterised some of the contributions to it, the overall cumulative gain was a new appreciation of the Bible as Bible.

The enduring contribution of the nineteenth century was in the area of source criticism. From 1918 what was called 'form criticism' sought to regain, through the written sources, contact with the developments that took place during the period of oral tradition. It was concerned with the process by which the beads (units giving, e.g., a saying, a story, a miracle of Jesus) of the gospel necklace were formed. Since the mid-1950s, 'redaction criticism' has been attending to the theological vision, the overall preoccupation of the creative editors that we call the evangelists. In these ways scholars have been developing and refining methodologies for approaching the Bible in all its rich complexity.

For many years this research was carried on solely within the Protestant churches. Gradually, however, the best insights of these approaches came to be accepted by the Roman Catholic church. The crucial documents here were the Encyclical *Divino Afflante Spiritu* (1943), *The Constitution on Divine Revelation* (1965), and the document published by the Pontifical Biblical Commission, *Instruction on the Historical Truth of the Gospels* (1964). This latter document accepts the validity of the approaches of 'source criticism,' 'form criticism,' and 'redaction criticism' in interpreting the Bible. It tells us that the interpreter must take careful note of 'the three stages of tradition by which the teaching and the life of Jesus have come down to us.' These are distinguished as the 'works and ... words of Jesus' (Stage 1); the apostolic preaching after Easter (Stage 2); the final editing and setting down of 'this earliest body of Instruction ... in the four gospels' (Stage 3).[6]

That Instruction provides us with the blueprint we will follow throughout this book. We will try to return to the words and deeds of Jesus of Nazareth (Stage 1). Then we will try to retrace the response to his preaching, his life, and his death which gave rise to the apostolic preaching (Stage 2). Finally we will try to move through the formation of the New Testament (Stage 3) into the reflection on the mystery of Christ that led to the Creed of the Council of Chalcedon.

We will draw on what is available to us from a rich variety of sources: the Scriptures and biblical scholarship, traditional and contemporary christological insights, a keen historical sense, praxis and praise, and above all the fleshy witness to the mystery of Christ, the lived discipleship of Christians in every age. It is extraordinarily difficult to hold all these elements together but if we emphasise one at the expense of another, our approach will be impoverished. The diversity of opinion among Scripture scholars can be bewildering and the rather dry categories of theology can be off-putting, but in our approach we need biblical insights if we wish to remain in living contact with the sources and we need the 'bias binding' of theology if we are to avoid ravelling at the edges. The cross-influence, we hope, will be enriching – a refreshed return to our common spirituality and the basic witness of other Christians will help to build up a more credible theology. We need, desperately, to have our imaginations fired without doing violence to our historical sense so that in prayer and activity we may contemplate in a transforming way the Christ of the gospels.

The results of such an approach should invite us to a new and enlivened following of the path of discipleship. Our basic mode of access to Jesus Christ will always be through the direction of our lives, through discipleship. Obviously, it is not some-

thing that can simply be gleaned from books but must be questioned, clarified, and sustained by the best scriptural, theological,
and historical insights available. Much of what has been emerging recently in writings about christology has been concerned
with drawing all of this together so as to build up a renewed,
living, engaging approach to the mystery of Jesus Christ. It is
concerned with the kind of person Jesus of Nazareth was, the
effect he had on people, the message he proclaimed, the lifestyle
he engaged in, the movement started by him in the context of his
time, what it was that led to his death, how the church began in
his name. This stress on history is indispensable. Through it,
these authors are trying to understand how disciples who were
engaged in these historical experiences came to confess this Jesus
as the Christ of God after Easter. They are concerned with the
correlation between historical experience and this profession of
faith.

We frequently tend to make a sharp distinction between
history and faith or between faith and theology or spirituality
and theology, and yet we forget that the statements of faith or
the outlines of our spirituality are always couched in the language of a particular theology and are culturally conditioned. We
must also realise that this underlying theology may not always
be as adequate as it might be. But as the people of God we deserve the help of the very best theology so that we may interpret
and live daily life to the full in terms of the God and father of
Jesus Christ and in the power of his Spirit. We are reminded that
we must 'Always be prepared to make a defence to anyone who
calls you to account for the hope that is in you, yet do it with
gentleness and reverence' (1 Pet 3:15).

To give a basis for the Christian hope that is in us means
that we cannot begin by appealing to the very conclusions that
are being called into question. Instead of begging the question
about our position as Christians we are asked to demonstrate the
reasonableness, the intelligibility, the plausibility of that stance.
In relation to the theology of Jesus Christ, which sustains and
directs our discipleship, our primary task must be to show the
intrinsic correlation between the person and history of Jesus of
Nazareth and our professions of faith in him. To do so means
that we cannot begin with these professions of faith themselves
nor indeed with the doctrinal statements of the church. Instead
we should begin with the apostolic witness to the life, the history,

the words, and the deeds of Jesus of Nazareth and attempt to retrace the steps of the journey undertaken by his disciples in arriving at the statements of faith that we find about him in gospel and creed and council. In other words we must show that our christology (discourse about Jesus as the Christ) can justifiably be founded in the concrete personal history of Jesus of Nazareth by following the path taken historically by his disciples. We simply cannot avoid the historical question or ignore the problem of the historical consistency of our approach.

However difficult such an undertaking may be, it becomes all the more pressing in a world that proclaims 'the death of permanence.' When talking about the New Testament communities we noted that what disposes us to believe in the first place – the whole social, mental and cultural climate – makes it very difficult for us to believe anything that is different from what we have always believed.[7] That total climate makes it possible for us to form an image of the Christ whose disciples we claim to be, but it also makes it difficult for us to modify that image or renew that discipleship.

Now that climate and culture have changed dramatically, especially in the last twenty-five years. We have been living through a period of profound change and upheaval with the resulting instability, insecurity, loss of identity, break-up of institutions, and the splintering of social life causing so much pain. And the trauma continues. Those who study these things say that our experiences have been traumatic because we have been living simultaneously through both the dying kick of a moribund culture and the gestation period of a new self-understanding of humankind that has not yet found adequate expression. The slow, gentle, almost imperceptible shakings experienced over the centuries finally had their effect and the very foundations of the 'classical culture' cracked dramatically. The assumptions on which that culture was built and which had gone unquestioned for so long could no longer sustain it; yet the secure foundations for the new future had not as yet been laid. We were literally caught between two worlds.

Since the life of the church is always culturally conditioned, this cultural fragmentation was bound to have a profound effect on the church. It would be tedious and unnecessary to try to catalogue the various ways in which the church was affected by all of this since we have had first-hand experience of at least part of it ourselves. Suffice it to say that even at this stage the 'Christian commonwealth' can no longer be assumed to exist anywhere, that the social and cultural underpinnings that once sustained Christianity have by and large vanished. So the preconditions for a certain kind of faith and a certain kind of Christianity no longer exist. The changed situation has saddened some people who lament the passing of the 'old ways.' Others have closed ranks against it and pretend it never happened. Still others see it as offering an exciting challenge to rediscover the Way of Jesus Christ. They maintain that this will lead us to a more personal, responsible faith.

When the 'residual Christian commonwealth' is no longer capable of sustaining the indifferent or cosseting the uncommitted, those who wish to be Christians will have to opt in or opt out. This new changed situation will impose a radical asceticism on those who come to this decision of faith. They will be called to a new kind of discipleship by the very nature of the situation in which they find themselves. In such circumstances they will be stripped of many of the cosy trappings, forced to jettison the non-essentials, get back to the heart, the core, of what Christianity is about and live it. Once more this quest for the heart of Christianity must begin with the Scriptures.

Summary

We have decided to adopt an approach to the mystery of Jesus Christ that begins with the Scriptures. We are making this choice because we hope it will help us to face the difficulties of discipleship in the world today.

To opt for this approach is to choose a starting point and a perspective that are at variance with those of the classical approach. This is not done arbitrarily or in order to disregard what is unquestionably valid and valuable in that approach. But it is done so that we may become bearers of the fruitful dialectic between the traditional approach and the one we now choose to follow. This dialectic will be with us in all that follows for although our discipleship has been shaped to a greater or lesser extent by classical christology, we are no longer unquestioningly satisfied to inhabit the confines of that approach. We carry the tension within us.

Because of the difference in starting point and perspective

we should not expect an exact correspondence in priority and preoccupation between one approach and the other. Indeed what is a serious problem within one approach may not present the same difficulty within the other. For example, if we start with the assumptions of classical christology we may feel obliged to 'prove' the humanity of Jesus Christ, yet no contemporary of Jesus of Nazareth would have dreamt of asking whether Jesus was fully human, whether he was a man. We need to return to the Scriptures and allow them to speak to us about the reality of his humanity while realising that the same scriptures proclaim 'that God was in Christ, reconciling the world to himself' (2 Cor 5: 19) .

If we could unravel something of that movement from knowing him as man to confessing him as Son of God, we would come closer to understanding the way in which disciples wrestled with that mystery. And we could then continue in contact with the centuries of reflections of later disciples that finally gave us the formula of Chalcedon (see appendix 2: *The Definition of Chalcedon*). In the process, I hope we will have come to appreciate the entire movement in a new way and come to a renewed understanding of Chalcedon.

This is the key to the approach that will be followed throughout this book. We will be trying to follow the movement in which the first disciples were engaged, the path they followed. Of course we are not forgetting that we, who have inherited 2000 years of tradition, cannot become contemporaries of Jesus' disciples, nor are we ignoring the fact that our faith embraces not only the earthly Jesus but the risen Christ. We may wish that we could approach the life of Jesus, the Scriptures, the question of discipleship for the first time. Such innocence, however, is not recoverable! Yet, while being aware of the problems of presuppositions, precomprehension, and the 'hermeneutical circle,' we will be attempting to *imaginatively* relive the life and death of Jesus as experienced by his historical disciples. Given their values, attitudes, and culture, how could they have followed a man who said and did what Jesus said and did? Given our values, attitudes, and culture, what are we to make of him? Who *is* this Jesus of Nazareth?

2. THE LANGUAGE OF JESUS

Words strain, crack
and sometimes break
under the burden.
T. S. Eliot

In attempting to answer the question: Who is Jesus of Nazareth?, we will concentrate first of all on the pages of the New Testament (Stage III) and struggle with our preconceptions so as to allow room for fresh, unbiased discovery. Such discovery should in turn raise, if not answer, some questions about the identity of Jesus. Even a casual perusal of these pages convinces us that Jesus was obviously a teacher (Mk 4:38; 5:35) who taught in a remarkable and memorable way, a teacher who captivated his audience, who impressed them with his authority and who had the knack of enshrining his insights in unforgettable language and discourse. So while it is true that the gospels are the products of a long history of oral tradition, of preaching, and of catechetical instruction, of collection and editing and translation, we can still be struck by the haunting quality of the language and ideas of this teacher, even in English translation. Despite the many differences between the final gospel accounts as we have them, we must accept that such a teacher is their ultimate source if we are to explain the unity, the cohesion, the inspiration they manifest. We must try to listen in to the language of this teacher.

Some Scripture scholars have translated the Greek text of the gospels into Aramaic and claim that this gives us a new insight into the way this teacher used his mother tongue.[1] They even maintain that they can detect ways of speaking preferred by this Jesus who spoke Aramaic with a Galilean accent. Without going into these studies, it is evident even from the gospels as we know them that we are dealing with someone who had a most profound vision of life and something of a poet's power over language. His use of language is distinctive, whether its purpose be to drive home some urgent message, to proclaim a call to decision, to announce what is radically new, to warn against danger. His use of parallelism, rhythm, and assonance push language to new levels. We see that whatever it was he wished to express must have been so radically new that he was forced to the limits of current usage in order to try to communicate it. A poet describes this problem with language as follows:

> Words strain,
> Crack and sometimes break, under the burden,
> Under the tension slip, slide, perish,
> Decay with imprecision, will not stay in place,
> Will not stay still ...
> Leaving one still with the intolerable wrestle
> with words and meanings.[2]

But beyond this usage of old forms in a new, vibrant, stretched way, there are characteristics in his speech for which it is difficult to find an exact analogy and a real parallel in the literature of that time. It is not that there is no analogy or no parallel whatsoever but that those analogies and parallels which are available do not adequately explain the newness of what Jesus is doing with language. In other words, it seems that he either took forms that existed on the periphery of Israel's tradition and brought them centre stage, or else forged new forms in an attempt to give expression to his message. Of course, this raises questions about the newness of his message and we will return to these in the following chapters. But for the present we will try to concentrate on the extraordinary creativity that marks his way of speaking and teaching. Obviously we can only refer to a few representative language forms from the wealth of material available. However, these should give us some insight into the language of Jesus.

I. The Kingdom/Reign Of God

This symbol was indisputably in use long before the time of Jesus. (We will examine its origins and content in Chapter 4.) But the frequency with which it is found on his lips and the meaning he gives to it is striking and unusual. To say that Jesus is preoccupied with the reign of God is to engage in understatement. The kingdom or reign of God is the central idea in his teaching. It is the main subject of his parables, of the collection of his teaching that is called the Sermon on the Mount and of the Johannine discourses. It is found in all five strata of the gospel tradition.

When we look at how Jesus uses the symbol of kingdom/reign of God we notice that he combines it with other words to form phrases for which it is difficult and at times impossible to find a parallel. He speaks of the kingdom 'approaching,' 'being at hand' (Mk 1:15, Mt 10:7, Lk 10:11); of 'entering into' it (Mk 9:47;10:15; 23-25;, Mt 5:20; 7:21;18:3; 23:13, Jn 3:5). It 'is coming' (Mk 9:1, Mt. 6:10, Lk 11:2; 17:20; 22:18). It is said to be a secret or mystery (Mk 4:11). People are 'to seek the kingdom' (Mt 6:33, Lk 12:31), some are 'not far' from it (Mk 12:34). Some will inherit it; some have made themselves eunuchs for it (Mt 19:12). There are 'keys to the kingdom' which can be given to some (Mt 16:19) while others 'shut the kingdom' against people. Jesus speaks of the 'least,' the 'great' (Mt 5:19), the 'greatest' in the kingdom. Above all, he says that the kingdom of God 'has come upon you' (Mt 12:28, Lk 11:20) or 'it is in the midst of you' (Lk 17:21).

Since we cannot discover precedents for these unusual forms, we ask who is this Jesus who uses the traditional kingdom symbol in such a highly creative way? Why does he find it necessary to transform traditional usage to the point of creating a new language? What kind of new reality exerts this kind of pressure on language? Are we in touch with some kind of creative genius who speaks about the kingdom/reign of God with such striking originality and freedom? Who is this teacher? If we had been among the crowds who heard him speak like this about the kingdom, would we have understood what he meant? Would we even have appreciated this radical departure from the 'received tradition'?

2. The Proverbial Sayings

We also find that Jesus makes use of the proverbial form. A proverb might be described as an insightful reflection on experience, challenging people to see things in a particular way. It is folk wisdom in pithy, aphoristic form. Every tradition has its share of such sayings: 'Far away hills are green;' 'A stitch in time,' etc. In Israel, especially within the Wisdom tradition, the ordinary, secular proverb form was used to reflect on God's involvement in the world, on life and death and to encourage people to act in a certain way. 'Do not despise the Lord's discipline or his reproof, for the Lord reproves him whom he loves, as father the son, in whom he delights' (Prov 3:11-12 and the entire book). It is against this kind of background that we must judge the sayings of Jesus.

In his discussion of Jesus as a teacher of wisdom, Bultmann gathered together fifteen proverbs which he maintained were authentic sayings of Jesus and which were without parallel. 'So here if anywhere we can find what is characteristic of the preaching of Jesus.'[3] All these sayings are most unusual and disturbing. These shattering aphorisms attack our efforts to weave the thread of life into a coherent and acceptable pattern. They jolt and jar and dislocate. They stand on its head what is taken as sure and certain and maintain that this is how it should really be. However, rather than attempt to comment on them, it is much wiser to let them speak for themselves.

i. The Most Radical Sayings:
'Leave the dead to bury their own dead' (Lk 9:60, Mt 8:22).
'If anyone strikes you on the right cheek, turn to him the other also; and if anyone would use you to take your coat, let him have your cloak as well; and if anyone forces you to go one mile, go with him two miles' (Mt 5:39-41).

ii. Sayings of Final Reversal:
'For whoever would save his life will lose it; and whoever loses his life for my sake and the gospel's will save it' (Mk 8:35).
'How hard it will be for those who have riches to enter the kingdom of God ... It is easier for a camel to go through the eye of a needle than for a rich man to enter the kingdom of God' (Mk 10:23, 25).
'But many that are first will be last and the last first' (Mk 10:31).
'Every one who exalts himself will be humbled, and he who humbles himself will be exalted' (Lk 14:11).

iii. Sayings of Conflict:
'No one can enter a strong man's house and plunder his goods, unless he first binds the strong man; then indeed he may plunder his house' (Mk 3:27).
'If a kingdom is divided against itself, that kingdom cannot stand. And if a house is divided against itself, that house will not be able to stand. And if Satan has risen up against himself and is divided, he cannot stand, but is coming to an end' (Mk 3:24-26).
'No one who puts his hand to the plough and looks back is fit for the kingdom of God' (Lk 9:62).
'Enter by the narrow gate; for the gate is wide and the way is easy that leads to destruction, and those who enter it are many.

For the gate is narrow and the way is hard that leads to life, and those who find it are few' (Mt 7:13-14).

'There is nothing outside a man which, by going into him, can defile him: but the things which come out of a man are what defile him' (Mk 7:15).

'Whoever does not receive the kingdom of God like a child shall not enter it' (Mk 10:15).

'Love your enemies and pray for those who persecute you, so that you may be sons of your father … for he makes his sun rise on the evil and on the good, and sends rain on the just and on the unjust. For if you love those who love you, what reward have you? Do not even the tax collectors do the same? And if you salute only your brethren, what more are you doing than others? Do not even the gentiles do the same? You, therefore, must be perfect, as your heavenly father is perfect' (Mt 5:44-48).

These sayings obviously retain at least the externals of the proverbial form. However, the intensification of insights, the sharpened paradox, and the profound antitheses expressed in them are quite extraordinary. The disconcerting questions they raise, the unthinkable possibilities they propose, and the total reversal of values they insinuate is not the stuff of which proverbs are usually made. What we find in these sayings of Jesus goes far beyond common sense, balanced judgment, and the accumulated wisdom of the ages. The accepted approaches to life are called into question and reversed by these sayings of Jesus. If we must use the word 'proverb,' it would be much more accurate to call them 'counter-proverbs.'

What do we make of these sayings, these counter-proverbs? What would we have made of them if we had heard them proclaimed by Jesus? Would we have taken them seriously when we heard them? Are we shocked by them today? Could we ever make our own the new vision, the radical new challenge they propose? Can we cope with their real purpose at all? Or have we discovered some subtle ways of neutralising them so that we can listen, nod in agreement, but qualify them by saying: 'He is exaggerating just to make a point,' and then proceed with our lives as before? Who is this Jesus who speaks these counter-proverbs, seeking to shatter the comfortable familiar world of his hearers?

3. *Abba Father*

A vitally important word found frequently on the lips of Jesus of Nazareth, especially in prayer was *Abba*, meaning 'father.' All Christians pray the Our Father, but our long-standing familiarity with it dulls our appreciation of its revolutionary character. The introduction to the Our Father in the Latin Mass contained the words *audemus dicere* (we dare to say) which caught something of the daring, astounding privilege that is ours in being able to pray to God as Father, through Jesus Christ.

One of the introductions proffered in the new Mass says 'Jesus taught us to call God our Father and so we have the courage to pray ...' This is true, but we need to try to appreciate what is compressed into these words. Christians are taught from childhood to pray to God as Father in a direct, personal, and intimate way. But the unquestioned ease with which we pray to God as father stands in marked contrast with much of what we find within Jewish prayer, piety, and spirituality.

The Jewish people had a profound appreciation of the fatherhood of God. In Jewish patriarchal society the father was the focus of the entire family, which depended upon him for sustenance, protection, and instruction. He cared for all members, exercised authority within the household, gave instruction, and expected love and obedience in return. When the word 'father' was applied analogically to God in a religious sense to disclose something of the relationship between Yahweh and Israel, it still carried many of these associations. Of course, it was further modified by being incorporated into a whole family of words, metaphors, and symbols which tried to speak about the profound relationship between Israel and this deeply compassionate God in language which had both masculine and feminine overtones. (In the psalms alone God is spoken of as fortress, rock, life-giving water, thunder, judge, shepherd, midwife, lover, helper, father, mother).[4]

Israel was convinced that God had chosen her and related himself to her as Father; that he had the concern and compassion of a father. However, she was terrified that this profound but delicately nuanced theological insight might somehow be misunderstood or debased. This danger was real because Israel was surrounded by pagan religions which tended to understand the fatherhood of their gods in mythological or biological ways. So we find that the Old Testament is always very careful in the way in which it refers to or describes God as Father. In line with this reverential care, we discover both in the Old Testament and in the material available to us concerning the spirituality of Israel and the liturgical and personal prayer of the people, that while God is spoken of as Father he is very rarely *addressed* simply as 'Father.' Almost always some more formal honorific title, e.g. 'Lord of the Universe,' 'Master of Heaven and Earth,' is used, or some qualification is introduced to avoid confusion or misunderstanding, e.g. 'Father in heaven.'

However, in the New Testament God is spoken of as Father with striking frequency, a frequency that would have scandalised many of those schooled in the mentality we have just noted. Given this background and the temper of the times, how is such a dramatic change or development to be explained? The New Testament is clear – this radically new usage was a consistent characteristic of Jesus' way of speaking. It exists because Jesus took the initiative and addressed God in this way, especially in prayer. It is clear from the gospels that Jesus preferred to get away from the crowds (Mk 1:35, 6:46; Lk 5:16) to be alone in his prayer (Mt 14:23; Lk 9:18; Mk 14:35); he sometimes went to the desert (Mk 1:35; Lk 5:16) or to a mountain (Mk 6:46; Mt 14:22-23; Lk 6:12, 9:28). Sometimes he would go off early in the morning (Mk 1:35) or he would spend part or all of the night in prayer in the lonely places (Mk 6:46; Mt 14:32-33; Lk 6:12). It seems that he had special recourse to prayer in times of critical difficulty and before moments of decision (Mk 1:35, 6:46,14:32-33; Lk 3:21, 6:12, 9:18, 28ff, 22:41-45). But what is most striking about the prayer of Jesus is that in all strata of the gospel tradition we find him not only frequently referring to God as Father but always actually *addressing* him *directly* as Father in prayer. His chosen word of address is found untranslated in the original Aramaic in Mk 14:36, *Abba*. Most scholars argue that in many other texts where we find the vocative of 'father' we are dealing with translations of *Abba* and should reinstate this word (Mt 11:25-26, 26:39, 42; Lk 10:21, 11:2, 23:24).

Now this way of addressing God is all the more remarkable when we consider that the Aramaic word *Abba* was not a formal 'religious' word but was in everyday use within the intimacy and familiarity of family life. Both children and adults would use this one word to address their fathers. In Jewish family circles it evoked all the authority, care, tenderness, intimacy and mutual trust experienced by children from the first moment of their existence. The warmth, the strong gentleness, the reassuring intimacy, the experiential depths of this word are difficult to translate into English. We need to allow the content we give to it to be deeply influenced by maternal experiences as well. Perhaps expressions like 'my dear father' or 'daddy' or 'poppa,' as used unselfconsciously by adults when they are giving expression to the profound love and appreciation that lie at the heart of their lives, come closest to communicating its meaning. This was the word that Jesus chose and used consistently in prayer to God and there is no doubt that in this word *Abba* we are listening to an authentic word, an authentic manner of speaking of Jesus of Nazareth.

Furthermore, scholars who have sifted through the liturgical and private prayers that have come down to us from the tradition of Israel maintain that *Abba* does not occur in the contemporary language of prayer addressed to God except by way of exception (three or four 'possible' instances). That this very unusual and distinctive way of praying sets Jesus apart to a significant degree from his contemporaries is unquestioned. It was precisely because of the familial and familiar associations of this word *Abba* that most Jews avoided using it in prayer. They would never have dreamt of using such an informal, unceremonious, almost disrespectful word of address to the great, all-holy, transcendent God of Israel. The vast majority of Jesus' contemporaries would have been shocked and scandalised by the thought that anyone would regularly pray to God in this way. Yet Jesus continually speaks of and speaks to the one God of Israel in the warm familiar tones of *Abba*.

We are forced to ask: Why did Jesus use this word, why did he think it right and natural to do so? The only answer must be that he did so because it alone adequately expressed the very heart of his experience of intimacy and familiarity with God. *Abba* is the one word that sums up the unaffected simplicity that lay at the core of Jesus' experience of his relationship to the God of Israel and it alone was the word by which to address and describe God as Jesus knew him. His experience of God must have been one of distinctive intimacy and only the word *Abba* with all its richness of overtones could bring it to speech.

Yet we must notice something very important: Despite this uniqueness, Jesus did not reserve this way of prayer for himself alone. He taught his disciples to pray in the same way (Lk 11:2; Mt 6:9). This is to be the prayer of disciples: When you pray, say Father (*Abba*) (Lk 11:2). Indeed it is possible to look on the rest of the prayer as spelling out what it means for a disciple to be able whole-heartedly to say *Abba* to God in childlike trust and confidence. The disciple prays to Abba for the coming of his kingdom and the petitions recognise the activity of this father king in the provision of 'daily bread,' in the forgiveness of sin, and in being saved from failure in the time of testing.

The *Abba* prayer is given to us in Luke 11:2-4 and Matthew 6:9-13, but there are noticeable differences between these two sources. Scholars maintain that Luke's directness ('Father,' without qualification) and brevity is more original; that Matthew has reverted to the more honorific 'Our Father who art in heaven.' This could indicate that Jewish converts found it difficult, perhaps shocking, to pray to God directly as *Abba* and reverted to a form more compatible with their own tradition. In Luke's version it reads:

Father,
Hallowed be thy name,
Thy kingdom come.
Give us each day our daily bread;
And forgive us our sins, for we ourselves forgive everyone
    who is indebted to us;
And lead us not into temptation.

The central petition of this prayer recalls the Jewish Kaddish prayer used at community prayer in the synagogues in the time of Jesus. It reads:

Magnified and sanctified be his great name
    in the world that he has created according to his will.
May he establish his kingdom in your lifetime
    and in your days and in the lifetime
    of all the house of Israel,
    even speedily and at a near time.

The parallels between both petitions are obvious, but so too are the marked differences – especially the simplicity, the brevity, and the intimacy of the *Abba* prayer. Each prayer envisages a substantially different kind of relationship between God and the person saying the prayer.

We should also notice that while Jesus encourages and urges his disciples to pray in the way he does (and it is disciples who are urged to pray constantly), he is never actually presented to us as including himself with his disciples in saying 'Our Father' (Mt 6:9, is somewhat peculiar to Matthew and Jesus is here teaching his disciples how they should pray). Indeed the distinction between 'my father' and 'their father' or 'your father' is rigorously maintained in the gospels. This would suggest that while Jesus was aware of a distinction between his experience of God and that of his disciples, yet he teaches them to pray in the same way as he does. The disciples' ability to pray in this way is seen as a consequence of the insight they have gained into Jesus' distinctive vision of God's relationship to human beings and is ultimately dependent on their relationship with Jesus. Two texts outside the gospels corroborate this: 'When we cry *Abba*, Father! it is the Spirit himself bearing witness with our spirit that we are children of God' (Rom 8:15-16), and because 'you are sons, God has sent the spirit of his son into our hearts, crying, *Abba*! Father!' (Galatians 4:6). They retain the original *Abba* Father form remembered vividly in the pre-Pauline tradition as characteristic of Jesus. It is a sacred prayer formula which can be used by Christians only because they possess the spirit of Jesus and are children of God.

While Jesus himself speaks of God and prays to him in this intimate way, and invites disciples to do the same, he does so with infinite respect. He wants this name reserved for God (and for one's own father). He wants it treated with great reverence. 'Call no man on earth *Abba* (referring to the current practice of extending this title to revered teachers and elders) for you have only one *Abba* who is in heaven' (Mt 23:9). He wishes it to be a genuine expression of their childlike trust in God who is truly their father.

Finally, if we remember that in the Jewish family the father is the one who exercises authority and instructs and that it is from him that the son receives everything ('All that is mine is yours' Lk 15:31), we will gain further insight into Jesus' sense of sonship as given to us in Mt 11:25-27.

Much has been written and debated about these verses in

39

Matthew. If they are the authentic words of Jesus – and they are credible as such – they once again speak to us of the nature of Jesus' sonship, of his praying to God as *Abba* and claiming to know the God to whom he surrenders himself. ('Father' directly, v. 25 and 'My Father,' v. 27). They tell us of his dependence on the Father who cares for him and for 'the babes' who say ab-ba; of his own thankful, devoted obedience; of his being a unique recipient of the 'mysteries of revelation'; of being commissioned to reveal the Father to whomsoever he chooses.

In summary, we can say that it is inaccurate to declare that Jesus merely helped people to realise that they are God's children. The Jewish people already knew that very well. What is remarkable is that a people who had been schooled to keep God at a respectful distance because of his supreme holiness and almighty power and therefore to approach him with awe and in fear and trembling, were, through Jesus of Nazareth, given the miraculous freedom to say *Abba* to this God. They themselves appreciated or were shocked by this astounding privilege. It is as if the central insights of the high points of Israel's experience of God had been lost sight of, but Jesus now restored all of these riches to them and added his own profoundly distinctive insights as well.

Jesus' use of this word *Abba* seems to give us, in condensed form, the very secret of his life, the core of what we understand by the originality of Jesus of Nazareth. God is known to him as *Abba* and he always responds to God as an obedient son – 'Not my will, but thine' (Lk 22:42; Mt 26:42), 'My food is to do the will of the one who sent me' (Jn 4:34), 'I have come to do your will' (Heb 10:9).

A threshold has been crossed, a new and fundamental breakthrough has been made. Jesus, basing himself totally on this foundation and this absolute conviction, allows his whole life to be shaped by this vision, this understanding of God as *Abba*. Jesus decided everything for the present and for the future, unwaveringly in the light of his consciousness of *Abba*. We could say that Jesus allows the future of the one whom he calls *Abba* to become his future. *Abba* is the focus of his life. *Abba* is his life project.

The gospels present Jesus to us as someone captivated by *Abba*, as being (if you like) literally in love with him. This seems to be the only way in which we can sum up what we hear when we listen to Jesus speaking to us of his father. Everything about him, his strength, his single-mindedness, his consistency, can only be explained in terms of his conviction about the active presence of this *Abba* in every moment of his life. This alone explains the source of his energy, his courage in the face of rejection and threat. It enables us to understand the driving force in his life that is seen in his dedication to the little ones in the name of the Father and in his assuring salvation to the hopeless and the lost. *Abba* is the father who cares for and cherishes all his children. Jesus is utterly convinced of 'the goodness and loving kindness of God' bent lovingly over humanity (Tit 3:4). In the gospels we see Jesus go off to lonely places to pray to *Abba*, 'a God who hugs humanity into his very person' (George Herbert) and to discover *Abba*'s will for him. In these lonely places of communion with *Abba* he found the strength to fail by human standards, knowing that *Abba* would be with him come what may. John (16:32) has caught this superbly: 'Yet, I am not alone. The Father is always with me.'

Yet even as we listen to all this we may tend to translate it into Trinitarian terms and say 'Why wouldn't Jesus pray to God as Father, isn't he the unique son, the second person of the Trinity, of one being with the Father?' These later dogmatic categories are not found in the New Testament and we are still 300 years away from the clarifications of the Council of Nicaea. We should not try to make more of this approach than it is capable of sustaining. On its own, it will not give us a new basis for apologetics or a 'proof' of dogmas. The church's conviction about the sonship of Jesus Christ is based on the totality of his life, death, and exaltation and not on individual words, however unprecedented or unique they may be. Indeed, it is not possible to say in *advance* what the real content of *Abba* is – that can only be discovered as it unfolds in his message and ministry, in his death and resurrection. Only then will we be able to appreciate all that is compressed into this single word. So far we have merely noted it as a linguistic form which is completely different from anything we find elsewhere in Israel.

On these grounds alone what it discloses to us by way of suggestion is remarkable and exciting. It speaks about the heart of an experience of God that is characterised by an extraordinary warmth and intimacy. This is enough for us. Instead of rushing to conclusions about who Jesus is, we should rather try to ponder imaginatively the mystery of his person and ask, as his contemporaries would have asked: What manner of man is this? Who is this man Jesus? What is there to justify the shocking originality of his claim? What kind of self-understanding must one have to claim this kind of intimacy and familiarity with the divine? What are the implications of this *Abba* word for practical living? If we had been contemporaries of Jesus, schooled in reverential awe of God, how would we have responded? With easy acceptance or with pious indignation or ...?

4. *The Parables of Jesus*

We must begin by saying that Jesus did not invent the parable form, which might be described in a general way as a short story with at least two levels of meaning, the purpose of which is to communicate a new insight. Parables had long been in use in Greece and Rome as well as in the stories and writings of Israel. Some of the more memorable biblical parables come to mind immediately – the story of the vineyard in Isaiah 5:1-7, or the book of Jonah, or Nathan's powerful parable to David:

> There were two men in a certain city, the one rich and the other poor. The rich man had very many flocks and herds, but the poor man had nothing but one little ewe lamb, which he had bought. And he brought it up and it grew up with him and with his children: It used to eat of his morsel, and drink from his cup, and lie in his bosom, and it was like a daughter to him. Now there came a traveller to the rich man and he was unwilling to take one of his own flock or herd to prepare for the wayfarer who had come to him, but he took the poor man's lamb and prepared it for the man who had come to him. Then David's anger was greatly kindled against the man and he said to Nathan, 'As the Lord lives, the man who has done this deserves to die; and he shall restore the lamb four-fold, because he did this thing and because he had no pity.' Nathan said to David, 'You are the man' (2 Sam 12:1-7).

The rabbis also told parables and used them to illustrate, explain, and defend their interpretations of the Law. Indeed, parables are still created and told. Yet when we look at the parables of Jesus it seems fair to say that he was one of the most brilliant exponents ever of this language-form.

A substantial proportion of the preaching of Jesus comes down to us in parable form. In fact, we find that parables are the most characteristic form of Jesus' way of speaking and that the synoptic gospels recount over forty parables. Scholars tell us that the parables are, by and large, authentic sayings of Jesus and so they put us in touch in a powerful way with his mind and, above all, his imagination.

These parables have so many common characteristics and they are so distinct in manner, style, and consistency that we must conclude that they are the products of a single, powerful, insightful imagination. Clearly, we are dealing with an incredibly persuasive but provocative teacher who teaches about what he calls 'the reign of God' active in the lives of people. He is a teacher who, with amazing clarity and incisiveness, succeeded in enshrining his message in the haunting and unforgettable poetry we call his parables. This poetry combines contrast and paradox, irony and humour, the similar and dissimilar, profound insight and concrete usage in a very powerful way. In the teachings of Jesus, parables are found more frequently than any other rhetorical form and with the parables we are at the bedrock of the tradition about Jesus of Nazareth. We are absolutely sure that he spoke in parables and, thanks to the work of scholars, especially Jeremias, in very many cases it is possible to reconstruct the original form of the parables as spoken by Jesus.

However, instead of being excited by all this, we are so frequently unimpressed by the parables. A fairly typical way of looking at them runs something like this: Jesus wished to tell the people about himself and God but they were simple, uneducated folk who were unable to grasp this sublime teaching. So he told them simple, innocent stories. A parable, in such a presentation, is a vehicle or medium for conveying divine truths or for teaching a moral lesson by moving from the known into the unknown and from the concrete toward the abstract. Each parable was intended to make only one rather obvious point which could be extracted quite easily later by teachers and preachers and expressed in more suitable fashion. The parable could more or less be discarded once it had done its job.

Such an approach lends itself to bland moralising by

preachers and teachers. The parable of the Good Samaritan is then told so as to exhort people to be nice to those around them and proclaiming the parable of the prodigal son may be an occasion for a sermon about emigration. This way of looking at parables has been severely criticised and rejected in recent times and the parables are now being freed to speak once again in their own absolutely unique way. What follows is an attempt to summarise these new insights.[5]

Critics insist that parables belong to the genre of religious literature and that they are carefully constructed, self-contained, literary units. Originally they were not written but narrated in dynamic interchange and handed on orally. They still retain their fresh, arresting style which invites engagement, judgment, and response. We must therefore appreciate them as narrative, as story, and realise that they draw their material and images from the everyday life of ordinary people engaged in the social, religious, and family affairs of first century Palestine. Like all narrative, they evoke a response and the listener is drawn into them as participant.

Because they are narratives, and must be read and heard as such, some scholars have dedicated their energies to reconstructing the original version of the parables from the gospel sources. They do this by distinguishing between the original version told by Jesus, the modifications it may have undergone during the period of oral tradition, the place given to it in the preaching of the community, and its present setting in the individual gospels. This undertaking has been very successful and scholars can now work with commonly accepted reconstructed texts of the parables. However, other scholars have maintained that we must try to see these narratives within the original life situation of Jesus' ministry where they were first spoken.

These scholars argue that if we do not do this, we run the risk of subordinating the parable to our own presuppositions and concerns. It is important, insofar as is possible, to try to rediscover the situation in which a parable was first told, Jesus' intention in telling it, and the experiences out of which and into which it was spoken. When this is done it becomes clearer that the parables are occasional narratives, spoken to specific groups of people on specific occasions. They presume a familiarity with a whole range of social, cultural, and historical experiences, yet it seems many of these parables are addressed to people who certainly did not share Jesus' vision of reality.

The parables have been approached even more recently by literary critics who, while taking account of these scholarly contributions, wish to address themselves first of all to what is distinctive about them from the point of view of language and literary form. Here the conclusion is unanimous: At the heart of the parables we find metaphor and the story extends this metaphor into narrative. This fundamental insight has had a most profound impact on the interpretation of the parables, as we shall see, and it continues to illuminate them.

To define parables as extended metaphors does not separate them from ordinary language and life. On the contrary, these critics insist that metaphorical thinking and imagining, the recognition of similarities in dissimilarities, have always been at the basis and the heart of human thought and language. However, we seldom recognise this now because we have grown so accustomed to the fossilised nature of our language and regard metaphor as the sole preserve of poets. Nevertheless, religious language at its best must always be quite self-consciously metaphorical. In that sense it is not at all surprising to find that Jesus' most characteristic form of teaching should be that of the extended metaphor. But good metaphor startles the imagination and disturbs the soul. So too we find that the parables of Jesus constantly surprise and frequently shock his hearers.

To understand why this is so we must remember that it is the very nature of metaphor to juxtapose two elements that cannot be simply compared. It is the 'deliberate yoking of opposites,' 'the transposition of an alien name,' seeing 'this' as 'that,' declaring that 'A *is* B.' To take an example from Aristotle, in a metaphor we do not say that 'Achilles rushed forward like a lion' but 'the lion rushed forward.' The simple comparison is suppressed and we are confronted by a dramatic new insight. Similes say A is *like* B so they can help us to clarify, to illustrate, to compare. Metaphor has a very different impact. We are challenged to see the similarities between realities previously unrelated in our minds and imaginations. This is so because in metaphor we find two disparate realities, active together in tension but sustained by a *single* word or phrase. The dissimilarity, the impropriety of what is brought together in metaphor, offers judgment, it opens

45

up a vision of new possibilities, it creates new meaning, it gives a glimpse of a new world. For metaphor does not simply refer to something else – it *bears* the reality to which it refers. In metaphor there are always two levels of meaning, the literal and what we can only call 'the new' ... for we cannot really say anymore. It is new, different, unexpected, revolutionary, tensive, on-going. At the literal level, metaphor begins within the given, the ordinary, the taken-for-granted world. But the introduction of the incongruous new element disturbs and displaces the old order, opens up a crack in the surface unity of our 'world' and lets us perceive reality in a new, heightened way.

The parables of Jesus begin within the everyday humdrum life of people as they go about their business at home, on the farm, in the family, on a journey, at a meal. There is nothing epic about the situations or characters they portray. The characters are familiar, they could be anyone, anywhere and they simply do what most people do in similar situations. The ordinariness of these narratives means that the hearers identify with these people. They feel at home. There is an immediacy, a directness, a relevance, a brevity about these narratives that is extraordinary. They make contact with all, no matter what their backgrounds, their circumstances in life, or their religious or political affiliation may be.

Since they are secular stories they do not presume shared presuppositions about God and his ways with the world, nor do they require a particular social background or expect a certain standard of education or moral rectitude of the hearers. They ask only that the story be heard and not just listened to. (To hear, in the Bible, is to obey). They call for involvement and response. They invite the hearer to become part of the narrative: 'This is the kind of situation you could find yourself in. These are the sorts of people you know. This is your life. This man/woman is you.' We agree. The indirectness of the approach seems innocent enough and we begin to relax into it and to go along with the story. But we have taken a bait and the barb soon begins to bite! (Jesus did speak of 'becoming fishers of men' (Mk 1:17; Lk 5:10), to catch or to 'hook' them!)

In these parables a metaphorical shift takes place, for something new and unexpected, an irritant that 'does not, yet does' fit is always introduced into the story, and the familiar, the certain, the comforting, the expected are at risk. The ground begins to open beneath our feet; a rift occurs in the old conventions; the fabric of our world is rent. What had been taken for granted as certain – the security of old ways, snug familiarities, inherited prejudices, unquestioned presuppositions – are now being stripped away and we are freed to stand before the new vision of truth that is disclosed. But this new vision is profoundly unexpected and surprising. It disorients and dis-eases and it may indeed be shocking and subversive. It is the *Samaritan* who is neighbour, it is the *last* who are first, it is the *lost* who are rejoiced over, the *stranger* who is at table, the *wastrel* son who is embraced and fêted. Jesus achieves this shift not by logical argument nor by an appeal to scriptural texts or any higher authority, nor by cajoling or brow-beating his hearers but by an absolutely brilliant use of extended metaphor which detonates the imagination.

These parables are symbolic probes that dig into each person's life and demand a response. Though there are no easy answers, people are freed to think for themselves. At most, the authentic parables of Jesus provide a framework which launches us and we must then complete what has been begun in us. Yet, paradoxically, we can never satisfy the demands of a parable even if we wrestle with it for our entire life. Conversely, to refuse to proceed is to renege on what we have already become involved in; to rid ourselves of the 'hook' within that can tear. Yet to try to go along with the parables involves confrontation with the new, the unknown, the frightening, the paradoxical, the illogical, that which affronts and reverses the accepted judgment of common sense.

Perhaps all this would become clearer if we looked at one of the parables that has been intensively studied from within this general approach.[6] However, we should be aware that the approach we are going to take does not take parable as parable seriously and so continues the violence done to it through the ages. The story in question is The Parable of the Good Samaritan, which has come down to us from the lips of Jesus virtually unchanged.

A man was going down from Jerusalem to Jericho, and he fell among robbers, who stripped him and beat him, and departed, leaving him half-dead. Now by chance a priest was going down that road; and when he saw him he passed by on the other side. So likewise a Levite. When he came to the place and saw him, he passed by on the other side. But a Samaritan, as he journeyed, came to where he was; and when he saw him, he had compassion, and went to him and bound up his wounds, pouring on oil and wine; then he set him on his own beast and brought him to an inn and took care of him. And the next day he took out two denarii and gave them to the innkeeper, saying, 'Take care of him; and whatever more you spend, I will repay you when I come back.' Which of these three, do you think, proved neighbour to the man who fell among the robbers? (Lk 10:36).

The prospect of looking at this parable again hardly appeals to us or promises a challenge. Familiarity has tended to neutralise it for us and domesticate its teller. Even the title is a give-away. We know the story. We could prompt the narrator once we get the first line. We know that it is about a man who fell among robbers, sought help from a priest and a Levite and finally received it from a Samaritan. Before the story begins we have identified ourselves with 'the good Samaritan.' The phrase has become part of our everyday language to describe helpful people. We have heard so many sermons exhorting us to follow this example or have based so many moralising lessons on it that the real depth, the real impact, the real challenge of this parable is lost on us.

However, in the historical situation in which Jesus told this parable, he was addressing a Jewish audience (it is set in the Jerusalem area and two of the characters are Temple functionaries embodying a whole social and religious order) who hated, loathed, and despised Samaritans. The reason for this intense hatred is historical and will be examined in the next chapter. Here it is sufficient to note that Jews despised their next-door neighbours as wretched, half-breed outcasts who had sold out on both their religion and their culture. To them the Samaritans were the scum of the earth. They hated them with that intensity of religious hatred which is found only among those who dispute each other's claim to be heirs to the one true faith. Orthodox Jews would have no dealings with a Samaritan (Jn 4:9), they would cross and re-cross the Jordan rather than enter that province; some rabbis believed that to accept any help from them would delay the redemption of Israel. With this in mind we must try to hear this story once again. It may be necessary to tell the story of how people might have heard the story!

The inbuilt dynamism demands that the hearers become involved. I am asked to identify with the man going down from Jerusalem to Jericho, (not with the Samaritan who has not yet appeared). 'That man is you.' So I walk that notoriously dangerous road. I am attacked, robbed, and stripped. I am left lying half dead in the ditch and I hope for help from the priest who approaches. The story tells me that the priest passes by on the other side of the road, presumably out of concern for his own welfare. But perhaps, as a good loyal Jew, I would begin to make excuses. I might say: Well he may have had some important functions to carry out in Jericho, he may have had religious duties to perform and if I were dead and he made contact with me he would become ritually unclean. I might begin to excuse the inexcusable by making religious excuses. Similarly, with the Levite I can make excuses for him. He is expected to observe everything meticulously and carefully follow in the steps of the priest who has preceded him. Again I excuse the inexcusable. Perhaps.

The hearers of Jesus, who would have expected the appearance of a third and final character (there are always three!) begin to anticipate. They *know* who is coming next and eyes begin to brighten. Jesus is a layman. Ah, now I see; he is being slightly anti-clerical! So a Jewish lay person will come around the corner and all of us will rejoice and applaud. But Jesus introduces a characteristic twist or shift into the story. The surface innocence of the language breaks and reveals the inescapable barb beneath. It is not a Jew who comes down the road, it is a Samaritan! No sooner had that unspeakable word (spit in contempt!) been mentioned than the antagonism of his hearers became palpable. But ignoring the reaction the story goes on to tell, in loving detail, about the Samaritan countering the action of the robbers and the non-action of the Jewish religious leaders, unselfishly picking up a beaten, good-as-dead man, caring for him and nursing him back to health. Then at the end, in Luke's account (v. 36) the provocative throwaway question of Jesus is found: 'Which of these three do you think proved neighbour to the man who fell among robbers?'

Jesus doesn't even put into words any conclusion he might

wish people to draw from it. The challenge is there as question and, even if it were not put into words, I cannot ignore its implications. I have listened to the story and must answer 'The Samaritan is his neighbour.'

But since I have identified with the injured man, I as a Jew must say what could not be said, I must say what has been ruled out as unspeakable – the Samaritan is my neighbour! So I am being forced/freed to say what cannot be said. I am to put words on what sticks in my throat, to voice what chokes me, to join two words never before united in the entire history of separation between Judea and Samaria – the words 'Samaritan' and 'neighbour.' This conclusion is revolting and sickening. It demands that my world view, my familiar horizons, my understanding, my whole value system be called into question. All my old familiarities, the lessons I learned from parents, grandparents, and religious leaders, my very faith itself is radically questioned and completely turned upside-down in and through this story.

But that is not the end of it. This story leads me further into what was previously unimaginable. If Jesus really had to tell a revolutionary story it would have been enough to have told it with the Samaritan in the ditch receiving help from me, a Jew. Now that kind of love of non-Jews would be sufficiently unthinkable! But this story says that my revered religious leaders, who should help me, refuse to do so and the Samaritan, who should refuse, comes to my assistance! I cannot cope with this utter reversal of expectations. It subverts everything I ever knew or held dear. The literal meaning of the story I have found to be quite incredible and yet shatteringly possible at the same time.

Now the tension it has generated within me disorientates me and yet seems to suggest something unbearably new at another level, at the metaphorical level. I know Jesus never mentioned God in this narrative. It is a thoroughly secular story about the interaction of certain characters. Even the man 'who proves to be a neighbour' doesn't seem to think about God. (Anyway the God of the Samaritans was just as sectarian as the God of the Jews!) He simply does what he has to do in a businesslike way. It is simply that his love and care for the other is lingeringly recounted. But this Jesus is always concerned with God and his reign so in the 'flash across' that can only happen through metaphor, I begin to think about God and the way he acts, about how he might reign in an utterly new way.

Could it be that it is only when my circumscribed world of closed options, set judgments, pre-determined positions, and guaranteed conclusions is torn asunder and turned upside-down, that there is room for God in my life? Is it true that his presence and his reign are so utterly different from what I expect that they spell the end of my world, certainly the end of the world in which I am master? Is it the case that, in the midst of confusion and upheaval, the reign of God is breaking into my life? Is it precisely through the shattering effect of parables that the reign of God takes root in my life and begins to grow and to take over? The ordinary conventional way of living, of knowing where I stand and what to expect must give way, it seems, to what can only be called a 'non-ordinary' way. It demands a revolution in perception to recognise the non-ordinary in the ordinary and an urgent revolution in living if I am to respond to it.

So we see that in telling this story Jesus challenges his hearers to re-examine all that had previously been taken for granted, to reverse the accepted judgments of common sense, to utter the unutterable, and to recognise that God's reign happens like this and in this. It shatters their 'small protective sanities' (Brendan Kennelly) and makes them vulnerable to God. It is an unbelievably powerful and *subversive* story, but so are all the parables. They suggest indirectly what this kingdom or reign of God is like and they re-define it by refusing to define it.

Parables alert us to what it might mean to live in the world in a radically new way. These narratives are about relationships. They are concerned with what people do, about new ways of being together because of their relatedness to what he calls the reign of God. They tease the mind and the imagination into new, extravagant, radical ways of grappling with reality. There is no substitute for parables nor can they be reduced to an idea or a bland generalisation. They function by holding in permanent tension two perspectives on reality; one ordinary, the other 'non-ordinary'; one, the place where I abide; the other, that which is inhabited by Jesus. We might describe them as threshold stories to hint at what is involved in belonging to the kingdom of God.

We may picture the circumscribed world of Jesus' hearers as a small closed circle centred on self. By contrast we can picture the world Jesus inhabits as a parabolic world that is limitless and extravagant but which subsumes the hearer's world. Its centre is God and God's reign.

51

In his parables Jesus tries to draw his hearers out of their closed, self-centred world toward the new world whose moving centre is the kingdom of God. His parables start within the world they recognise but, through the power of metaphor, he then confronts them with the paradox: This is not our world after all! This shattering of the everyday world brings them to the threshold of the new world of Jesus, which they perceive as both possible and impossible at the same time. The parables dislocate and disturb, as they seek to draw the hearers away from the old and toward the new. A challenging alternative is presented. Only the hearers can decide which world they will choose.

The latter choice is frightening, for the old 'centre cannot hold' (Yeats) and the new is not yet known. There are no guidelines, no landmarks. The parable merely suggests that the image of the present world turned inside-out and upside-down is the nearest you will come to glimpsing this radical newness until you actually cross the threshold into the way of life where God is God. A shift in perception alone will not suffice, a pondering of the parable is not enough. We will never really know a parable until we cross the threshold into the world opened up for us *by* parable, a world of paradox and mystery, the antithesis of our everyday world.

Finally, while we may justifiably compare the parables of Jesus with those found in other sources and traditions, we must also acknowledge their uniqueness. Even the rabbinic parables, which are most nearly contemporaneous with those of Jesus, are quite different. Paradox, metaphor, and hyperbole are not commonly found in them. Their characteristic link with a scriptural text, the typical application and explanation they offer, are missing from the parables of Jesus. His parables are religious stories, theirs are theological.

Jesus does not use parables to illustrate his teaching as the rabbis did. They are not some kind of teaching aids that help to communicate his 'real' message. His parables *are* his teaching, *are* his message. In fact they are so personal that they are the very mystery of Jesus in narrative form. Jesus has so poured himself into the parables that he is prepared to die for the truth they unfold. It is because he himself *is* parable that his parables are remembered. Who is this Jesus of Nazareth who tells these dislocating, threshold stories that seem to threaten all that is held dear and sacred? How dare he! What right has he? Those who heard his parables for the first time had to decide either to accept them, with all that they imply, or be prepared to destroy Jesus so as to regain the security of the old ways. If we had heard them, how would we have reacted?

3. SETTING THE SCENE

*And whatever happens began in the past
and presses hard on the future.*
T. S. Eliot

We have looked at a few aspects of the language of Jesus and have contrasted certain language forms used by him with those current at that time. Thus we were referring to the wider context in which Jesus' ministry took place. We must now turn our attention to some of the factors that shaped that context. The ministry and message of Jesus must be understood as interacting with the social, religious, political, and economic circumstances of that time.[1]

The kingdom of Israel had been split in two at the death of Solomon in 922 BC. The Assyrians had conquered the northern kingdom in 721 BC. Then in 587 BC the southern kingdom fell to the Babylonians who destroyed the Temple in Jerusalem and took the king and the aristocracy of Judea into exile in Babylon. This catastrophe shocked the Jewish people and raised very serious questions about their understanding of God, his relationship to his people, and the promises made about the everlasting throne of David.

While in exile, however, they survived this crisis and began to see themselves as the remnant of the true Israel and to realise that their sufferings could be redemptive for all (Ez 11:15-21; Is 53). Because they were in 'a strange land,' far from the ruins even of their Temple, they sought alternative ways to continue to sing 'the Lord's song' and to preserve their identity. They began to collect and interpret the old traditions which had welded them together as a people. The synagogue emerged as a significant institution within Jewish life, becoming an important meeting place for prayer, for the study and collection of the sacred traditions, and for education and hospitality.

In 539 BC Cyrus, the Persian Emperor, defeated the Babylonians and allowed the Jews to return to their homeland. Many chose to remain in Babylon. Those who did return began to rebuild the Temple, the walls of Jerusalem, and their homeland, while at the same time ensuring that developments which had begun during the years of exile continued and intensified. In fact, the next two hundred years was a period of extraordinary literary activity. The law (Torah) also began to take on *the* central role in Judaism and even the major prophets were subordinate to it. The scribes, who were scholars and experts on the 'Scriptures,' took over the prophets' function of interpreting God's will. And so Israel became a 'People of the Book.'

These returned exiles brought with them a new understanding of their faith, a passionate concern for preserving their identity as the people of God, and a violent opposition to any dilution of their racial purity. Yet, just across their northern border was a people who claimed to be Jewish in faith and race but who did not share the same concerns. These were the Samaritans. After 721 BC, the Assyrians had deported many of the original Samaritans and 'planted' colonists in their place. In time these colonists intermarried with the native population, something which was anathema to the Jews who had returned from exile and who regarded themselves as the only faithful interpreters of Israel's religious traditions. In their eyes the Samaritans were half-breeds and half-pagans and they would allow them no part in the rebuilding of the Temple.

Hostility and friction developed into schism and the Samaritans built their own rival Temple on Mount Gerisim. The Jews, however, destroyed this Temple before the Christian era. Josephus the historian tells us that during Passover between AD 6-9 the Samaritans defiled the Temple court in Jerusalem by strewing it with human bones.

Hostilities between Jews and Samaritans had reached an irreconcilable level. The policy of separatism, religious and racial purity, proposed by the returned exiles and their descendants, seems to have caused difficulties and tensions within Judea itself. We hear of conflict between 'the men of the exile,' 'the holy race,' and 'the people of the land,' who had not been deported, concerning forms of worship, purity laws, intermarriage, contact with Samaritans, etc. These internal dissensions deepened as Judaism came into contact with the Hellenistic culture which spread across the East after the conquest of Alexander the Great (333-323 BC). The richer, more aristocratic Jews were willing, indeed anxious, to accept this but the rigorists and the ordinary people opposed it. As always, political developments deepened the crisis.

After almost 200 years of virtual independence the tiny Jewish theocracy, ruled by the High Priest in Jerusalem, came under threat. Again, Syria to the north, ruled by the Seleucids, and Egypt to the south, under the Ptolemies, began to vie for power. From 300-200 BC the Ptolemies controlled Palestine. Some of the more aristocratic families were given positions of power and the Greek culture and way of life continued to spread.

The Jewish state became part of the Seleucid kingdom in 200 BC and these overlords became interested in Hellenising the Jews and in controlling the appointment of high priests. Antiochus IV executed this program so aggressively that the Jewish religion was persecuted. Determined to turn Jerusalem into a Greek city state, he set up an altar to Zeus in the Temple ('the abomination of desolation in the holy place'). The Jewish people, especially the Hasidim or pious ones, could take no more and they revolted in 167 BC under the leadership of Judas Maccabeus and his brothers, and eventually achieved independence in 164 BC.

The Maccabees cleansed and re-dedicated the profaned Temple and, in recognition of all their achievements, they were allowed to assume the High Priesthood. Thus, from 143-63 BC the Jews enjoyed complete independence and, under their priest/kings (Hasmoneans), the state was extended to roughly the same area as that ruled by David and Solomon. Ironically this movement, which began as a reaction against extreme Hellenisation, itself became infected by the same disease. Indeed the Hasmonean rulers were in many ways scarcely distinguishable from Hellenistic kings and they were certainly very different from the high priests of Israel's golden age! And while the ordinary Jewish people were proud of their new-found independence they were, nevertheless, deeply unhappy about the political ruthlessness and religious ambivalence of the Hasmoneans.

In 63 BC the Romans, under Pompey, overran the country and incorporated it into the Roman province of Syria. In 37 BC, in accordance with the Roman policy of appointing native rulers, Herod (the Great) became king of the Jews, answerable only to Rome. All Jews were united in hating him for many reasons, not least of which was the tax burden he imposed. When he died his kingdom was divided between three of his sons but the situation in the South became so bad that in AD 6 the Romans again intervened and began to rule Judea and Samaria directly, while the

North remained relatively independent and open to new influences.

To view this as a mere potted version of the very difficult and complex political history of the Jewish people, and of little help in trying to understand their religious situation during those years, would be a grave misconception. For no matter how easily we tend to separate religion and politics, the Jews could not. Every Jew would have had to take a definite stance on the events of the time and such a stance would have had profound religious significance. In fact it was these historical events that shaped the religious hopes, expectations, and movements of those centuries.

From the time of the exile it was felt that the prophetic voice was silent 'since the time when the prophets ceased to appear' (Macc 9:27). With the changed emphasis and preoccupations of the post-exile world, the scribal expert had replaced the prophet and now only 'the echo' of God speaking to the prophets was half-heard in the land. The threats to life, religion and property, experienced during the constant political upheavals under successive overlords, led the people to wonder about God, his involvement in their history, and his plans for their future.

The newly-returned exiles were convinced that 'the Lord is among you as king, O Israel; never again shall you fear disaster' (Zeph 3:14-15). Later, in very changed circumstances, the people who were praying, struggling for justice, seeking to follow God's will, the Hasidim, gradually became disillusioned with the course of events and with political and religious processes. They experienced oppression and injustice from both the foreigner and from their fellow Jews. So far as official religion and political organisation were concerned, they experienced only the desire of the powerful to hold onto their power. Some even began to despair of history as they experienced it, and became convinced that things were now so bad that the end of the world must be at hand. God would have to intervene and put an end to the old wicked order of things which had become so suffused with evil. Then the 'new order,' 'the new age,' 'the new world,' could be ushered in, bringing about radical transformation of the old into the new.

This is the general picture portrayed in the literary genre

called apocalyptic which grew out of situations of extreme crisis and succeeded in inspiring hope in the anguished so that they might 'endure to the end' (Daniel). The authors wrote in the name of great men from Israel's past and declared that they were privileged to describe 'the last battle' from the vantage point of the future in heaven. In this literature, and in the many popular movements of the time, we find a growing conviction that some definitive (eschatological) saviour figure(s) would appear before the end. Such figures were modelled on various historical persons and projected onto the future. They were given many names. Some groups expected God tc send the great eschatological prophet, and possession of the *pneuma* (spirit) was to indicate the beginning of the last days. Others believed that the coming one would be a Messiah figure like David (2 Sam) who would defeat Israel's enemies but would also be just and righteous. The king of Israel, and later the priests and prophets, were anointed and called *mashiach*, 'God's anointed one,' the Messiah, or *Christos* in Greek. Through this common rite-name, these previously distinct functions of king, prophet, and priest began to merge and the Messiah was understood as the one near to God, mediator between God and his people, filled with God's spirit.

Because of the different meanings of the title, different aspects of it could be highlighted in order to give expression to the hopes and expectations of the various groups. Some spoke of an ideal future Messiah-King like David who would rule the people in God's place. Others looked forward to a king who would combine Davidic and Mosaic traits. And of course there were those who based their hopes on the coming of the eschatological prophet (Is 42:1-6, 49:1-3, 52:7, 59:21, 61:1-2). These passages speak of the coming one who will possess the spirit, offer the true interpretation of the law, announce the approaching reign of God, and bring the liberation, justice, and peace that constitute salvation. Some groups drew on Deut 18:15-18 and spoke of a latter-day prophet like Moses. Still others, basing themselves on texts from Malachi: 'Behold I send my messenger to prepare the way before me ... I will send you Elijah the prophet before the great and terrible day of the Lord comes' (3:1, 4:5), began to speculate about Elijah Redivivus as the prophet of the last times who would prepare the way for God himself.

There were inevitable shifts and shadings between these

various figures as speculation and writing developed. But by way of generalisation we could speak of two underlying trends.[2] One was preoccupied with the Davidic dynasty; the other was more in harmony with the prophetic tradition (always critical of the kingship) and Wisdom theology. It seems that hopes for the former developed among Hasidic groups because of the conflict between the Hasmonean priests-kings and themselves. This Messiah would be of the house of David and would destroy all enemies of the true Israel, bring about the final deliverance and usher in the kingdom of God. Hopes for the latter developed among those who had become disillusioned with many aspects of kingship as they had experienced it and who began to look for an ideal saviour figure who would embody what was best in the prophetic and Wisdom traditions. He would be all-wise like Solomon, a miracle worker, an exorcist, a true servant and Son of God. This all-wise, non-dynastic, eschatological prophet would be responsible for carrying out judgment on those who opposed him. It was expected, especially in the Book of Wisdom, that he would be misunderstood, rejected, suffer a martyr's death, and be vindicated by God, and so receive a royal crown (Wis 2:19). He would be a suffering Messiah.

Finally, another stream of expectation developed around the 'coming Son of Man,' a heavenly figure who would pass sentence on the godless and the just according to their response to the law. Daniel 7:13-14 played a vital formative role in the development of this concept, especially as we find it in the non-canonical Book of Enoch. There the Son of Man is the end-time saviour of the just who has existed in heaven from the beginning but who will be revealed to the saints of God only at the last hour.

We should notice that none of these messianic or apocalyptic expectations of salvation, despite their great fluidity, were universal in intent. They concerned the deliverance of the Jewish people from their enemies so that the eschatological community of peace, ruled over by the Messiah, might come into being. Then, and only then, could the definitive kingdom of God, the utterly 'new heaven and new earth,' begin.

The complexity and variety of these strands of tradition would probably have translated themselves in the minds of the majority into the simple conviction that there was 'one who is to come' and he would bring deliverance from all that did not allow them to make and keep life human.

However, certain very important groupings within Judaism saw these developments in a much more definite way – yet in ways that differed radically from each other. Let us look at four of these:

1. The Pharisees: These were an extraordinarily powerful group within first century Judaism. They have had a bad press in Christian sources being regarded as legalistic fanatics – a judgment which will certainly be deemed unfair, if not simplistic, when we begin to understand what they really stood for. The Pharisees who stand in the tradition of the Hasidim, were convinced that the Law revealed God's purpose and will for all people and that it should always be followed meticulously. Accordingly, they were dedicated to studying the Scriptures and they also elaborated an immense commentary which showed how the minutiae of the law applied to each and every situation. For them, these traditions were just as binding as the Pentateuch.

The principal concern of the Pharisees was the reform of Israel itself. Their ideal was to live in the everyday world as close to God and as ritually pure as the priests in the temple. Whether the movement was begun by priests is uncertain; more important is the fact that it became a lay movement, obviously responding to genuine needs within the community, especially the need to oppose the erosive pressures of Hellenism. In reaction to Hellenisation, the Pharisees, while they paid taxes to Rome under protest, tried to make people aware of the presence of God in every moment of every day. With this in mind they legislated for every aspect of life down to the most minute detail. In particular, they were preoccupied with paying tithes on the fruits of the earth, rigorously observing all facets of the Sabbath observance, keeping themselves ritually pure, and avoiding contact with people who did not observe the law as they did. They looked forward to and felt they were preparing for the coming of a Davidic-dynastic-Messiah who would restore the kingdom to Israel.

Because of the obvious difficulties of this way of life, the Pharisees formed closed communities and co-operatives of their own. (Their name means 'the separate ones,' that is, the holy community of Israel.) While this did not endear them to some sections of the population, neither did it prevent them from becoming the more popular moral and religious leaders, exercising immense authority over the people who were impressed by their genuine devotion and prayerful sincerity. Indeed, many were convinced that to be pleasing to God they would have to strive to emulate the Pharisees and their way of life. Although this was impracticable for most of them, failure to do so guaranteed the creation of guilt complexes. The Pharisees prided themselves in keeping the laws and the traditions and they tended to despise those who were lax in these matters, referring to them as 'sinners, unbelievers, and men without religion.'

The highest rank within the Pharisees was held by the scribes, scholars or lawyers who were experts on religious questions and on the traditions of the elders. Some of these scribes were powerful members of the Jewish Sanhedrin or Great Council of 72.

2. The Sadducees: These also had a very powerful membership in the Great Council. By and large they represented the wealthy Hellenised aristocrats of Jerusalem, many of whom were rich landowners. The chief priest together with the elders and other priests were members of this group. In addition to the offering of sacrifice, they were concerned with the control of the Temple and its wealth and with the organisation of the Jewish state. (The Temple was the religious and political centre of Judaism.) All Jews over twelve years of age, even if they lived abroad, were obliged to pay an annual Temple tax and contribute a tenth of their possessions toward the maintenance of the priests. When we also remember the livestock market associated with sacrifices and the currency exchange for payment of tax, we realise that those in charge of the Temple really controlled a vast financial and administrative empire. Indeed, the Temple cult and administration practically supported the whole city of Jerusalem.

Unlike the Pharisees and the Hasidic groups, the Sadducees were quite willing to collaborate with the ruling authorities in the land. They had worked out a compromise which meant that they would accept foreign domination provided their own position remained undisturbed. Because they held a leading position within the country, they were committed to maintaining the status quo, so the Romans, with whom they collaborated, did not interfere with them.

Their conservatism in these matters was based on and reflected in their conservative attitude to Scripture. They are remembered from the New Testament for their rejection of hope in the resurrection of the dead (Mk 12:18-23; Acts 23:6). Unlike the Pharisees, they accepted only the Pentateuch which legislated for the Temple and the priesthood, which they controlled, and they rejected any later developments such as resurrection of the dead or the traditions of the elders. They were therefore opposed to new ideas, to changes in 'Temple' religion or political structures, to anything which would threaten their self interest. The high priests who ruled during this troubled period belonged to the party of the Sadducees.

3. The Essenes: It would be difficult to imagine a group more opposed to all that the Sadducees stood for than the Essenes. They are not mentioned in the New Testament and most of our information about them comes from the writings of the community living at Qumran on the shores of the Dead Sea. Their name seems to be a Hellenised version of Hasidim and they certainly stand four-square within that tradition.

We have seen how the Pharisees were intent on recognising and responding to the presence of God in the everyday affairs of life, with making the 'ordinary' holy, while still being devoted to the Temple and its ritual. The Essenes went much further in their pursuit of perfection. They rejected Temple worship as impure. The priests in their view were illegitimate and so they withdrew to the wilderness to live ascetic and celibate lives apart from society. (The wilderness recalled Exodus, the 'honeymoon period' of history when Israel was without kings or corrupt ministers and Yahweh alone was Lord). The Dead Sea scrolls (discovered in 1947) tell us that the 'teacher of righteousness' formed loose-knit groups of wilderness dwellers into the kind of highly developed community that we know existed at Qumran. He was remembered as the supreme teacher, the definitive interpreter of the will of God, who translated it into a way of life that set the Essenes apart from all others. The life of the community – its prayer, its study, its renunciation of private property, its ritual worship and common meals of brotherhood, its rigid observance of the many precepts of the 'rule of the community' – was understood to be the true, indeed the only authentic way to live and to worship God. They were unashamedly sectarian in their approach.

Their writings and lifestyle were profoundly influenced by apocalyptic and they looked forward to a high priestly Messiah (perhaps two Messiahs). They hoped that God, in response to their suffering and way of life, would be provoked to act and would purify the priesthood and establish the true Temple where they alone would worship. It was for this reason that they went through the rites of purification prescribed for sacrificing priests each and every day. They considered themselves to be the only faithful remnant of God and looked to God to destroy all the wicked and save only them when the final battle between 'The Sons of Light' (the community) and 'The Sons of Darkness' would be over.

4. The Zealots: It is this final reference that links the Essenes most closely to the last movement we will look at, the Zealots. They too believed that they were engaged in the holy war of the end time against Israel's enemies and that God would intervene and bring his work to completion. For them, Israel's only Lord was God, she was his very own possession and any form of occupation of the land was a crime against Yahweh himself. The same impulse felt by the Pharisees, the Essenes, and indeed the vast majority of the people, to see Israel restored as an independent, truly Jewish kingdom, was carried to the point of violent resistance by the Zealots and the Sicarii (dagger-carrying assassins).

Zeal for God, for his Temple, for his land, for the freedom granted by him to his people, was what motivated them to rid the country of the foreigners and their collaborators. They were fanatical in their opposition to intermarriage, contact with gentiles, the eating of 'unclean,' food and the use of graven images. The secret resistance groups which characterised this movement seem to have been founded by Judas the Galilean (Acts 5:37), who opposed the paying of tribute to Rome. In AD 6 he led a revolt that was savagely put down by the Romans. His last stand was at Sephoris near Nazareth when Jesus was still a child. The Romans crucified two thousand of the rebels but the movement continued and engaged in sporadic guerilla warfare with the occupying forces.

John the Baptiser

The preceding pages have allowed us to glimpse something of the turbulent history of the Jewish people, the complex and fragmented hopes and aspirations to which such a history gave rise, and the movements it fostered. Once we understand the tensions and hopelessness experienced by so many, the almost universal desire for 'a coming one' who would right all wrongs, we will be in a better position to appreciate the kind of world within which John the Baptiser began to preach.

He is not a lone voice. He stands in the line of those older Hasidic and baptismal movements which proclaimed the need for *metanoia*, a change of heart and lifestyle, and which insisted that there had to be repentance, conversion, and a return to God after disobedience and denial if the people were to hope for salvation. To neglect this call would be to incur the threat of God's judgment. Hence the note of desperate urgency which characterised their preaching.

Around this time the conviction began to grow in apocalyptic circles that just before the End, Israel, through the ministry of the eschatological prophet, would be offered the grace of conversion for the last time. So when John appeared on the scene expectations would have quickened and questions would have been asked. The spirit was stirring, the prophetic voice was once again heard in the land, God's messenger was speaking, the last chance was being offered, the end times were at hand. This *could* be the arrival of the Coming One. This strange, unconventional, ascetic figure provoked reactions among the scribal establishment and was doubtless seen as a threat.

This prophetic preacher, 'a man sent by God' (Jn 1:6), appeared on the banks of the Jordan, 'in the wilderness,' far away from the Temple, the priesthood, and the ritual of sacrifice. He proclaimed a message that was at variance with what was happening in the 'holy place' and he stood apart from any of the groups or movements we have seen so far; his name was linked in a special way to the ritual action of being baptised.

John's vision and approach were clearly not that of apocalyptic. His message, his mode of proclamation, his images of fire, axe, and winnow, his lifestyle, his very garb were those of a prophet. He drew the crowds out into the desert, out to the place that recalled the original excitement of Israel's first love, and continually offered the hope of a new future (but also the threat of disaster) in preparation for the End. He was a living sign of contradiction and in prophetic style he proceeded to destroy the cozy cocoons that Israel had spun for herself.

John's Preaching

To the people of this time who were looking forward to the Day of Yahweh, John's message (Mt 3:7-12; Lk 3:7-15) sounded like a revival of the preaching of the prophet Amos, and it was equally full of fire and gloom. We saw that around the time of John's appearance many people were looking forward to a definite intervention by God that would destroy the enemies of Israel and establish her as the great messianic people. Like Amos, John reversed this expectation, declaring that God was angry with the Jewish people and that through certain events which were to come he would sift them like wheat and destroy them like chaff in the fire. The end time was at hand and no one could escape the judgment of God. There was no point in protesting that they deserved salvation simply because they were heirs to the promises of God to his people – 'We have Abraham for our father' (Mt 3:9; Lk 3:8) – John maintained that it is only those 'who bear the fruit that befits repentance' (Mt 3:8; Lk 3:8) who could be saved. In other words, without such good works as should flow from a changed way of life, Israel would be judged to be worse than the pagans and God's punishment would not be turned aside. Furthermore, this transformation must happen in the life of each individual, for no one can repent on behalf of someone else.

Thus John forcefully unites the transformation of one's life now, with its consequent commitment to social justice (Lk 3:10-14), and one's position in the face of the judgment that is 'even now' (Mt 3:10; Lk 3:9). But this *metanoia* (repentance) proclaimed by John is an absolutely free gift from God which demands the dissolution of the old and the birth of the new. This repentance is symbolised by baptism by John in the waters of the Jordan. Other baptismal movements employed the same ritual action but it is remembered as being especially characteristic of John the Baptiser (Mk 1:4). Only by repenting can people have any hope of salvation.

However, John offers no guarantees. He is very clear about judgment, about the future crisis, about the oncoming catastrophe. This is primary; any hint of salvation is merely tentative and secondary. We remember Amos speaking in a similar vein: 'Perhaps you may yet have a future, it may be that God will be gracious to the remnant of Joseph' (5:15). This preaching carries the power of fear in it – by no stretch of the imagination could it simply be called 'good news.' One thing is certain though, if this call goes unheeded disaster will follow. Any possibility of salvation will be mediated through this baptism of repentance by John. Only those who repent and are baptised can hope to pass unscathed through the fearful fiery calamity of the day of wrath and judgment.

John has no crisis of identity about his prophetic ministry and mediatorial role! Yet he does speak of 'a coming one,' mightier than himself, who will baptise with wind and with fire and who is already 'among them' (Jn 1:26). So God's future, to which John is so passionately committed, is certainly not closed. God must be allowed to be God. The future is in his hands.

Jesus Meets John

We are told that crowds came out from all over Judea and the Jordan region to hear John and be baptised by him. Soldiers, tax collectors, and prostitutes came. Pharisees and even Sadducees came (Mt 3:7). Among the multitude who gathered to hear him and to be baptised was Jesus of Nazareth.

We sometimes picture the scenario like this: John is on stage heralding the dramatic entry of Jesus, whose coming he awaits. Jesus enters. There is immediate recognition. Jesus asks to be baptised. John protests that this action should be reversed, but Jesus says: 'Let it be so for the edification of the people.' John baptises Jesus. A voice from heaven acclaims him as 'my beloved Son.' Jesus begins his ministry; John fades out.

It is highly improbable that it happened like that. It would have been very odd indeed if Jesus had suddenly appeared and asked for baptism without listening to John's preaching. John's baptism is inseparable from his preaching. By accepting baptism from John, Jesus was affirming the basic truth of what he had heard John proclaim, that Israel was on a collision course with catastrophe unless all the people became converted and lived in a radically new way.

Jesus was undoubtedly drawn, as others were, by the strong persuasive personality of John. He was convinced that the prophetic spirit was active and the voice of God was to be heard clearly through John's preaching. He accepted the prophetic authority of John without question. The gospel accounts of what Jesus said about John show that he was greatly impressed by the message, the ministry, and the destiny of the Baptiser. There is admiration and love in his words about the single-mindedness of John. He is prophet and more than prophet; no man is greater than John the Baptiser (Mt 11:7-11). Mark's gospel confirms this significance and presents John as part of the gospel of Jesus Christ.

The Baptism of Jesus

All four gospels, and the summaries in Acts 1:22, 10:37, 13:24 tell us that Jesus was baptised by John. The gospels proclaim Jesus as the sinless saviour of the world, so to present him as sharing in John's 'baptism of repentance for the forgiveness of sin' (Lk 3:3) could raise questions or cause embarrassment. Yet this reference to his baptism is consistently retained because it happened and because it was of more than ordinary significance for Jesus of Nazareth. The gospel accounts perceive this moment at the Jordan as a decisive one for Jesus; they agree that the Spirit came upon Jesus and that he was hailed as Son of God. A retelling of an historical happening is joined to a post-Easter proclamation of Jesus as the Christ and Son of God in the texts as we have them. We must work with them as they are, in all their complexity, if we are to understand what this experience meant for Jesus and for his ministry.

If we try to do this by listening to what the biblical scholars and theologians tell us about the baptismal scene, we may become aware of different nuances in interpretation. Let us look at the approaches taken by Jeremias, Dodd, and Schillebeeckx.

Interpretations

For Jeremias,[3] Jesus, by being baptised, is taking his place among the eschatological people of God who are being assembled by John. The descent of the Spirit means prophetic inspiration, being grasped by God and called to be his messenger. But this is the advent of the long-quenched Spirit, so this event foretells the inauguration of the end time of final salvation and grace. Jeremias understands Jesus as experiencing a call to be the prophet-messenger through whom God speaks for the last time. From then on, he is in the grip of the Spirit and is confronted with the full implications of what it means to call God *Abba* as he carries out his mission. Finally, he suggests that Jesus' awareness of his mission, his consciousness of being the unique recipient and mediator of knowledge of God (according to his interpretation of Mt 11:27), could be traced back to his baptism.

Dodd[4] sees Jesus' baptism by John as an act of solidarity with the soldiers, tax collectors, and prostitutes whom Jesus saw as potential members of the New Israel. 'But at his baptism something happened which altered the current of his life.' 'It was a turning point in the career of Jesus himself and a crucial moment in that traffic of two worlds.' 'This was the moment at which Jesus accepted his vocation.' 'For him ... it was the act of God by which he was anointed for his mission.'

Schillebeeckx[5] sees it as 'a disclosure experience, that is, a source experience that was revelatory.' However, he refuses to psychologise about it and points out that Jesus' baptism was not his first religious experience, nor do we really have any explicit knowledge about how he understood himself up to that moment.

But because Jesus' ministry as prophet is linked with his baptism, Schillebeeckx wonders whether his baptism might not be his first, public, symbolic act as a prophet. Is Jesus, he asks, thereby declaring in concrete action and acted parable that apostate Israel is truly in need of a profound change of heart, as John maintains, and is he at the same time proclaiming that the salvation and grace about which John is reticent are really at hand?

In the light of Schillebeeckx's contribution, it does seem that Jeremias and Dodd have tended to consider the baptismal scene somewhat in isolation. They have thereby read it as a sudden, unprecedented call or revelation. However, we can hardly build elaborate theories about Jesus' inner religious life on such brief and densely theological texts. So it is important not to isolate this moment but to see it in the context of his life and development and within the hopes and expectations of Israel. We must always recognise the Jewishness of Jesus. It is vital to understand the part played by his upbringing, environment, and schooling, which were the same as those of any Jewish child. So, although we do not have factual details about his 'hidden life,' we can look on it as the time when he became the kind of person he was during his ministry. No doubt the highly accurate but empathetic observation of people and events that we find in his parables and teaching are funded by experiences gained during these years. He saw 'life steadily and saw it whole.' In a word, the person coming for baptism at the Jordan River is the workman of Nazareth.

In that sense, then, Schillebeeckx is right in what he says about the life of Jesus up to that time, but his own suggestion about the significance of his baptism would seem to go beyond the evidence of the text and beyond what John's baptism signified in itself. Yet it appeals, because it would harmonise with much that follows later in the ministry of Jesus and help to clarify some difficult questions. When Jesus wishes to sum up all the final implications of his unfolding ministry he speaks of it in terms of a 'baptism with which I am to be baptised' (Lk 12:50).

He understands his ministry as bounded by two baptisms, one by John, marking the beginning of his prophetic ministry; the other, the death he will suffer. This baptismal reference indicates that the time of association with John was of decisive significance for Jesus. Again we find Jesus making a similar appeal to John when the question of his own authority is raised (Lk 20:1-8; Mk 11:27-33). Jesus asks: 'Was the baptism of John from heaven or from men?' They refuse to answer so he refuses to tell them about the source of his own authority. But it is clear that he regards both his own and John's prophetic authority as interlinked and as being 'from heaven.'

Jesus Leaves John

Jesus does not question the mission, the authority, the *metanoia* preaching, and the baptism of John and they were obviously significant for his own ministry. Jesus understood John and admired him greatly. Still, whatever the precise relationship between them, Jesus parted company with John and with John's way of life. He did not continue John's mission, for despite the agreement between them there was, above all, a disagreement so fundamental that it led to a break between them.

What divides them is what appears at first sight to unite them – their vision of God and his way of acting. Both are dedicated to God and his future, but who is this God? Is he John's stern, wrathful God of Judgment, or is he the God of Jesus' message and ministry? They appear to be working with essentially different visions of God and his activity. So if John spoke of 'a coming one' it is hard to imagine him easily recognising the fulfilment of his expectations in what we shall discover about the life and ministry of Jesus. Jesus and his ministry, as we shall see, are quite simply not what John expected.

Jesus is convinced by his own vision of God that something radically new is beginning so he can no longer be satisfied with John's preaching and way of life. He experiences the beginnings of a new creation which demands a new way of life, a new ministry, and a new mission, a new struggle with self, with tradition, with expectations. A wrestling with symbols, concepts, words, a quest for language to give expression to this newness, and a unique lifestyle to enflesh this vision are called for.

So they part company. Their approaches to life are contrasted in Mt 11:16-19 and Lk 7:31-35 in the characterisations used by the people to play off one against the other in order to ignore both. 'For John came neither eating nor drinking, and they say "He has a demon."' The Son of Man came eating and drinking, and they say 'Behold, a glutton and a drunkard, a friend of tax collectors and sinners.'

The gaunt ascetical John and the worldly Jesus. John nibbles at the snails and honey of the wilderness. Jesus enjoys food and drink. John shuns society. Jesus moves freely in high and low places. There is nothing odd or affected or strained about Jesus. His normality must strike us and yet the haunting mystery is there.

In retrospect, the gospels see John balanced between two eras. He is the last and the greatest in the old, and he heralds the new. But the fulfilment of what he pointed toward will be surpassed in the life and ministry of Jesus.

Armed with this kind of hindsight judgment, it is easy to opt for the way of Jesus. But suppose we too had gone out in fear and trembling to hear John and be baptised by him. Suppose further that we had returned to our livelihoods determined that if we had two coats we would share with him who had none and if we had food we would do likewise (Lk 3:11) and were convinced that our baptism and new way of life would ensure our salvation in the days of final trial. Would we be prepared to let go of this new-found conviction and follow Jesus? Would we even listen to him? Even today, are we more at home with the preaching and exhortations of John than those of Jesus?

The Motif of Testing

In the synoptic gospels Jesus' baptism is followed by a story about his being tempted – 'the temptation in the desert' as we call it. More accurately, this is a story about testing, *peirasmos* in Greek, and it tells of a struggle, an ordeal. The gospel narratives of this test evoke many Old Testament stories and typologies. One thinks of Abraham's test in the story of the binding of Isaac, or the testing of the people in the desert, or 'the day at Massah in the desert when your fathers put me to the test.' But at the core of this complex gospel story lies a very primitive tradition about Jesus. The tests narrated by the evangelists all call his sonship into question and so we are told that Jesus' consciousness of sonship was the driving force behind his decision to begin his public ministry. Toward the end of the last section we were already using words like 'struggle' and 'wrestling' with this in mind.

But to understand what is being said here, it is better if we do not take these accounts of the testing of Jesus in isolation. Perhaps we should try first of all to see the whole of Jesus' ministry as a *peirasmos*, or struggle, as a wrestling with opposition of various kinds, and then return to review this story of testing which is placed at the very beginning of his ministry. In doing this, we are obviously anticipating much of what is yet to be unfolded and thereby breaking the proposed sequence. On the other hand it can be argued that this is the best way into this story and that we may in fact need this kind of framework to hold things together. So readers who wish to follow the proposed sequence may pass over this 'interlude' to Chapter 4 and return to it later.

An Overview

The letter to the Hebrews says: 'Therefore he had to be made like his brethren in every respect ... For because he himself has suffered and been tempted/tested he is able to help those who are tempted (tested)' (2:17-18). 'For we have not a high priest who is unable to sympathise with our weakness, but one who in every respect has been tempted (tested) as we are, yet without sinning' (4:15). The approach proposed here should highlight his solidarity with us, that he is 'like us in all things,' that 'he learned obedience through what he suffered' (5:8).

To attempt to view the entire ministry of Jesus under the rubric of 'test' or 'trial' is in harmony with much of what we find in the gospels. In fact, Jesus himself uses this language to describe his ministry when he speaks of his disciples as 'those who have continued with me in my trials/tests' (Lk 22:28). References to 'testing' are also found in Mk 1:13, 8:11, 10:2, 12:15. What these 'trials' and 'tests' were becomes apparent from other passages in the gospels, many of them authentic words of Jesus.

It seems that Jesus spoke of both an accomplished victory over the forces of evil, achieved before he began his ministry, and an ongoing struggle, or *peirasmos*, with these forces of evil in daily life. His words often take the form of reassuring confidence spoken to his disciples who were themselves facing difficulties. Think for example of an obviously authentic saying like 'But no one can enter a strong man's house and plunder his goods, unless he first binds the strong man; then indeed he may plunder his house' (Mk 3:27; see Mt 12:29), or 'When a strong man, fully armed, guards his own palace his goods are in peace; but when one stronger than he assails him and overcomes him, he takes away his armour in which he trusted and divides his spoil' (Lk 11:21-22). Jesus intimates to them that he has wrestled with the 'strong man' as he calls him, that he has overcome and bound him, that he has ransacked his citadel. He presents this victory as the basis of his own power over evil and demons.

To the seventy disciples returning in joy from their mission, he says that he has seen Satan 'fall like lightning from heaven' (Lk 10:18). Jesus maintains that he has already overcome the basic opposition, that he will not waver in the face of evil, that he has made the fundamental choice to follow *Abba*'s will no matter what the cost. But the cost is real and it takes its toll. So while there is an accomplished victory, there is also an ongoing struggle in which he is trying to bring God to humankind and humankind to God. He must search for *Abba*'s will and future as they emerge out of everyday occurrences. He must wrestle with the possibilities that confront him. He must be on guard for the tester is always awaiting 'an opportune time' (Lk 4:13). He must set his face against easy solutions. Nor is this a purely internal struggle, for although the 'strong man' may be bound, the synoptics present the accounts of Jesus' exorcisms as struggles and duels fought with the evil one.

Indications – Family

There are many indications of this theme of ongoing struggle in the gospels. Let us take a rather random overview of such hints. At times the burden of Jesus' unique vision, the loneliness, the isolation of being set apart, the pain of misunderstanding become almost too much for him and they force a pained response from him. His family and his friends, it seems, do not understand him. In fact, they think he is out of his mind: 'They went out to seize him, for they said he is beside himself' (Mk 3:21). It is a hard thing to be misunderstood by your own, to be unable to explain yourself to those who are nearest and dearest to you, not even to your own mother. And Jesus cries out, 'A prophet is not without honour except in his own country and among his own kin, and in his own house' (Mk 6:4), no doubt reflecting on his own anguished experience.

Again, it seems he had to set his face against the current conventions of family life, even against family ties, if he were to be free to preach about *Abba*. Many of his sayings about relationships within family and clan must have given scandal in the closely knit society of that time. Individualism in the sense in which we understand it was unknown. Loyalty to one's family, one's friends, one's group was regarded as a sacred duty. Heretics, informers, renegades, and enemies were excluded, and it was a popular saying that 'You must love your neighbour and hate your enemy' (Mt 5:43).

For them, being sister or brother to some might necessitate hostility toward others. Jesus contradicts this saying that there are to be no outsiders or no enemies; all are neighbours. Sayings like these, found in Luke 6:27-36, must have been unbelievably shocking to Jesus' contemporaries and perhaps especially so to his extended family. This startling kind of non-exclusivity would disrupt everything and make life as people knew it unlivable. It would spell the end of family and group solidarity as they understood it. Jesus is aware of the disruptive consequences of all this:

> Do you think that I have come to give peace on earth? No, I tell you, but rather division; for henceforth in one house there will be five divided, three against two and two against three; they will be divided father against son and son against father, mother against daughter and daughter

against her mother, mother-in-law against her daughter-in-law and daughter-in-law against her mother-in-law (Lk 12:51-53).

(Compare with Micah 7:6 which deplores such a breakdown.)

Jesus himself left Nazareth. He no longer had 'a home,' no longer had 'a place on which to lay his head,' and in line with this experience he preached that disciples had to leave father and mother, put them in second place, 'hate them' as the gospel text (Lk 14:26) puts it. Disciples were even told to refuse to mourn their death, to refuse to bury them or offer sacrifice for a year (the supreme filial duty of a pious Jew), if the call of God's kingdom came upon them. They had to regard all those who accepted *Abba*'s call as their new family, as being closer to them than their own kith and kin, even their own mothers. 'Who is my mother and who are my brothers?' he asks (Mk 3:33), when he is told that his mother and his brothers are outside, and he goes on to say that those who sit listening to his preaching are his real family now. 'Looking around on those who sat about him he said: "Here are my mother and my brothers! Who ever does the will of God is my brother and sister, and mother"' (Mk 3:34-35). It is not simply the womb that bore him or the breasts he sucked that are blessed, but those who hear the word of God and keep it (Lk 11:27).

All this is very demanding, very difficult, and very painful. The path that he treads alone is far from easy but this is the path that he consistently takes.

Suffering

Again, the blinding clarity of his vision, the suffering involved in carrying it through, make him cry out spontaneously with fierce smouldering intensity and determination in words like 'I have come to cast fire on the earth and how I wish it were already kindled. I have a baptism to be baptised with and how constrained I am until it is accomplished.' (Lk 12:49-50) And yet the words of a deeply disappointed man come through in phrases like 'What an unbelieving and perverse generation! How long am I to be with you? How long am I to bear with you?' (Mk 9:19). There are fourteen extreme rebukes in the gospels about this evil, adulterous, peevish, and unfaithful generation, some of which reflect Jesus' own historical experience rather than that of

74

the community. Jesus does not mask his failure or his disillusionment. He wept over Jerusalem, was angry at the abuse of the Temple, was annoyed by the pettiness of the Pharisees, and pained by the myopia of his disciples.

The gospels give us a picture of Jesus as being constantly spied upon (they watched him to see if he would heal him on the Sabbath [Mk 3:2]), under suspicion, hounded from one place to another. Smart people tried to trick him in his words. 'And they sent to him some of the Pharisees and some of the Herodians to entrap him in his talk ... Is it lawful to pay tribute to Caesar or not?' (Mk 12:13-17). People are sent from the capital to test him in what he says: 'And Sadducees came to him, who say there is no resurrection: and they asked him a question' (Mk 12:18). Again they had objected, like spoilt and peevish children, to John's call to repentance because it was too demanding. Now equally they complain about Jesus' prodigal offer of salvation because it is too easy! (Mt 11:16-19; Lk 7:31-34). The best lack real conviction and when he preaches the word of God to them they look for free bread. The worst are 'full of passionate intensity' (Yeats) and reject both his message and himself.

Faced with the selfless and lovingly compassionate works of Jesus on behalf of the poor and the sick and the maimed, they explain it away by the diabolically perverse assertion that he is in league with Satan (Mk 3:22-27)! They are willing to opt for the absurdity of evil divided against itself, rather than admit that these actions of Jesus might point to the presence of a gracious God. Or again, they ask the biting small-village question, 'Where did this man get all this?' (Mk 6:2). Who does he think he is anyway? He is a nobody, they said. He is the carpenter or the son of the carpenter or perhaps the illegitimate son of Mary. We know the family and the background, how could such a one be anything? Anyway he is from up the road, across the hill, he is from Galilee, the back of beyond, we have his measure. With ironic understatement Mark says 'they took offence at him' (Mk 6:3).

Faced with such abuse, with such rejection, with so much misunderstanding, Jesus would have needed to have the unshakable confidence that there was someone somewhere who understood him, someone who would stand by him when all others misunderstood him, rejected him, or abandoned him. He needed this assurance if he were to remain dedicated to his mission. Jesus had precisely this trust and this confidence in *Abba* and it alone can explain the awesome compulsion, the dedication, the single-mindedness which drove him on even against such opposition. *Abba* knows. 'Yet I am not alone. The Father is always with me' (Jn 16:32).

And if we had been disciples of this Jesus who was being called in question and rejected by so many people, including our spiritual leaders, how would we have reacted? Would it have been enough to say '*Abba* knows'?

That, briefly, is something of what we mean by the ongoing test, the trial, the ordeal in the life of Jesus that would end only in the garden and in the abandonment on the cross. But the garden and the cross are the climax of a way of life characterised not only by joy and peace but also by ordeal and agony and real struggle.

The last petition of the *Abba* prayer, 'Protect us from the *peirasmos*, save us in the hour of trial and testing,' was doubtless prayed by Jesus himself out of the struggle of his own life before he taught others to do likewise.

Messiah?

Before leaving this section about the on-going test, we must consider one thing in particular which seemed to bring recurring anguish to Jesus. It seems to have been the source of constant testing for him, if we are to judge by the sharpness of his reaction to it. We are thinking here of the way in which many people seem to have tried to link him to current expectations of the Messiah.

The concept of Messiah was a multivalent one which, as we have seen, had been interpreted in a variety of ways by various groups during Israel's history. But given the social and political circumstances of the generation or so before the time of Jesus, most people tended to interpret it in a predominantly political fashion. Hope of a Messiah was running very high around the time of Jesus. We know that some people claimed to be the Messiah and they found a hearing and gathered a following. A prayer of the time asks that God's Messiah may come very soon.

Despite the many differences in ideology and strategy between the various movements and groups in the country regarding the coming of God's Messiah, all were convinced that it would involve a special calling and destiny for Israel. Jesus too was understood to be concerned with the final gathering of the new Israel and with calling the people to a new destiny. Some of the kingdom language he used sounded a familiar note, so he was open to misunderstanding. His mission, despite his best efforts to explain its distinctiveness, could be given the overtones of current Messianism. Many people did give that meaning to it and it seems that Jesus was plagued by precisely this misunderstanding of his message and ministry and had to set his face firmly against it. Still, it persisted.

Perhaps some of those who shared the Zealot vision were attracted by a selective hearing of what Jesus said and attached themselves to him for a time. We do know that at least one ex-Zealot, Simon the Canaanite (Lk 6:15), was numbered among the Twelve. The reputation for being a revolutionary dies hard even if your new leader is opposed to the way of violence. And Jesus was opposed to it. He spoke of loving enemies, of turning the other cheek, of not resisting evil-doers; he refused to be drawn into the debate about tribute to Caesar. All this shows that, despite the political implications of his message, he in no way identified with Zealots and their tactics.

Jesus in effect declares himself to be against any violent revolution. The stories he tells about the slow growth and patient expectation of the kingdom, and perhaps the warnings against 'false prophets,' may well have had the views of such extremists in mind. Yet, what he had to say, and the whole trend of his ministry, is much more revolutionary than anything proposed by Zealots or other revolutionaries. When Jesus cleansed the Temple he was no doubt acting in his role as prophet and pointing to the contradiction between theory and practice at the heart of Israel's religious life. But the Temple was a vast power complex and to question what took place there was bound to have political implications. People could see it as a Messianic action and be either delighted or suspicious, depending on how they viewed the Temple practice. It does seem to have brought a certain notoriety to Jesus and to have fanned the flame of Messianic expectations.

Popular opinion wanted to cast him in this role of political Messiah and Jesus seems to have suffered greatly from this frustrating misinterpretation of his work. Some of the disciples also seem to have cast him in this role. On the road to Emmaus, two of them say, 'We had been hoping that he was the man to liberate Israel' (Lk 24: 21). This seems to be a fair summary of the way in which some of his followers would have misunderstood his ministry. Again the question is asked, 'Will you at this time restore the kingdom of Israel?' (Acts 1:6). We should note also the amazing and explosive tension that comes across in all four gospels after the account of the multiplication of the loaves and fishes. It tells us that they wanted to take him by force and make him king, that is, anoint him Messiah.

He had to force the people to disperse and compel the disciples to get into the boat. These are strong words. It was clearly a moment of crisis, a test. The people were behind him and he could have gone the way of public political endeavour. But he held fast and set his face toward *Abba* and the mysterious future to which *Abba* was calling him. This meant that many of his followers turned away and those who remained were more confused than ever. It is suggested that this was a turning point in his ministry.

Jesus' extreme sensitivity toward this kind of misunderstanding comes across to us in his stunning rebuke to Simon Peter, 'Get behind me, Satan' (Mk 8:33). Peter had just answered Jesus' question to the disciples: 'Who do you say that I am?' by confessing, 'You are the Christ' (8:29). But when Jesus goes on to say that the Son of Man must suffer, be rejected, and killed, Peter rebukes him. This does not fit in with Peter's notions of a glorious Christ/Messiah. But Jesus rebuked Peter and said, 'Get behind me, Satan.' Any disciple who asks Jesus to play the role of a non-suffering glorious Messiah is 'testing' Jesus, is voicing a Satanic temptation. In line with this we should notice that in Mark's gospel it is the demons who hail Jesus as the (Messianic) Son of God (Mk 3:11, 5:7).

It is significant too that the synoptics never present Jesus himself as laying any claim to the title of Messiah or to any of its equivalents. At most he accepts it only when it is offered by others. Even then that acceptance is usually characterised by a certain reluctance and ambiguity or a corrective emphasis is added. The classic example of this ambiguity and reticence concerning the title of Messiah, is his reply to the high priest: 'I adjure you by the living God, tell us if you are the Christ, the Son of God'? Jesus said, 'You have said so' (Mt 26:63-64). In Mark's gospel he replies to Pilate's question, 'Are you the King of the Jews'?

(the Messiah) with the same phrase: 'You have said so' (Mk 15:2-5). In Luke he answers the Council's request, 'If you are the Christ tell us,' by saying, 'If I tell you, you will not believe and if I ask you, you will not answer.' To their further question, 'Are you the Son of God, then'? he replies again, 'You say that I am' (Lk 22:67-70).

It is difficult for us to hear these nuances because of pressure from a line in apologetics that ran: 'He claimed to be Messiah and proved that claim ...' However it does seem that although the community proclaimed Jesus Messiah after Easter, it also remembered the ambiguity of this title and the painful misunderstandings to which it exposed Jesus during his ministry. Finally, we must also remember that it was beneath the inscription 'King of the Jews' that Jesus died on the cross. His opponents actually succeeded in convincing the Romans that he was a political pretender to the kingship and they must have been able to point to some 'plausible' evidence for the charge. So far as the Romans were concerned, he was just another Messianic pretender to the crown, a rebel rejected by the Jews. So his opponents were finally able to confirm this misrepresentation of Jesus' message and work.

Clarification

It is important to realise that the foregoing does not in any way exclude the certainty that Jesus thought of himself as the one through whom God was acting to save. That this was the case will become obvious in the following chapters. What is being said now is simply that Jesus could not accept the popular connotations of the title of Messiah as applying to himself, yet the people tried to foist them on him. This was part of his pain. The popular conceptions of Messiah were, as he understood them, distortions of the true meaning of what he was saying and doing. So Jesus refuses to lay claim to such a title because it would distort what God wished to communicate through him. He will not delimit God's freedom and he must struggle to keep his disciples open always to the newness and the surprise of God. Dodd[6] puts it this way: We should ask not 'Did Jesus claim to be the Messiah?' but 'What kind of Messiah did he intend to be?'

The Temptation Story

Now that we have seen something of the pervasiveness of

this theme of *peirasmos* in the gospels, we can see more clearly what is compressed into the simple precision of the words 'one tempted/tested as we are in every respect.' We should also be in a better position to situate and understand the temptation or testing story (outlined in Mt 4:1-11 and Lk 4:1-13 and mentioned in the brief summary in Mk 1:12-13) where Jesus' constancy to *Abba*'s will is tested. The setting and the story recall the testing of Israel in the wilderness, but the testing continued daily in the land and Israel failed. She courted other gods; she hankered after novelty and sought proofs; she chose the past and refused God's future; she was selfish and preoccupied with immediate needs; she longed for world domination. Jesus bears within him the seeds of the new Israel. He too is to be tested. Will he stand firm?

All three interludes are concerned with one and the same thing, the temptation to avoid, to shrink from the implications of what he understood his mission and his vocation to be. They are tests aimed explicitly at his consciousness of sonship. In all these scenes he is called on to 'prove his sonship' by demonstrations of power rather than to let it unfold in quiet dedication, weakness, and hiddenness. So together they symbolise all that could obstruct him or divert him from following through the role he saw for himself in relation to Abba. They draw together in a dramatic way the nub of what we have seen as the on-going test in the ministry of Jesus.

Would he align himself with the 'other kingdom,' connive with the evil within people, play on their desires, harness this force to gain power and prestige for the self? Would he try to overcome the scandalous ambiguity, impotence, and ordinariness of his chosen ministry by vast dramatic gestures that would leave people in no doubt about who he was and what he was about? Would he try to wield the power of God in the face of Israel's enemies and bring the longed-for liberation? Would he force the hand of destiny and somehow galvanise God into acting as his people wanted him to act? Would he dazzle the people with miracles, satisfy their immediate needs, manipulate them by promising an absolute end to all suffering, conflict, and limitation? Jesus yielded to none of these temptations. He would allow God to be truly God and would 'worship and serve him only.' He had sufficiently hoped in this God not to try to force destiny, to look for proof, or 'test' God. He would live only by 'every word' that is uttered by this God.

The Other Way

This narrative gives us the core convictions that we will discover everywhere in the ministry of Jesus. Here we have the secret of his ministry. God, as Jesus understands him, is at the centre of all we hear him say or see him do. This God and his reign among his people is Jesus' burning concern. So he goes away from the wilderness, perhaps taking some of John the Baptiser's disciples with him (see Jn 1:37-42). Unlike John, the Essenes, and various ascetical movements in Israel, Jesus leaves the desert behind and goes back into the thick of life. He goes neither to Judea nor the Temple but to Galilee where the Diaspora influence was quite strong and the people reasonably open to new ideas.

There, this unknown workman from a small provincial village, untrained in the formal theology of the day (Jn 7:15, cf Mk 6:2) and uncertified by any rabbinic faculty, begins to preach an extraordinary new message and engage in a ministry which shocks and scandalises the best religious people of the time. Then, adding insult to injury, he insinuates that in all this he is acting as the prophet of God!

If we place him in the socio-religious context that we have seen so far we realise that the odds are stacked against him from the start. The question is not so much 'How will he succeed?' as 'How can he even begin?' We may find it difficult to think like this, cossetted as we are by the achievement of the New Testament communities and by the whole span of our tradition. And so we do not want to let go, to experience the pain, the agony, the heart searching, the uncertainty, the not knowing of Jesus's historical disciples. But we must let go if we are to take the path of discipleship.

As his ministry begins, the disciples do not know who Jesus really is. They cannot be sure how exactly he is to be related to God. It is at most a question. They do not know how things are going to turn out in the future. They do not know that he will be crucified and they certainly do not expect that he will be raised from the dead. In trying to take this path of discipleship we should try to think our way back into this mentality and keep asking: If I had been there and heard this or saw that, how would I have reacted?

4. THE MINISTRY BEGINS

Here the impossible union
of spheres of existence is actual.
T. S. Eliot

'Now after John was arrested, Jesus came into Galilee, preaching the gospel of God and saying, "The time is fulfilled, and the kingdom of God is at hand; repent and believe in the gospel"' (Mk 1:14-15). Thus Mark dramatically introduces the ministry of Jesus of Nazareth.

Bultmann captured Jesus' historical appearance superbly when he referred to him as 'The Proclaimer of the Kingdom/reign of God.' This is indeed who he is. We noted earlier that the kingdom of God is the central subject in Jesus' teaching and that the gospels are shot through with this theme. He proclaims the kingdom of God with unshakable conviction and provocative originality from the very beginning of his ministry. It seems to spring from the very core of his being and it determines the content of his message and the direction of his ministry right from the start. It is rooted in his own conviction that something new and final was happening in and through him. He claims to be the one who definitively announces and, in fact, ushers in the kingdom of God.

The Jewish world, as we saw, was tensely awaiting God's final salvific action or the final coming of his reign or kingdom. Into this Jewish world comes this enigmatic figure, Jesus of Nazareth, preaching the imminence and indeed the in-breaking of this kingdom or reign of God.

What did Jesus mean by this kingdom/reign of God? He never gives us a handy, once-and-for-all definition of the kingdom. So we are left with many questions. Did he differentiate his vision of the kingdom of God from that found in the books of the Bible, in ancient Jewish prayers, and in the writings of the apocalyptic sects? Why did he link it with new, strange words? How would his hearers, who were already familiar with the kingdom symbol, understand or misunderstand this preaching? How do we understand or misunderstand it today? What do we make of it? Do we simply glide over it, having ceased long since to notice its strangeness? Do we translate it as church or heaven or the next life, make our own sense of it and move on?

When we begin to think about it we may find ourselves facing great difficulties. For us, kingdom or reign may well recall 'old, unhappy, far-off things' and we begin to form images of a realm or territory ruled over by a king. We remember too that rule or reign connotes servitude for many people. It is difficult to shift from the literal level and everything we know about symbols and metaphors seems to abandon us.

When we turn to the vast body of literature on the subject of the kingdom of God we may still face difficulties. We are told that in the Bible the kingdom of God is 'not an office but a function. It is not a title but a deed.'[1] We may still be confused because this is far removed from our Western way of thinking. Even when we try to think of kingship rather than kingdom, reign rather than realm, it is not easy for us to appreciate the biblical view. However, the Bible insists that the kingship of God refers to the totality of God's activity in creating the world and his constant activity on behalf of his people.

> The primary and essential reference is to the sovereignty of God conceived in the most concrete possible manner, i.e. to his activity in ruling ... The kingdom of God is the power of God expressed in deeds; it is that which God does, wherein it becomes evident that he is king. It is not a place or a community ruled by God. It is quite concretely the activity of God as king.[2]

Or again, 'God's being and existence cannot be conceived apart from his rule ... the deity of God is his rule.' So to speak of the coming of the kingdom in the Bible means calling forth 'a vision of the unity of each being, the unity of all men and the whole world as flowing from the future ... God in his very being is the future of the world.'[3] Salvation is communion with him.

This vision is obviously not yet realised, for the present state of things is characterised by injustice and anguish, by hunger and death, by lack of freedom, disunity, and sin. And human beings certainly cannot bring it about unaided. So if God's reign is to be effective, it will involve overcoming all that opposes the lordship of God, it will involve liberation from all injustice and the establishment of God's own justice in the special sense of help and protection for the helpless, the weak, and the poor.

> To hope for the coming of the final reign of God is to hope for a future act of God which will be decisive for the salva-

tion of the people in a way in which his past acts on their behalf were not ... that final and decisive all-transforming act of God wherein he manifests himself as he visits and redeems his people.[4]

There is a clear connection between this understanding of the kingship of God and the 'Day of Yahweh' spoken of by the prophets, and ultimately 'the coming of the kingdom means the coming of God, the final self-revelation of God.'[5]

If these quotations have done nothing else they should have convinced us of the strangeness of the expression 'King-dom/reign of God' and made us realise how foreign it is to our mentality and thought processes. Yet we have heard it over and over again since childhood and for that very reason we need to spend much time and thought trying to appreciate what it really means. It is, after all, the root metaphor of Jesus of Nazareth.

Leaving aside now this search for definitions or descriptions of the reign of God, we will look at the work of one of the theologians just quoted. This should help us toward a renewed appreciation of this profoundly biblical expression. Norman Perrin devoted a great deal of time and energy to researching the whole question of the meaning of 'the Kingdom of God.' Toward the end of his life he began to think of it in a new way, as a symbol. At first this might appear to be an attempt to explain the less obscure through the more obscure, for our grasp of symbol may be at least as hazy as our understanding of kingdom. But let us try to listen to what he says.[6]

Perrin draws his definition of symbol from *Metaphor and Reality* by Philip Wheelwright,[7] who says, 'A symbol, in general, is a relatively stable and repeatable element of perceptual experience, standing for some larger meaning or set of meanings which cannot be given or not fully given, in perceptual experience itself.' So a symbol represents something other than itself; the way in which it represents it is what is vitally important. Symbol is evocative of and actually embodies much more than can be articulated rationally. (See chap. 9.)

This new definition and language may seem a little bewildering, so it may help if we first try to apply it to another symbol that is inseparable from kingdom and is at the very heart of Israel's consciousness, namely, covenant. It seems that the development of the covenant tradition pre-dated the tradition associated with the kingdom symbol. Indeed, much of what was compressed into the covenant symbol was later subsumed into the kingdom symbol.

In order to grasp something of the reality of covenant as symbol, we would need to trace its development in the Bible. Let us begin by picturing the following scene: A boy is playing in the long grass of open pasture land. He hears the sound of a great herd of goats and cattle being driven toward him. Two herdsmen walk out onto the open ground. They talk a lot but he cannot hear what they are saying. They gesticulate, point in various directions, slap hands frequently. Then they take a beast from each of their flocks, slaughter them, divide them in two, and pass between them. How strange! More gestures, more words. He moves closer and hears them saying: 'That part of the grazing is yours, that part is mine. May we be split apart like these animals if we dishonour this pledge.' The boy has never witnessed anything like this before and he decides to call this a covenant.

In this story something happens in 'perceptual experience' and it is named by using the word-image, covenant. It is used in a literal sense.

When we turn to the Bible we are told that the same kind of actions take place in Genesis 15. What is happening here? Scripture replies: 'There is a covenant here.' But we say: 'You need two partners for a covenant and only Abram and some animals are to be seen.' Then we are told that here covenant is being used to convey a deeper meaning, to disclose something of the mysterious relationship that exists between Abram and his God which 'cannot be given ... in perceptual experience.' The deep mystery here cannot be fully named and our only attempt to disclose its significance is to label it as covenant. So while there is a naming, there is also a regret about the inadequacy of the naming. It both is and is not a covenant.

In effect, the biblical authors are saying that we speak of it as *covenant* because it has *something* of the character of covenant. But it is not a covenant in the usual literal sense of the word. What we have discovered is new depth, a new potential, in covenant that somehow matches this new experience, that conveys the religious meaning of this experience, that discloses its larger meaning ... There is a many-to-many relationship involved. So covenant here is used evocatively as a symbol according to our definition.

In Deuteronomy we find covenant used again, but this time to interpret a very different set of experiences. Here it has a new and expanded meaning, for it is now used to interpret the experience of the whole people and to disclose the religious significance of what is happening to them. In effect, it is saying: We cannot describe the real significance of what is happening here in an exhaustive way because it is of ultimate significance, it has to do with mystery. We try to open up its religious significance by saying that God has covenanted himself to the entire people. So it is not a covenant in a literal sense. Nor is it a covenant in exactly the same sense as that of Abram's experience. The whole people are now involved in what is happening. However, this new experience is understood to be a further expression of the promises made to Abram. So the content, the meaning, the intent of covenant is both deeper and broader than they realised previously.

We find that it continues to be used after the people settle in the land of Israel as a way of interpreting their entire history and also their present experience. Thus, we begin to appreciate how symbols involve us in an ever-expanding and deepening many-to-many relationship. We may picture the relationship between the symbol and the religious meaning it communicates as two equal sets of ripples constantly spreading outwards.

Covenant is used in a new set of circumstances under the Davidic dynasty to speak of the everlasting throne of David and to warn that the covenant could break down. After the fall of the Northern Kingdom, it is still used with all its evocative power. But stranger still, even after the exile, when everything that had been understood to derive from the covenant relationship has been destroyed, we still hear people speaking of covenant. When there appears to be no justification whatsoever for speaking of covenant, the prophets use this powerful master-symbol to rally the hopes of the people. They *must* use it because it is the root symbol which contains and evokes their entire history and hopes as a people. If the prophets are to inspire hope in the hopeless they *must* use this symbol. Quite simply, if covenant ever lost all its evocative power for the people, Israel could no longer exist. For her very self-understanding is expressed in terms of covenant.

But how are the prophets to speak of covenant in a situation that seems to contradict the received meaning of the symbol? They revive the evocative and transforming power of covenant by re-telling the Exodus story. The exilic prophets say: 'Just as Yahweh brought us out of Egypt, so now he will bring us home.' They are re-handling the symbol of covenant in a creative and imaginative way by giving it a new future content. Yahweh will covenant himself to the people in a way that will far surpass the old covenant of Sinai. In this way they inspired hope in the people, 'when hope had grown grey hairs, hope had mourning on' (Hopkins) and made them realise that God was indeed 'Father and fondler of heart thou hast wrung' (Hopkins: *Wreck of the Deutschland*).[8]

Turning to the New Testament, we find that the covenant symbol continues to be used to speak of the *new* covenant of Jesus – in the Last Supper narratives and in John's farewell discourse. It is used to reveal the ultimate religious meaning of Jesus' ministry, death, and resurrection.

So we see how the symbol expands as it is used to reveal the religious meaning of very different historical experiences and how it must not be understood to refer to or interpret one series of events only. To attempt to do this is to freeze the symbol and make it refer only to the past. We must not 'read the symbol too sharply.'[9]

The example just given should have in some way contributed to clarifying this approach so we can return to what Perrin has to say about the kingdom as symbol. Among many Near Eastern peoples we find a myth about God's creating the world by over-coming and slaying a primeval monster and then renewing the fertility of this world each year. Perrin says that it is here that the roots of the kingdom-symbol are to be found.

The basic image is probably that of a walled city ruled over by a king, where disorder has been overcome, where people are safe and protected, and sustenance is provided. This is then taken up and used as a symbol 'to stand for what is not given ...,' namely, the activity of the gods (understood to be acting as kings) to overcome chaos, bring about creation, and renew the fertility of land and flocks.

Israel's understanding of *creatio ex nihilo*, and of God's providential involvement with his people is very different from that world-view, yet they too could use this symbol to celebrate

Yahweh's kingship as they understood it. This probably began to happen in the days of Israel's own monarchy.

So we find the constant refrain 'Yahweh has become King' in Psalms 47, 93, 96, 97, 98, 99, 145. Of course, characteristic modifications are introduced, leaving one in no doubt about the uniqueness of their God and his demands 'for justice and righteousness and equity.' This is the language of the covenant tradition, which scholars believe was worked out before being translated in terms of the new kingdom symbol. But we find both brought together in Psalms 99:6-7, 136, 145:10-14 and in Exodus. These passages recall the mighty acts by which the Lord has shown that he is king and that 'he shall reign forever and ever.'

For Perrin the symbol functions by evoking the story of God's continuous activity in creating the world and saving his people and the story 'is effective because it interprets the historical experience of the Jewish people in the world.'[10] To use this symbol in creed or song of praise was to evoke a whole complex of stories that told them who they were as a people. The real meaning of their lives was revealed to them in stories of what God had done and would continue to do for them as a people. But what would happen when the events of history seemed to contradict their belief that God was king? What could be said when the northern kingdom fell? Above all, what could one say in the face of the fall of the southern kingdom and the Babylonian exile?

As in the case of covenant, prophets arose who retold the story of what God had done in creation and history and explained that he had acted in recent history to pass judgment on their sinfulness, but that he was still their God. So they retell the Exodus story and apply it to their present experience. They have discovered new depth, new possibilities within the symbol. By using it in these drastically changed circumstances, they can challenge the people to conversion, they can thereby inspire vibrant new hope in a people on the edge of despair. They speak of an excitingly new act of God as king, on their behalf, whereby he will deliver them from captivity as surely as he had delivered their forefathers from Egypt. And so he did and the exiles came home. 'The Lord is among you as King, O Israel, never again shall you fear disaster' (Zeph 3:14-17).

But disaster struck again and again in the centuries that followed; in disturbed, anguished, straitened circumstances the apocalyptic seers use this kingdom symbol once more and evoke the ancient stories. But the ways in which they do so are very different.

The dualism and determinism that characterise these writings seem strange to us after reading the prophets. We wonder if they are really talking about hope. However, if we remember the intense suffering and oppression of these times, we will understand why the expansion of symbols no longer seems adequate to interpret history. These writers, who lived through such painful times, felt they could inspire hope in the people, could enable them to cope with the unbearable anguish of their experience, only by speaking of two mutually antagonistic forces, one good, the other evil. So the symbols no longer simply expand, they split (which is still a form of expansion): the kingdom of light and the kingdom of darkness – the present evil age and the blessed one to come. The faithful Jews will belong to the kingdom of light and, after the destruction of their enemies, they will live forever in the blessed age to come. So it was now no longer a matter of development *within* history, as in the prophetic literature, but of liberation *from* history. Their hope now is that God will act definitively on their behalf by destroying the kingdom of evil and delivering them permanently from all the evils of history.

Finally, we recall the Kaddish prayer for the establishment of the kingdom (quoted in chap. 2) which was used in the Jewish synagogues immediately before the time of Jesus. This meant that the whole community was regularly using this symbol in prayer and evoking the whole complex of stories associated with it. Because it was used by the whole community, the range of meaning and expectations concerning God's activity would have varied very considerably even from individual to individual.

In this world, at this time, when the people are looking forward in a particularly intense way to the coming of God's kingdom, to a final, eschatological act of God, Jesus begins to preach about the kingdom of God. Speculations about the form that God's kingdom would take, and the phenomenon that would accompany its arrival, were legion at that time. The kingdom was in a real sense an open symbol without any fixed content or meaning, so each hearer would supply his or her own content. Therefore all who spoke of the kingdom would have to clarify what it evoked for them, what exactly they meant by it, how they understood God's activity. Its concrete content and meaning would emerge from the message and activity of the preacher. Jesus is no exception to this.

The content Jesus gives to it, the vision it evokes for him, emerges from his message and activity as a whole. It becomes known only when we listen to his stories about how this king acts and when we understand that Jesus acts as he does because he is convinced that he is mirroring God's activity. But it is obvious that if he means something special by it, he would have to distinguish his concept of the kingdom from that found in the Bible, in the Jewish prayers, apocalyptic literature, and in current interpretations. In other words we would expect both continuity and discontinuity here. This is what we find.

Jesus carried on the process of ongoing re-interpretation that characterises the use of this symbol in the Old Testament, with the freshness of an original mind and a new spirit, with a brand new imagination. He took up the symbol of kingdom, which had evolved throughout the history of Israel, which had been used by prophets and priests and apocalyptic seers, and he re-molded it, re-created it, gave it a new content in the light of his own basic experience of God and his way of acting. He used this symbol to evoke all the old stories that were compressed into it but, through his unique handling of it, he evoked an entirely new set of relationships and suggested extravagantly new possibilities. So on the lips of Jesus, we hear a different, distinctive kind of language.

We have noticed already that he used the kingdom symbol in conjunction with words which had never or hardly ever been linked with it previously. For example, he regularly spoke of the kingdom as 'coming' and 'approaching' (Mt 12:28; Lk 17:20) and tells disciples to pray that 'it will come.' This is virtually without parallel. In fact, he uses a whole list of words in reference to the kingdom for which there is no known parallel.[11] Again he differs from both Judaism and the early church by using 'kingdom of God' to refer both to God's decisive saving activity in human history and the state secured for his people by this activity. Judaism spoke of the 'age to come' and the church spoke of 'the coming of the Lord Jesus.'

On this point we must also notice the differences between

the apocalyptic speculations of that time and Jesus' own approach. In contrast with the seers, Jesus is remarkably reserved and reticent. He uses parables and images to hint at what the kingdom means; they offer guided tours. Unlike them, he refuses to be drawn into speculation about 'when and where' and what signs would precede its coming. He offers no signs (Mk 8:11-12) and warns against thinking that the kingdom was 'coming with signs, to be observed'; nor will they say, 'Lo, here it is! or There! For behold, the kingdom of God is in the midst of you' (Lk 17:20-21). To think as others do, he says, is to believe that God's activity can be limited to one place or one set of meanings or one pattern of life. It is a mystery and Jesus invites his hearers to enter deeper and deeper into it and not think that it can be grasped once and for all. That is why Jesus speaks about the reign of God in symbol and metaphor, because the only adequate, non-distorting way of relating to mystery is through symbol (see chap. 9). Any other approach claims to know too much, it grasps, it diminishes, it destroys. The kingdom, for Jesus, is not a realm nor a concept or a programme – it is a symbol bearing the reality to which it refers, the activity of God as king. When he evokes this symbol or narrates the parables of its presence, the kingdom gains symbolic shape. People can be invited to 'enter' this symbol, experience its transforming power, inhabit the radical alternatives it proposes. In this way they begin to get a feel for new ways of perceiving reality, of imagining new possibilities, living new alternatives, because, through the power of symbol, they have been put in touch with God's activity in our world.

We notice one final characteristic of his use of kingdom of God sayings in this context. Apocalyptic sources tended to talk about the salvation and destiny of the whole nation or the whole group of righteous ones. John the Baptiser had emphasised instead the vital importance of individual conversion so that God might not punish the whole people. With Jesus too the emphasis shifts from the group to the individual, but then it moves back to the group again in a radically new way. So, while there is a deeply personal quality about his preaching of the kingdom/reign, its implications for the web of relationship in which people live is constantly stressed. It is always related, as we saw in the case of the parables and counter-proverbs, to the living experience of each person.

By introducing contrast and incongruity, Jesus challenged the accepted patterns of the individual's thought and action. It is only the multivalent language of symbol and metaphor and story which can disclose something of the reality of the kingdom. The kingdom/reign gains symbolic form in these stories when some critical change comes about through a startling but credible development. As the hearers struggle with paradox, with the overturning of certainties, with the discovery that they have been looking for the wrong thing in the wrong place, Jesus claims that the kingdom is drawing near, in fact, 'is in their midst,' that they are entering into it.

Again, we see its personal quality in a saying like 'If it is by the finger of God that I cast out demons, then the kingdom of God has come upon you' (Lk 11:20). He is claiming that this exorcism is a manifestation of the kingly activity of God in the experience of those present. This exorcism, the healing of this individual, evokes and makes present all they know about the God who heals and makes whole and they are challenged to respond to it. However, God's activity cannot simply be confined to this moment nor to the life of any individual as we shall see.

The similarity we have just noted between the preaching of Jesus and John should not mask the real difference between them noted earlier. Even if John did use the words the 'kingdom of God' as the summary in Mt 3:2 suggests (many scholars question this), this does not mean that Jesus repeated John's message. Even if John did use these words, the similarity exists at the verbal level only, not at the level of meaning or content. There is a fundamental and unbridgeable difference between Jesus and John. It is the most basic difference of all, a difference in their understanding of God and his activity among his people. In other words, it is their understanding of the kingdom/reign of God that is different, even if both use the same concept! The question then is: Is God truly the God John preaches, a God of judgment, or is he God as Jesus proclaimed him? First we must ask: How did Jesus proclaim the kingdom/reign of God? How did he tell the story of this king and his activity?

All that follows will attempt to answer this question but we may need, even at this stage, to be put in touch with the main themes of his preaching. A fruitful way of attempting to come into contact with the core of his message is to attend to his parables of the kingdom. If we try to listen again to the most striking of these parables, the parable of the prodigal (father or son?), we may begin to appreciate the kind of kingly rule of God that Jesus had in mind.

Of course it is very difficult for us really to hear this story. Our familiarity with it has robbed us of the possibility of its having a real impact on us. We know it only as a story about God and so do not hear it in the first instance as a story about an earthly father. Acknowledging this difficulty, let us now try to hear it at the literal level so that, through the urging of metaphor, we may be startled into a new realisation of who God really is. Once again we will have to strive to inhabit this story as the first hearers did. This is how Jesus told it to them:

There was a man who had two sons; and the younger of them said to his father, 'Father, give me the share of property that falls to me.' And he divided his living between them. Not many days later, the younger son gathered all he had and took his journey into a far country, and there he squandered his property in loose living. And when he had spent everything, a great famine arose in that country, and he began to be in want. So he went and joined himself to one of the citizens of that country, who sent him into his fields to feed swine. And he would gladly have fed on the pods that the swine ate; and no one gave him anything. But when he came to himself, he said, 'How many of my father's hired servants have bread enough and to spare, but I perish here with hunger! I will arise and go to my father, and I will say to him, 'Father, I have sinned against heaven and before you; I am no longer worthy to be called your son; treat me as one of your hired servants.' And he arose and came to his father. But while he was yet at a distance, his father saw him and had compassion, and ran and embraced him and kissed him. And the son said to him, 'Father, I have sinned against heaven and before you; I am no longer worthy to be called your son.' But the father said to his servants, 'Bring quickly the best robe, and put it on him; and put a ring on his hand, and shoes on his feet; and bring the fatted calf and kill it, and let us eat and make merry; for this my son was dead, and is alive again; he was lost, and is found.' And they began to make merry.

Now his elder son was in the field; and as he came and drew near to the house, he heard music and dancing. And he called one of the servants and asked what this meant. And he said to him, 'Your brother has come, and your father has killed the fatted calf, because he has received him safe and sound.' But he was angry and refused to go in. His father came out and entreated him, but he answered his father, 'Lo, these many years I have served you, and I never disobeyed your command; yet you never gave me a kid, that I might make merry with my friends. But when this son of yours came, who has devoured your living with harlots, you killed for him the fatted calf!' And he said to him, 'Son, you are always with me, and what is mine is yours. It was fitting to make merry and be glad, for this your brother was dead, and is alive; he was lost, and is found' (Lk 15: 11-32).

As soon as the story begins, the audience is asked to identify with the father of these two sons. These three characters (verifying 'the law of the three' found in stories and folkloric material) would evoke other stories about a father and two sons from the Bible, from story tradition, and from their own experience. Already their minds and imaginations move into inevitabilities. One son would be good, the other would be bad and as fathers they feel confident that they will know how to exercise judgment when the time comes.

A Jewish father could pass on his property by will or as a gift during his lifetime. Here instead the younger son takes the initiative and demands that the father divide his property while still alive. (Would Jesus' audience have heard this as a suggestion that the son is treating his father as if he were merely an obstacle to his youthful dreams, as if he were already dead?) Anyway, this father divides the property between his sons. This settlement gave the son a legal right of possession of the property divided in his favour but he could not dispose of it during his father's lifetime. The younger son here does in fact dispose of the property (v. 13) and hurries off across the threshold of home and homeland to sow his wild oats in the far country of the Diaspora. His actions so far would hardly have endeared him to those who had become his father by proxy through hearing this story. He has turned away from his father and his future in his father's house. His preoccupation is with himself and with the present. In the far country of his exile, after the mindless squandering of his wasteful days, he finds himself in dire straits.

The hearers of the story would be alert to all the implications of what is hinted at here. He is experiencing the depths of degradation, he does the work of a slave, he is in contact with unclean animals, he cannot practice his religion. (If he did not eat the food being given to the swine did he steal the food he ate?) No doubt those listening to this story would have argued that, since, effectively, he had turned himself into a gentile, he should be disowned by his father and declared legally dead. (Remember the action of the fathers in *Fiddler on the Roof* and *The Jazz Singer*?)

But this story goes on to say that 'he came to himself.' He takes a gamble and decides to put hunger and hardship behind him by returning to his father and asking for employment as a hired hand. His hope is that his father will still be prepared to meet him and that he will be able to coax him into allowing him to earn a living as a servant. He has his confession lines prepared. He knows he has done wrong. He feels guilty and is convinced that he must be punished and he expects that if the meeting takes place his father will harp on his sin and highlight his guilt and shame. They will become permanently institutionalised in the change of status from son to hired servant ('He was son and heir once, you know!')

The audience would not have been impressed by the motives proposed by this son for his return to the margins of his father's house. They are selfish and calculating. Indeed the hearers may well have been incensed to think that he should have the cheek to expect anything after all that he has done. Could the father dare to offer employment to one who is legally dead? This father, however, is very different. He is watching and waiting for the first signs of his son's return. He does not hold himself aloof and wait for the boy to come to the threshold of his circle of power and beg. In his fatherly longing, he cannot wait to be reunited with his son. So he does not stand on ceremony or pay any heed to rights. 'While he was yet at a distance ... his father ... had compassion and ran and embraced him and kissed him.'

The father has loved this boy unconditionally even in his exile but he knows that forgiveness cannot be forced on someone. It must be accepted as a gracious gift. So he is held in a father's arms and he is kissed with a father's kiss. The son stammers out his prepared self-accusation, his confession of guilt, but he never reaches the words 'Treat me as one of your servants.' The father will not let him speak these words. He cuts short his recital of the past. Astoundingly, he does not think within these categories at all. Indeed, everything he says and does is the very opposite of what was anticipated. He is thinking only of what he can do so that his boy will know that he is a son. How can he convince him that he is loved as a *son* and not because of what he did or did not do? So in addition to a father's embrace and kiss, he prodigally piles up symbol upon symbol of sonship. No one, least of all his son, is to be in any doubt about the reality of his sonship. He is given the best robe to show that he is held in the highest esteem, the ring bestows authority, the shoes emphasise that he is a free-born son and not a slave. Finally, the fatted calf is killed and he is brought across the threshold of homecoming to take the place of honour at the festal meal celebrated round the family table.

The father's love has cut through the awful circle of guilt and punishment, hatred and self-hatred, that human beings so frequently contruct for themselves and others and demand to see implemented. Love stands opposed to these destructive categories. The meeting between them makes visible, incarnates, the father's love. It is not that a new love comes into existence but the father's actions are the necessary expression of a love that has always been there and which alone makes this meeting possible. It is a genetic moment of transformation.

The son sees his father as he truly is for the first time and makes the overwhelming discovery that he has been loved even in his sin. The depth of the father's unconditional love is revealed and simultaneously the son becomes aware of the seriousness of his offence for the first time. It is not simply that he has been insolent or has broken conventions or commandments, but that he has turned away from this indescribably loving father. His awareness of his true state does not come from checklisting commandments or legal requirements. It is the direct consequence of experiencing compassionate love and gracious forgiveness. In that moment of transformation he knows with certainty that he is simultaneously far worse than he ever believed and far better than he ever imagined. He is changed from being a slave who calculates to being a son who for the first time can appreciate and rejoice in the pure gracious privileges of sonship. This transformation is so radical that it is like the lost being found and the dead coming back to life again.

The father wishes only that his child will have life and have it to the full. This author of life stands for life and is opposed to death in any form. He longs for home-comings and dreads exile. We are not told that the son said anything but this is not surprising. 'At such times we find ourselves silent and without adequate words because homecoming does not involve coming to know any new facts about the world but merely a changed perception.'[12]

His only possible response to such an experience of changed perception could not be translated into words. It must be incarnated in life. His response could only be one of pure joy, embodied in a life of transformed sonship lived toward the future in the secure space of the father's life-giving home.

If those who had taken on the father's role as the story unfolded were unhappy about what this son had done, how would they react to what is said about the father's initiative? The father that Jesus speaks about replaces the just demands of the law by a love that ignores the past, that does not judge or condemn but can only rejoice in a child's safe return home. How could they cope with the response of this prodigal father? Perhaps we may find the answer to this question in the other half of the story where we are told about the other brother.

The family feast is in session and everyone, servants and hired hands, but above all family members, are expected to come in and join in the festivities. The elder brother, who was in the field, hears the music and dancing and asks what it means. When the servant tells him, 'he was angry.'

There we have the answer to our question. He is resentful and angry. The hearers are angry. He refuses to go in. He will not cross the threshold and be party to this celebration. Sadly we are learning that joy is not the only response to graciousness. Then the prodigal father leaves the place of celebration, crosses the threshold, and goes out to this son too and entreats him. How can a father have a family reunion if one of his two sons refuses to take part in it?

This apparently loyal son, in his anger, searches for targets and names grievances. His complaints sound understandable, reasonable, and justified. He has kept the letter of the law, he has stayed close to his father, he has always done what his father wanted. But as we listen more closely we hear the voice of someone who is a victim of his past and his calculations. He knows better than his father how things should be. This son has done what he thinks his father should also have done: kill the younger boy off completely. We notice that he will not call him 'my brother' but refers to him contemptuously as 'this son of yours.' He was convinced that by doing the right things, by engaging in an ethic of achievement, he would merit the privileges of sonship and by his obedience have a claim against his father.

To someone with this kind of mentality, self-worth is determined by achievements, so another's misfortune or sin allows them to maintain his or her superiority by contrast. But such a basis for self-esteem, since it relies on externals, is constantly in danger; it is not secure or guaranteed. There develops a constant pathological need for reassurance. In their quest for reassurance such people may well end up asserting themselves, calculating, and begrudging others their good fortune. This is how the elder son reacts. He is locked into a small world of his own making and is preoccupied with himself. He does not know what a father is or what love means and so he cannot appreciate that being a son is a pure gift. He does not realise that he has a father who has two sons and that both of them are equally sons to him, simply because they are sons and not because of what they achieve. This is what the father now tries to communicate to him.

There is no condemnation for him either. The father speaks in warm affectionate tones, 'My dear child,' and goes on to reassure him by acknowledging the real situation that exists between them: 'You are always with me and all that is mine is yours.' This is how things really are. Yet what this son needs is not to have the facts of the situation set out, but a radical shift in perception so that he can share in his father's vision, enter into his parabolic world. Can he be brought to realise that what he seeks to achieve by grasping must be lovingly accepted, for all that and infinitely more besides is already given? Will he come to realise that his father's love for him is in no way diminished because he loves his other son equally? This is the shift called for, the threshold to be crossed. The father can only invite the son to accept the full implications of this with a brother's heart. The one he had scornfully referred to as 'this son of yours' is now referred to by his father as 'this your brother.' How can he say that he has a father without acknowledging each child of that father? Will he not recognise and respond to his brother as brother?

In the final verse (32) the father offers the older son the same motive for making merry as he had offered previously in verse 24. We are left wondering whether this second half of the story may yet end with the words found at the end of the first half which alone can fully gladden this father's heart: 'And they began to make merry.'

Having listened to this story at the literal level and having tried to guess the reaction of the hearers, we must now listen to it as an extended metaphor about the kingdom/reign of God. Once again we must try to allow ourselves to be jolted into an appreciation of the God Jesus proclaims through the power of this metaphor and the vividness of its disclosure of God's care for his child-ren. This disclosure will concern us throughout the following pages.

Here we simply note that it confronts us in a dramatic way with the major themes of Jesus' preaching that we will hear over and over again. His proclamation and ministry are about a God who is an utterly gracious and compassionate father. So while it does violence to the parable as parable, we might schematise the core themes of Jesus' preaching:

1. The prevenient, gracious, and forgiving love of God as *Abba* is offered as pure gift to all. This is good news for all, but especially for those who are classed as 'the poor and the sinners.'

2. The transforming revelation of *Abba's* love is mediated through a personal meeting with Jesus and the hearers realise that outcasts are really children and can say *Abba*.

3. Repentance is joy and a new life as a child of *Abba* begins and grows out of thankfulness for this experience.

Jesus' preaching is always concerned with these themes. We observe them refracted through all that he says and does. If we are to judge from his use of language in describing the kingdom/reign of God active in life, Jesus' own deepest foundational exper-ience of *Abba* must have been an overwhelming experience of being loved and being heard. He constantly speaks of the absolute graciousness of God and of his own total, yet gracious, dependence on this father. If we pay attention to the images and metaphors he uses in the parables to describe the inexhaustible bountifulness, the superabundance of God's goodness and mercy, we come into contact with this experience. *Abba* is in love with him and he is in love with *Abba*. And because Jesus appreciates *Abba*'s graciousness and gives thanks for his own absolute dependence in this way, we can understand something of the wonder of Jesus himself, his enthusiasm and his passionate commitment to doing the will of *Abba*. In other words, what he lived and preached was his own experience of God as *Abba* – Jesus spoke out of the fullness of the heart.

He is enthralled by the love and graciousness of God but is convinced that *Abba* is passionately in love with *all* his children. Jesus is forever struggling to communicate this insight to those around him. He is trying to implant a new imagination in his hearers – if only these women and men could catch a glimpse of this mystery! (To change the imagination is to achieve a most radical change.) If only they could be brought face to face with it, even for a moment, all would be achieved! As he sees it, if they caught even a glimmer of it, they could not but be overwhelmed by the sheer, prodigal generosity of the father's love.

In the parables we can see Jesus struggling to find the most adequate, the most satisfactory, the most impact-filled image to reveal the mystery that he calls by the familiar name of *Abba*. 'How shall I describe the kingdom of God, to what shall I liken it?' He is like someone lost for words in the presence of wonder. And despite the incredible power of the images he uses, he is never satisfied with any of them and he begins to search again, for each image can suggest only one facet of this profound mystery. God, he says, is like a dotingly prodigal father; he is like a foolish shepherd who risks all to save one, or a foolish housewife who, with amazing single-mindedness, spends her time searching for what others regard as worthless and then spends the forty worths of it celebrating when she has found it, or the employer who repays workers according to calculations based not on what they deserve, but on his own prodigal generosity. All these succeed in getting across to us the overwhelming surprise, the ecstatic joy of encountering the absolute prodigality of *Abba*'s love and mercy for humankind. Surely, this is *good* news. His primary concern always, as we shall see, is to proclaim that the coming of the kingdom is about the revelation of God's love and graciousness and compassion to all.

Here Jesus is to be distinguished from all those we have seen so far, even John. It is necessary to keep this in mind lest we think that 'the judgment' preaching of John translates the 'kingdom' of Jesus. Nothing could be further from the truth. For John, what was to come was the judgment of God and some might perhaps be saved. The preaching of Jesus, in contrast, is primarily about God's love and compassion for all. Here the stress is on the sovereignty of God's love. This is to be a reign characterised by all-embracing compassion. By contrast, Jesus' predecessors and contemporaries fail to take account of God's all-inclusive compassion. 'The Law and the prophets were until John; since then the good news of the kingdom is preached and everyone enters it violently' (Lk 16:16). Jesus acts in the name of a king who is utterly gracious in his way of acting and he speaks in the name of a father who is infinitely compassionate.

Yet some will not accept the reign of a God who can only be compassionate or the love of a father who can only forgive and who pleads with his children for a return of love. His love and compassion cannot be forced upon them. They are free, they must 'come to themselves.' If they do not respond positively, then they are choosing not to be one with this father-king who passionately desires to have all his children with him and with each other. To take this negative option means that they, and not this father, are passing judgment on themselves.

This prospect terrifies Jesus, so he sets out to convince them that the final prodigal kingly act of this compassionate father to save all his children is happening *now*. The kingdom of God is becoming present, the offer of unconditional love is being communicated now and must be accepted *now*. He declares that the shift of aeons is taking place, that the fullness of time has come, God's kingdom, his reign, is taking definitive shape now. It is upon you, it is among you, in the midst of you as a reign of clemency, compassion, and reconciliation that can finally heal the rupture between people and God. It is happening now, it must be responded to now. It is this conviction that gives to his preaching its note of fierce urgency and directness. Now, it must be now, only at this moment. Each moment is precious and vital, live every moment to the full, wring every possibility from it.

For God's sake always be ready since no one knows the day or the hour. Keep wide awake, proclaim it to everyone; don't take time off to chat to people on the road. 'Let the dead bury their own dead.' The kingdom is coming at an hour you do not expect. It can sneak up on you like a thief in the night and come as suddenly as labour pains on a woman. Stay alert. Be ready. Respond.

None of this is said to frighten or threaten people. Far from it. Jesus is alerting people to what is happening. He is saying that today, now, this moment is the privileged time of merciful salvation. God, he claims, is not to be thought of as remote, transcendent or waiting 'beyond,' nor as stern judge or wrathful punisher. Rather in his chosen metaphors, he is the father-king of all, who is very near, is always present and is coming now. Abba is making himself present now as kingly saviour. He is graciously active. He is transforming the human situation. No wonder then that he urgently calls on people to respond to this stupendous invitation and allow it to invert their values, change their lives, and then live the difference that it makes. He asks them to take a gamble, risk everything. Their real life hangs in balance. It is really a matter of life and death. Something staggeringly new and exciting is taking place. The reign of *Abba* is dawning. God's future is penetrating the present.

These are extraordinary claims. 'What does it really mean?' his contemporaries would have asked. What basis is there for it? Is it too good to be true? Could God be so completely different from all I have ever believed him to be? Am I to accept that others have misunderstood him and that Jesus' revolutionary way of speaking about him is right? Can I believe something so different? Is it all an illusion? What am I to believe?

5. PREACHING GOOD NEWS

God must be allowed to surprise us.
Patrick Kavanagh

Luke tells us that Jesus came to Nazareth, where he had been brought up, and went into the synagogue, as was his custom, on the Sabbath day. And he stood up to read, and there was given to him the book of the prophet Isaiah. He opened the book and found the place where it was written:

The Spirit of the Lord is upon me, because he has anointed me to preach good news to the poor. He has sent me to proclaim release to the captives and recovering of sight to the blind, to set at liberty those who are oppressed, to proclaim the acceptable year of the Lord. And he closed the book and gave it back to the attendant, and sat down; and the eyes of all in the synagogue were fixed on him. And he began to say to them, 'Today this Scripture has been fulfilled in your hearing' (Lk 4:16-21).

The text from Isaiah 61:1-2 goes on 'and the day of vengeance of our God' – significantly this is not included in Luke. What is included is Jesus' programme, his life's project. He is going to proclaim the acceptable year, the jubilee year of the Lord's favour. In Israel every fiftieth year was a jubilee (Lev 25) when all debts were cancelled, slaves were set free, and a new social order was introduced. Jesus is going to extend this to all people, especially the poor and the oppressed, and it will last far beyond the dawn of the next new year. All debts will be cancelled and all bonds broken by the father-king. Jesus is being sent to 'evangelise' the poor (as the Greek text has it), to bring them the good news that will set them free from slavery. He is going to bring tidings of a new event that is so hopeful and encouraging that it will make all of them glad and happy. It will speak of the reversal of their present situation, of new freedom, of longed-for liberation. It will truly be *good* news.

This concentration is also present in the reply to John's disciples. And he answered them:

Go and tell John what you have seen and heard: The blind receive their sight, the lame walk, lepers are cleansed, and the deaf hear, the dead are raised up, the poor have good news preached to them. And blessed is he who takes no offence at me (Lk 7:22-23).

Again we find the same basic message in the reversals that will make people happy or blessed:

And he lifted up his eyes on the disciples, and said: 'Blessed are you poor, for yours is the kingdom of God. Blessed are you that hunger now, for you shall be satisfied. Blessed are you that weep now, for you shall laugh. Blessed are you when men hate you, and when they exclude you and revile you, and cast out your name as evil, on account of the Son of Man! Rejoice in that day, and leap for joy, for behold, your reward is great in heaven; for so their fathers did to the prophets (Lk 6:20-22).

Jesus sets out to proclaim the father's kingly rule as good news in word and action. He does this because he knows that God is a compassionate father whose heart goes out to his children and that he has compassion for all of them. That is *the* characteristic of Jesus' message and ministry. Notice how often the phrases 'compassion,' 'suffering along with,' 'being moved,' 'reaching out' occur in the gospels to describe Jesus' reaction to people or to describe a reaction of key characters in the stories he tells.

The root meaning of compassion (*rahimin*) in the Bible is tender, vulnerable love. It speaks of the visceral attachment of parent and child or sister and brother or the tender response of those who feel for and with another, whose hearts go out, who are moved in the depth of their being. In the Old Testament, Yahweh is said to turn toward his creatures in this way. The gospels tell us that Jesus is 'moved with pity' for a leper (Mk 1:41), that 'He saw a great throng and he had compassion on them' (Mk 6:34), and 'I have compassion on the crowd because they have nothing to eat' (Mk 8:2).

He enters into the fears and the pain, the tears and the worries and the anxieties of people in order to transform them. 'Do not fear, only believe' (Mk 5:36), 'Why do you make a tumult and weep?' (Mk 5:39), 'Take heart, it is I, have no fear' (Mk 6:50). This phrase 'Do not be anxious' recurs (Mt 6:25-33).

He responds to infirmity and sickness in the same way: 'He

had compassion on them and healed their sick' (Mt 14:14). When he meets the widow of Naim on her way to bury her son he is moved and enters into her grief, and 'he had compassion on her' and said to her 'Do not weep' (Lk 7:13). Again, in the context of grief at another death we are told: 'When Jesus saw her weeping, and the Jews who came with her also weeping, he was deeply moved in spirit and troubled (these are equivalent to the root meaning of what we translate as 'compassion') ... and Jesus wept. So the Jews said, "See how he loved him"' (Jn 11:33-36).

In his stories, the Samaritan 'when he saw him ... he had compassion' (Lk 10:33), the king 'has compassion' but the unmerciful servant has none (Mt 18:23-25). Similarly, Jesus is moved to compassion and reaches out to and touches the untouchables. He touches the lepers and the beggars and the blind, he grasps the hands of the palsied and the crippled and the insane. He draws all into himself because he is compassionate as his Father is compassionate.

Perhaps we too can assent to this as an ideal that we might some day follow. But Jesus goes further still out of compassion and here we may find it difficult to follow him. He brings good news to 'the poor and the sinners,' with all that it implied in the circumstances of that time and that place.

What did it imply? What did it mean? Who are the 'poor and the sinners' in whose company Jesus is found and whose friend he is said to be? It is important to try to tease out these questions because of the significance of this evangelisation for Jesus himself and therefore for us, his disciples.

In his reply to John we are told that 'the blind see, the lame walk ... the dead are raised up.' What is happening now involves a total transformation, a total reversal. As we listen we would expect that the 'raising of the dead' would be the climax, that it should be *the* sign of the kingdom, but no, in Semitic sentence structure the emphasis is placed on the last clause and so the climax is 'the poor have good news preached to them' (Mt 11:5). This is what is singled out.

For Jesus this is *the* sign that God as kingly saviour is active here, not only in healings or exorcisms or miracles but above all in the evangelisation of the poor. Nor is his reply simply a cataloguing of miracles. It is the ecstatic joyful cry of someone who knows with absolute certainty that the reign of God is active already. He knows that it is active because the power of God is now realising the signs of the times of salvation prophesied by Isaiah. Above all, then, God's presence as kingly saviour is manifesting itself in and through Jesus' preaching of good news to the poor.

But who are the poor? It is difficult for us to appreciate what this term means in the New Testament world. We have inherited a tradition that has maintained confusion in people's minds about the real identity of the poor. This was accomplished mainly by playing off Matthew's 'the poor in spirit' against Luke's 'the poor' (without qualification) so as to serve the interests of those who were not poor. So it has even been said that people may be as rich as kings provided they are 'poor in spirit'! Others stressed that 'the poor' were those who did not appreciate the 'things of God.' Indeed, those who experienced some of the problems that affluence brings were said to be the 'real poor'!

Such statements strive to make the one word 'poor' refer to both the poor and those who have made them poor, the wealthy. This is non-sense that ensures that we will once again evade the challenge offered by the Bible in the name of the poor, and it oppresses the poor to the point of depriving them of their very last possession, their name. Given this 'tradition,' if we are to recognise the poor in the Bible (or in our world) we must think first of all of real, material poverty, of the destitute.

In the Old Testament 'the poor' is part of the massive vocabulary used to describe oppression. It refers especially to those who are economically deprived, those without health or wealth or social status because they are victims of injustice or oppression. The word most commonly used to speak of the poor is *ani.* The root meaning of it is to be bent over, to be pushed to the ground, that is, to be humiliated. God is said to be on the side of such people. He liberated his people from slavery and oppression in Egypt when they were afflicted. Yahweh is 'father of the fatherless and protector of widows ... he gives the desolate a home to dwell in; he leads out prisoners to prosperity' (Ps 68:5-6). This people, who had themselves been liberated, must never pervert justice in dealing with resident aliens or orphans or widows (Deut 24). His prophets fulminate against injustice and proclaim God's special care for the poor (Amos 2:6-7; Job 24:2-12).

After the Exile 'the poor,' while retaining these roots, sometimes develops a more explicitly religious or spiritual connotation and refers to those who trust entirely in God for protection and deliverance (the *anawim*).

In the New Testament 'the poor' (*ptokos*) reverts to its original meaning and refers to those who lacked what was necessary to make life human. It renews the emphasis on 'the bent over,' the 'heavily burdened,' the victims of 'man's inhumanity to man.' The 'poor' included widows and orphans, farm labourers and those without a trade, the un-employed and the unemployable, beggars and the mentally disturbed. These unfortunates were unable to support themselves, were at the mercy of others, and were not treated as persons but as 'objects of pity' or 'cold charity' or 'loved for God's sake,' not their own. They felt shamed and humiliated, deprived of their self-esteem. They were the marginalised, the pariahs of that society. We come across partial lists of them in the gospels: 'the poor and maimed and blind and lame' (Lk 14:21); they are the oppressed, the broken-hearted, the simple-minded, those on the edge of despair, the lonely and lost, the victims of the dominant. They were ostracised, marginalised, were excluded from the socio-religious communities of that day. How could this come about?

We saw already something of the structuring of that society and the preoccupations of key groups within it. It is necessary now to look at the consequences of such a structuring for the masses of the people if we are to understand what the gospels mean by 'the poor and sinners' or perhaps more accurately 'the poor who are sinners.' It is fair to say that the Sadducees, the Pharisees, Essenes, and the Zealots, despite all the obvious differences among them, all share a sectarian mentality. The conviction that this group, these people, this community are doing things the right way and that the others are wrong or misguided is a presumption common to all of them. In this view, God loves those who control the Temple and offer sacrifice more than those who do not; God loves those who know and obey the Law, pray frequently, fast regularly, tithe their possessions, live carefully, avoid contact with sinners, more than those who do not; God loves those who have this body of truth and knowledge, belong to this community, take part in these rituals, shun outsiders, are preparing for the end, more than those who do not; God loves those who burn with zeal for his law and his land, who hate infidels and foreigners, who wish to establish a theocracy and impose God's law on everyone, who long for the holy war between the children of light and the children of darkness, more than those who cannot and do not.

All of these programmes are saying: If you belong to this group, if you do this rather than that, if you have this special knowledge, these traditions, then you are more important, you are closer to God, more loved by him than those who do not. So God loves the Jews more than he loves the pagans, he loves one group of Jews more than the others, he loves those who obey the details of the Law more than those who do not, he loves the educated more than the illiterate, those who are ethically good more than those who are not, those who pray more than those 'who will not go away and cannot pray' (*Eliot*).[2]

So we have a religiously-sanctioned rigid division between one or other privileged group and the others, especially 'the rabble,' 'the crowd' (Jn 7:49) who do not belong and who do not have these privileges. And what is to become of all those 'who do not belong.' 'the others,' 'the rest'? The answer is very simple: If they change their lives completely and become like those 'who do,' those who 'belong,' then God will love them too! Until such time as this happens (and it is highly unlikely) they can be written off as non-persons whose ignorance and misfortune serve only to confirm the rightness or righteousness of those who were not numbered among 'the poor and the sinners.' So we see that 'the poor and the sinners' is a wide category and embraces, first and foremost, the sociologically poor (and must always be firmly anchored there). But, by way of extension, it could include those who were uneducated in religious affairs or whose way of life was thought to make them unclean or dishonest or immoral. As distinct from the 'authorities or the Pharisees,' we hear them referred to as 'this crowd who do not know the Law, who are damned' (Jn 7:48-49).

In that religious society the illiterate, those who had to struggle for subsistence, those who had not been schooled in the Law, could not avoid breaking some of the many laws and customs and were therefore *presumed* to be sinful. Tax collectors, although they were financially secure, belonged because it was taken for granted that they were well off because they had dishonestly and sinfully taken more than their due share. Prostitutes might not be economically destitute but they were 'outcasts' because they promoted sinfulness and were shunned by the respectable people. Even shepherds were classed as immoral because it was presumed that they would range too widely with their flocks and would swap weak for strong lambs or kids!

We need to clarify further something that is implied in all of this, namely the assumption that 'the poor' are sinners. Sometimes we work with a rather narrow understanding of sin as 'any thought, word, deed or omission...,' as being about the state of the soul. The people of Jesus' time did not understand sin in this private, internal way. 'As he passed by he saw a man blind from birth and his disciples asked him, "Rabbi, who sinned, this man or his parents, that he was born blind?"' (Jn 9:1-2). The presumption here is that there is an intrinsic connection between sin and being blind, that the blind man carries in his body the marks of sin, that his blindness means that he is marked out by God as a sinner. This conviction about the link between sin and one's way of life applied in many ways to many situations. It was thought that a spirit, not of God, but an evil spirit, could take possession of people and manifest its presence in all sorts of ways. The people might be deaf or dumb (Mk 9:17-25) or prone to convulsions (Mk 1:26) or they might possess a 'spirit of infirmity' (Lk 13:11). Thus it was assumed that people are handicapped or have to beg for a living because of their sinfulness. And a sinner is one who is cut off from God. To be cut off from God is to be cut off from the community.

So sin is not a purely internal thing. Its presence will show itself in terms of health, wealth, status, prestige, and social integration. If you were sick or handicapped, poor or oppressed, lacked public esteem or were an outcast, then you were a sinner. If you were a sinner it was because ... Obviously this is a vicious circle. Those who are not like the]righteous' people are sinners because sinners are not like the 'righteous' people!

Within this system it was theoretically but not practically possible for some of 'the poor and the sinners' to alter and become like the respected people. An individual tax collector might go through the necessary procedures; perhaps someone whose lot was improving might try to study the Law ... perhaps.

But what about the 'rest of the rest,' the untouchables, the forgettables, the non-persons, the oppressed, the marginalised, the broken, 'the sat-upon, the spat-upon, the ratted-on' people?

They were kept in their wretched condition by the very structures of this religious system. They were necessary to it, for they carried its pain so that the few might carry its glory. The poor were fated to be like that, the respected people said, and the poor accepted this fatalistically. They could not change within this system nor could they change the system itself. It could only continue to work as it did, to the benefit of the elite, if it kept the poor from changing. The system is based on the calculus, If X then Y; If I do this, that will follow; if I behave in this way, God will be pleased; if I do these things, God will love me. Such a value system, such an approach to salvation and merit, breeds massive guilt and fear and hopelessness in those who cannot work the system or benefit from it. These are 'the poor' who stand hapless and hopeless before the social, political, or religious power structures.

Of course, it is not seen as a 'system' but as the way God really wanted things to be. The learned theologians and holiness teachers of that system sat in judgment on the poor and declared them unfit for salvation and at the same time continued to heap legal burdens on them that broke their spirits and their hopes (Lk 11:46; see Mt 23). So 'they labour and are heavy laden' (Mt 11:28). They were being written off now and forever. Because they were incapable of X, Y could not follow. They were incapable of coming close to God and so they could not be children of God. The effects of sin were obvious in their lives so, in the name of God, they must be cut off from God. It is not surprising that they were without hope and steeped in despair. They had ceased to expect anything from themselves, from others, or from God.

'The poor' are always those who, in their way of life and in their very selves, carry the wounds inflicted by political or religious systems. They are exploited, dehumanised, scandalously oppressed as non-persons, degraded as worthless. Jesus cannot canonise their poverty because it is in fact an expression of sin; it is the hand of death laid on them through the oppression and injustice of other people. Rather he protests against it because he sees it as incompatible with the kingdom of justice and love. So he declares the poor to be blessed because his Father's kingdom will put an end to all this evil that has congealed into structures and systems. The religious and moral system that Jesus opposes is not characterised by compassion or forgiveness. Those who are not compassionate do not experience the pain of others. Those who do not forgive, condemn people to eternal failure. This confers enormous power on those who are not compassionate and do not forgive. They are in control. Consequently, to be compassionate, to offer forgiveness in this system, is to shake it to its very foundations. To claim to do so in the name of God is to blaspheme.

Yet within this system, Jesus speaks and acts in the name of a king who is utterly compassionate, who does not make distinctions or exact vengeance. He acts in the name of a Father who loves all his children equally, without exception. So he calls all to himself (Mt 11:28ff) for he knows what the theologians and religious leaders have forgotten, that those whom they classify as 'the poor and the sinners' are truly loved by God as God. *Abba* is not sectarian, he is not exclusive, he does not court favourites to him, there are no outsiders.

Jesus proclaims a revolutionary message by insisting that the system which condemned the poor, the little ones, the sinners was being overturned. God's love and compassion and care enfolds and suffuses all. He proclaims that each one of these 'beggars and sinners' who are regarded as being cut off from God eternally are all cherished by him. He is not like the God of the Scribes and Pharisees, the Essenes or the Zealots – not even the God proclaimed by John. He is the Father of tender compassion.

All are loved by this father-king 'who makes his rain fall and his sun shine on the just and the unjust.' This is the creator God who can only love his creatures. No group can assert itself over against others because of its culture or virtue or insight or prayer or piety. The humanity of all is at risk because of their estrangement from the love of *Abba*, which alone enriches and which so passionately pursues their enrichment through love.

This message about this kind of God is 'good news to the poor.' Such a message alone can make them glad, for it makes contact with their one remaining hope: The poor feel so wretched and hopeless, so humiliated, so bereft of human help or hope that their only hope is to throw themselves completely on God for help. Thus they may 'come to themselves'; they may understand their true condition before God. They may be so empty of self that there is space for God in their lives. They could be surprised by joy, overwhelmed by mercy. But they are so aware of their 'sinfulness' (it is screamed at them every moment by the structures of this society), of their need for forgiveness, that even this final stage of hope seems futile. If God is as the spiritual leaders say he is, if he expects them to first change their lives before he forgives them, then what is the point of continuing to hope? Of themselves alone they cannot rise up, bearing the whole weight of this system, and transform it and themselves.

But suppose God is not as they have been taught, suppose he is utterly gracious and merciful, suppose he does not wait for them to repent but takes the initiative and enables them to repent by drawing on his love? Such a message of pure graciousness would make contact with the only hope they could have. And this is precisely what Jesus teaches. God, he says, is a gracious God of justice and love and compassion. He wills to put right all that is not right; he is infinite love and wishes to draw all humanity to himself through tender compassion and forgiveness. No one is excluded.

In his preaching to the 'poor and the sinners,' Jesus reverses the 'If X, then Y' calculus completely. His consistent approach is: *Show* them they are loved unconditionally, that the prodigal Father loves all, reaches out to all in forgiveness, passionately longs to reinstate them as his children, and then they will repent. They will be so overwhelmed by this new insight into the Father's boundless love and their own sinfulness that they will realise that they are simultaneously worse than they ever believed and better than they ever imagined. They will be so empowered by this new vision that their lives will be transformed. 'Y, therefore X.' The world of his contemporaries is turned upside down. Jesus scandalously offered the Father's forgiveness and salvation to sinners before they repented, because he was convinced that, face to face with such graciousness, people couldn't but repent. If they would cease seeing God as an implacable task-master and realise that he is Abba, all would be different. This Father is not standing apart, sternly awaiting their repentance, but is on their side, is most intensively active within their lives, and by his own love is enabling them to respond to his love of them. This is how he reigns.

But there is nothing automatic about this, nor are we to imagine that all poor persons responded instantly to what Jesus preached. In itself, poverty is no guarantee of openness to God or neighbour. It can warp hearts, deaden sensibilities, distort outlooks, kill humanity, breed resentment and hatred, just as wealth can. But we can see how such a message would have an extraordinary appeal to many of 'the poor.' When their personal distress and their absolute need for forgiveness combine with Jesus' indifference to the sins of the past, it makes them fit hearers of Jesus' proclamation. They can hear it as good news. 'God must be allowed to surprise us'.[3] They can appreciate and understand Jesus' scandalous message that if God is the kingly Father of all, then his care is directed to all (and all really means all): the 'poor and the sinners,' The scribes and the Pharisees, the Jews and the gentiles. The lost sheep is loved by this shepherd-king precisely because it is lost, but he cares for the ninety-nine no less.

Because the poor are poor, they are blessed and the kingdom is theirs, not because they deserve it, but because *Abba* is that kind of God. Those who are 'sinners' receive the gospel. It concentrates on them in order that *all* may be evangelised and, through conversion, come to know the one Father.

Such a message is shocking to those who feel that their observance of the Law and the traditions give them rights with God; that they have the measure of him, that they have a claim against him, that he owes them something, that they could calculate, bargain, and demand their rights. They have done what was demanded, therefore God must love them. But they do not trust. They do not understand that love is a pure *gift*, that being a child of *Abba* cannot be merited. It is *given*.

The elder brother in the parable of the prodigal typifies this approach and mentality. He stayed at home, obeyed the rules, did all the 'right' things and so felt he could calculate his rights. If X, then Y. But he did not do the one thing necessary: He failed to see his father as father and his brother as brother and respond to them in love. He did not trust his father or entrust himself to him. He held on to what he had, did what he was good at, and watched. He did not appreciate the privilege of being a son and had only the calculating mentality of a slave.

Jesus sees that many people do this. They parade their good deeds before God and trumpet their virtue before those who can never emulate them so that, by contrast, they may feel righteous. Jesus says they cannot continue to maintain moral or religious superiority. They react strongly. How dare Jesus suggest that God's activity can be recognised whenever extravagant or unexpected behaviour subverts the certainties they live by? Is single-minded passion to replace the law of God? Above all, how dare he suggest that those whom they avoided as a religious duty might be loved by God just as much as they were? They who strove so hard to ensure that they would be loved by God! Such people are the great begrudgers (Mt 20:15). Jesus' message is absolutely shocking to them (note how often they 'murmur') because it concerns the freedom of God to love and to forgive all equally, without distinction or dictation; to love both the sinner and the pious, the weak and the strong, the rich and the poor, the Pharisee and the publican. It is intolerable to them to declare that the kingdom of God belongs not just to the 'righteous' but to those they have branded as outcasts and sinners.

This is the incredible paradox of Jesus' message; it decentres the righteous, re-integrates the excommunicated, and puts the sinner at the centre of the gospel. This is what makes it good news for ears that can hear and hearts that are open. Conversely, it is why offence was taken against Jesus. It is the cause of his scandal. It shook the establishment of his day to its deepest foundations. It is without parallel. Jesus was not attempting simple reforms. In his own words, that would be as foolish as putting a new patch on an old garment or new wine into old wine skins. Instead, he was announcing and ushering in a new creation.

We are told that Jesus is known as a 'friend of tax collectors and sinners.' He is in solidarity with them. He 'opts' for them. But is this option not itself sectarian? No. Because it is a stratified society, one may contribute to oppressiveness, not only by unjust decisions, but also by merely maintaining one's position. So, within that system, if Jesus opted to be in solidarity with the religious leaders and the 'respectable' people and their worldview, he would be making a sectarian choice, *even if* he used non-exclusive language and was genuinely concerned with the poor. He would not be doing anything new but merely confirming the divisiveness of the status quo. He would still be with those on the 'inside,' the privileged, and would simply be underwriting the old injustices of the system. He could not opt for the poor and at the same time opt to be in solidarity with those who benefit from the system which holds the poor in a state of poverty. Jesus cannot face the oppressors with the results of their oppression and yet be one with them. The only way he can be really inclusive in his approach is to be in solidarity with those who are outcast, excluded, excommunicated, the poor and the sinners. Structurally, systemically, he must do this so that he can draw together the excluded and those who excluded them, as children of the one Father who cherishes all equally.

But Jesus does not play down the difficulties that the wealthy face in entering the kingdom nor does he underestimate the seductive power of riches. 'Jesus said to his disciples, "How hard it will be for those who have riches to enter the kingdom of God," and the disciples were amazed at his words. But Jesus said to them again, "Children, how hard it is to enter the kingdom of God! It is easier for a camel to go through the eye of a needle than for a rich man to enter the kingdom of God"' (Mk 10:23-25; Lk 18:24-25; Mt 19:23-24). 'Woe to you that are rich for you have received your consolation' (Lk 6:24). The rich young man who wishes to inherit eternal life is told to give his wealth to the poor and then come and follow Jesus, but 'he went away sorrowful for he had great possessions' (Mk 10:22). In the parable of the rich man and Lazarus, the rich man, by his lifestyle, excludes himself from the bosom of Abraham. Very significantly, the only words that God ever utters in any parable are addressed to a rich man: 'Fool! This night your soul is required of you and the things you have prepared, whose will they be?' (Lk 12:20).

There is simply no point in trying to explain these texts by pushing very thin camels through very broad needle eyes! They mean what they say. If Jesus tells parables of reversal to hint at the kingdom's presence, the most obvious reversal for the rich is to be deprived of their riches.

Perhaps we can now begin to understand more fully why Matthew places 'preaching good news to the poor' in the final and emphatic position. For Jesus, this is *the* sign that God's kingdom is breaking in. In this absolute paradox of his proclamation the reign of God is active. The dream of Isaiah is being fulfilled by being surpassed. In the Old Testament, God's steadfastness, his covenant love, his sheer benevolence, his pure graciousness, his tender compassion, and his dedication to justice are understood to be lavished above all on the weak, the underdogs, the defenceless. God is on their side to overcome the evil and the manifold forms of death they experience. So if these unfortunate people are now experiencing acceptance, wholeness, forgiveness, healing, human dignity, and responsibility through the words and at the hands of Jesus, it must mean that the gracious God of tender compassion and right-making justice is active here, that his kingdom, his reign, is making itself present. Here his voice speaks infallibly, so Jesus can pronounce the poor to be eschatologically blessed. 'Blessed are you poor for yours is the kingdom of God. Blessed are you that hunger, who are hated, excluded, reviled, and cast out ... for yours is the kingdom.' How God-filled are you, the poor, the hungry, the sorrowing; God will bring to fulfilment what he has begun in you. If you are not blessed, God is not *Abba*.

Perhaps now we too can begin to understand what Jesus means when he says that it is only those who 'become like little children' who can 'enter the kingdom of heaven' (Mt 18:3), or 'Let the children come to me ... to such belongs the kingdom of God. Truly I say to you, whoever does not receive the kingdom of God like a child shall not enter it' (Mk 10:14-16), or 'Whoever received one such child in my name receives me' (Mk 9:37). The mystery of God as *Abba* and his ways can be accepted only by those who have the hand-in-hand dependence, the unquestioning sincerity and trust of children. This God offers his revelation not to 'the wise and understanding' but 'to babes' (Mt 11:25). We understand too why Jesus refers to his disciples as 'little ones' (Mk 9:42), and 'servants' (Mk 9:35) and 'the least' (Mt 25:40). They are people without status in that religious society.

As we attend more closely, we notice that he speaks and acts as if the kingdom or reign of God is active now, present in their midst, effective in him and his followers. He promises the kingdom as if he has authority to do so. He declares that those who really hear his message and experience his ministry are forever blessed by God. It is a privilege that has not been granted to prophets and kings. The difference is encapsulated in the breathtaking change from 'Thus says the Lord' in the teaching of the prophets, to the 'But I say to you' of Jesus.

Jesus claims that God is graciously active through his preaching, that he is offering grace and forgiveness *now*. We remember how people had been looking forward to eschatological salvation which was to come at the end of time. Jesus now declares that it is present by anticipation and is being offered to all through the mediation of his fragile and questionable and therefore shocking message. Familiarity once again keeps us from recognising the astonishing and shattering implications of all of this.

We tend to neutralise it by saying, 'He was the Son of God and this is what he had come to do.' But if we had been contemporaries, we would have seen and heard a man who preached a message and engaged in a ministry. We would have been in touch with this non-academic, itinerant preacher who had entered into solidarity with the poor, the tax collectors, and the sinners, who shared the very life of the homeless little ones. Would we have been convinced by what we have seen? Would we have been overwhelmed by it? Yet he is claiming that this is the shape of the incipient fulfilment of the best things hoped for by Israel and, indeed, people everywhere. The God-given transformation, the new beginning, is taking place already, now. Such a message from such a person would arouse curiosity, even excitement, and provoke uncertainty. Would our response place us among the ranks of 'the poor' or the righteous? How would we respond? Would we take the risk of accepting what the people of learning and insight and prayer reject?

When Jesus spoke of the kingdom, at first many people would have related it to their own convictions about God and his ways. They would have accepted the language. God was king, yes, and would show himself as king in one glorious final action on behalf of those he loved and against those who did not love him. But this Jesus proceeds to tell parables about kings and householders who act so differently that it overturned all their certainties! On behalf of this king, he enters into solidarity with those whom they knew were not on the side of the king! 'What is happening here?' they would have asked. Jesus would have replied, 'The kingdom of God is taking shape within our world.' As they wrestled with this, they would ask, 'What can he possibly mean?' They would have recalled all they heard about the coming of God's final kingdom, the signs that would precede it: the cosmic convulsions, the final battles, the messianic woes, the triumph of the nation, the judgment by fire, above all the messianic peace. How could anyone talk about the coming of the kingdom when none of these things were happening?

Yet Jesus is saying that this kingdom is making itself felt as he preaches good news to the poor. What he experiences is God's kingly activity working in him and through him, in response to those around him. So he proclaims that the kingdom is among them already even if the consummation of the end is not yet.

The debate about 'the already or not yet' of the kingdom need not concern us here. Jesus spoke of the kingdom as already present but looked forward to its *definitive* coming – in that sense it is both 'already' and 'not yet.' His contemporaries would have found this difficult to understand, much less accept. It seemed to say that the end of all history was present in the midst of history! He claimed that the power of the end time was present, but the end was not yet. Jesus spoke like this because, since the kingdom is God's kingdom, it is total paradox for those who think only as the world does. But the kingdom involves a total revolution of the structures of the Old World. So it is possible 'to take offence' at Jesus as Matthew 11:6 continues.

And they did take offence. There is nothing absolutely compelling or self-authenticating about what Jesus is saying. It can be called into question. Indeed, it is so unconventional and subversive that it *should* be rejected. He is making an absolute claim, but what is its basis and its proof? If God were really active here, you would certainly expect more than this clever but confusing talk that would turn everything upside down if you accepted it. God's reign cannot be about associating with outcasts and those cut off from God! The hard facts, the sordid lifestyle of his rabble followers and uneducated disciples, disproves everything.

How would we have reacted when so many good and holy people were taking offence at the preaching of Jesus of Nazareth? Why was his message such a stumbling block to so many people of his own time? Would we accept this preaching of good news to the poor or would we hear it in the voice of the antichrist?

6. GOOD NEWS IN ACTION

Suffer me not to be separated
And let my cry come unto thee.
T. S. Eliot

Jesus does not simply speak about love or compassion or forgiveness or good news. He translates this message into a way of life that is absolutely consistent with his preaching, thus confronting his contemporaries inescapably with the implications of his message. We see the test of what he says in what he does. He engages in a whole range of activities which concretise the content and meaning of the reign of God. His preaching and his activity, his message and his ministry are inseparable. The deeds of this man speak, for they are good news, his message is active. Jesus is searching for ways to reveal to others the superabundant prodigality of God's love so that they may know the Father as he is. He is aware of the constant presence of this boundless love and he struggles to extend this consciousness to others, to mediate this presence to them.

Table Fellowship

To make this happen he can only use his bodily presence as a medium of communication, but throughout the gospels we realise that extraordinary things happened in his presence. Through what he did people came to recognise the force of love that pulsed through life. In the company of Jesus, they became so aware of love's graciousness toward them that they learned to entrust themselves to it and to celebrate its presence constantly. Again and again, we notice references in the gospels to gratuity, extravagance, and superabundance. There is an opposition to all that is incomplete, niggardly, tight-fisted, or lacking and there is a celebration of gracious excess.

In reading the gospels we might be forgiven for thinking that Jesus is always coming from, going to, or talking about banquets, feasts, and meals. He is remembered vividly as a companion at table and as someone to whom meals were very important. Opponents coined a catcall and flung it at him: 'Behold a glutton and a drunkard, a friend of tax collectors and sinners' (Lk 7:34). At table he once told his host, 'When you give a dinner or a banquet do not invite your friends or your brothers or your kinsmen or rich neighbours, lest they also invite you in return and you be repaid' (Lk 14:12). He invited himself to be a guest of Zacchaeus, the tax collector and notorious 'sinner' whom people avoided (Lk 19:5-7). He annoyed people because he excluded no one from his meals. 'This man, they said, receives sinners and eats with them' (Lk 15:2).

Do these references simply mean that Jesus liked food and drink, was very hospitable, extended invitations, and did not mind who joined in the celebration? No. Through these meals Jesus is extending to others both himself and the mystery at the heart of his life. He chooses this medium to proclaim and celebrate God's all-inclusive love. What was the significance of eating and drinking in the presence of Jesus?

Our self-service style meals have none of the significance that meals had for the Jews at that time.[1] A companion was one who broke bread with you (com-panion) – for a Jew, sharing a meal was a very intimate expression of friendship and communication and was much more than a social occasion. To take part in a meal meant fellowship with God and with those who sat at table. It meant sharing peace, brotherhood or sisterhood, and forgiveness. They understood meals in this way because those who took part in table fellowship shared in the blessings of God, pronounced by the host or head of table. Because of this, people would never eat or drink with those who did not belong to their stratum of society or did not share in their vision of God and his involvement with the world. Those who strove to become the pure and holy remnant of Israel assiduously avoided contact with the unholy and to share table fellowship with them would be tantamount to sacrilege.

Jesus cuts through these distinctions, stratifications, and taboos in a scandalous way we find difficult to appreciate. He accepts everyone, no matter what their background or social standing. Jesus insists on unrestricted table fellowship. He invited the 'righteous and the sinners' to share meals together where Jesus either serves as host or is himself a guest. He invites rich and poor, Zealot and tax collector, Pharisee and prostitute to share a table. To eat with Jesus was a risky business. You might become ritually unclean as a result of mixing with the wrong people or, more frighteningly, you might experience a change of heart!

Barriers were broken down in the presence of Jesus. He accepts people as they are, and can be. He reaches out to them as fellow human beings and so they feel forgiven, reconciled, part of a wider community – they feel human again. They can accept themselves and each other and lose their guilt, and in this way he created a new kind of relationship among people. He liberated them by his bodily presence. People were given the space to enable them to begin to see themselves and each other, not through layers of prejudice, but as Jesus sees them.

We begin to realise that eating and drinking in the presence of Jesus is not simply a matter of giving food to the hungry. Nor is it a question of gathering together disadvantaged members of society in order to inaugurate social change, nor is it a question of offering group therapy. It is a question of theology and eschatology rather than biology, sociology, or psychology. By seeking to draw together in table fellowship the so-called sinners and self-styled righteous, Jesus is making an unbelievably powerful statement about God and his ways of bringing about final salvation. Without asking people how they stand in relation to God he offers them, peace, wholeness, and forgiveness. His self-righteous contemporaries were extremely scandalised at this offensive behaviour of offering integrating fellowship and communion to those whom they avoided as a sacred duty. In their eyes, it was blasphemous and sacrilegious to invoke the blessings of God on notorious sinners and to offer divine forgiveness to the outcasts of religious society.

Jesus gathers around him, in inclusive bread-breaking, the very people who were excluded from temple and community in Israel. Nothing broken or unclean or enfeebled could be present where God communicated his holiness. At Qumran they refused to allow the blind and the deaf, the lame and the feeble to join the community. Jesus refused to accept that there are any outsiders. The parable of the great feast (Lk 14:15-24) catalogues some of these unwanted people, insisting that they be seated at table. 'Bring in the poor and maimed and blind and lame' (21). And when there is still room (and there is always room in abundance) the servant is sent out to bring in people who are even more unfortunate. 'Go out into the highways and hedges, and compel people to come in, that my house may be filled' (23). This is exactly what Jesus is doing. He reminds those who had received invitations that the time for in-gathering is at hand, but the real surprise is that those whom no one, least of all themselves, expected to be invited are being asked to share the feast.

The shock of all this intensifies when we recall the chasm maintained between the sinners and the righteous and how carefully the righteous avoided contact with the despised 'sinners,' lest they be defiled or corrupted. We remember, too, that in that world sinners could expect to receive acceptance only when they had repented and become righteous. So the pious contemporaries of Jesus would understand the full implications of his open table fellowship and would be extremely scandalised by this action. They were outraged by his acceptance of sinners, his identification with them. (We might wonder how we would have reacted then or, indeed, how we would react to modern parallels.) It was plain to them that Jesus was overturning the values by which they lived their lives. By valuing those they despised, he was calling into question the system that devalued, and those whose interest it served. They were appalled and insulted and they took offence at him ... 'Behold a glutton and wine bibber, friend of tax collectors and sinners.'

Some commentators say that some of his parables were spoken to 'explain' and vindicate this communication of good news to the poor through table fellowship. Through these narratives Jesus is saying in effect: 'I am acting like this because this is what *Abba* is really like.' In other words, he ironically tells parables about the kingdom of God, to the people of God who prided themselves in knowing all about God, to explain his own godless conduct! He maintained that in his preaching and in his bread-breaking with outcasts he was anticipating the messianic banquet of the last times when the love of God for all would be revealed. So those who sit at table with him are accepted now and are offered forgiveness even before they repent. Eschatological forgiveness is being offered here and now. 'And when Jesus heard it, he said to them, "Those who are well have no need of a physician, but those who are sick; I came not to call the righteous, but sinners"' (Mk 2:17). This is his own scandalising summary of his ministry.

Often when we think about forgiveness and sin we are inclined to look for texts where Jesus explicitly says, 'Your sins are forgiven.' But we ought to look instead to the much more pervasive and more striking theme of acceptance, table fellowship, and festivity and try to understand their implications for forgiveness. His self-righteous contemporaries caught the full implications and they never forgave him for this attack on their ethical system and their understanding of merit. Jesus turned it upside down. His approach was subversive: 'The first are last and the last first.'

This good news for the poor, in word and in action or in active words and in actions that speak, is the great pre-Easter scandal. We cannot attach too much importance to it in our attempts to understand Jesus and to understand who it is we are asked to follow and imitate. His message met with violent opposition because it was literally too good to be true, and so it was labelled as heresy. But Jesus stood by his words. He stood firm for 'He had the knack of making men feel as small as they really were, which meant as great as God had made them.'[2] Jesus was demanding that pious persons break the idols they worshipped and acknowledge that they were sinners. He continued to demand this and would not water down the demand. On the other hand, through his acceptance of and solidarity with them, he gave sinners the courage to do what they had regarded as impossible, namely, to believe in God's boundless goodness and to repent through love. 'Because you have loved me, you have made me lovable' (*St Augustine*).

But Jesus was painfully aware that this message, the best news that humankind had ever heard, was being met with incomprehension and hostility. The news was so good, so great, and yet it was impossible to break through to them, that he felt faced by an almost complete failure which wrung from him the cry, 'And you would not' (Mt 23:37) – I have done my utmost and you have still refused and I cannot save you against your will.

But he stood firm and told them that the prostitutes and the tax collectors and the sinners they disdained would enter the kingdom and they would not. He declared that the very sinners they avoided were just as loved by God as they were. To their faces he maintained that they could not enter the kingdom because they were so puffed up with their own importance that they would not let the kingdom enter them. It could have no place in their lives. They had to understand what love is, allow it to show them their need for transformation, before even a saviour could save them.

These people were so full of the arrogant intolerance of the self-righteous that they believed that they could be their own saviours. They were convinced that they were responsible for their own rightness. Jesus tells the parable of the Pharisee and the tax collector to 'some who trusted in themselves that they were righteous and despised others' (Lk 18:9). It is an irrefutably accurate description of what is found so often in the heart of the 'best' people.

Human beings find it so difficult to recognise love in all things and to return love for love. We want to control, to impress, to ensure that we are appreciated. We have a pathological need to know that we are loved and we use our energies trying to wheedle this affirmation from others and from God. We spend so much time trying to prove it or win it that we come to believe that there is no other possible approach. We see mercy and compassion as exceptions and cannot imagine a world founded only on compassion. We cannot believe that what we are looking for is already given to us before our search begins. If we could come to believe that we are sustained by an infinitely compassionate love that gives itself to us with gracious abandon, that suffuses all our frantic activities, that wills only what is best for us, our quest would be ended. We would 'arrive where we started and know the place for the first time ... a condition of complete simplicity costing not less than everything ...'[3]

Peace would come at last and all our frustrated energies would be released for deployment in a new way which trusts the self and others because we can entrust ourselves to God. This is Jesus' hope. This is his struggle with the righteous. He offers the same vision to all. He tries to convince the self-righteous that they, like those they despise, need to accept the love of God and allow it to transform them as it seeks to transform all others.

This is difficult because they believe they must make themselves perfect. They are terrified to entrust themselves to the weakness and vulnerability of love. In their preoccupation with achievement, they have forgotten that God's love is pure gift, that it cannot be won because it has already been given. Nor can they accept that in responding to his love they cannot hide behind a web of formalism. They are convinced that their laws and traditions are the same as God's demands, a fatal but often repeated mistake in the history of religions. They have no genuine understanding of their own preoccupations, of their own abject need before *Abba*, who alone can enrich.

Because they lack understanding, they cannot allow God to be truly a kingly father. They diminish him, reduce him to a keeper of accounts who must deliver according to their demands, their calculations. They cannot stand open-handed before God and therefore they cannot accept the forgiveness he so prodigally offers. They rely on themselves and so make themselves impervious even to God's graciousness. Jesus struggles with them because they are preventing not only themselves but the poor, the true heirs of the kingdom, from coming to their father. 'They shut the doors of the kingdom of heaven on people' (Mt 23:13). They have made people feel guilty so that, compared to the failure of others they can believe they have achieved something and impressed God, and can therefore feel self-righteous.

Jesus says that they had cut off the poor from their Father by barriers of casuistry. They laid intolerable loads of useless, God-concealing legalism on these poor people. They are denying them their true future. In short, they are distorting the true image of God as *Abba* and they are turning him into an implacable task-master. 'Woe to you Pharisees for you tithe mint and rue and every herb and neglect justice and the love of God' (Lk 11:52). 'Woe to you lawyers for you have taken away the key of knowledge; you did not enter yourselves and you hindered those who were entering' (Lk 11:42); also see Mt 23 (*passim*). And Jesus calls the oppressed to himself in that tender passage, 'Come to me, all who labour and are heavy laden, and I will give you rest ...' (Mt 11:28-30). He invites all who are tired from carrying heavy loads, mostly from being despised by their fellow humans, to come to him and he will give them rest. The yoke he will put on them is easy, the burden he will put on them is light.

This 'come to me' of Jesus is reminiscent of the call of the prophets, calling Israel back to God. But they would only use such words as coming directly from God himself. The prophets did not call the people to themselves but to God. But Jesus calls them to himself with all the authority that that implies. If we had been contemporaries, how would we have reacted to Jesus' indiscriminate table fellowship? Would we have taken God at his word? Would we have taken on the yoke of Jesus or continued to break the poor with our yoke?

Healings, Exorcisms, Miracles

Another way the kingdom takes concrete, visible shape is through the activity of Jesus 'going about doing good' (Acts 10:38; Mk 3:4). His solidarity with the broken and the poor, his *healings*, his *exorcisms*, and his *miracles*, confront us in the gospels.

We have already seen that some people felt the world had become so evil that God would have to intervene and put an end to its wickedness. Evil could have many manifestations: oppression and lack of freedom, possession by evil spirits, illness or lack of prestige or prosperity. Disorders in nature, storms, crop failure, anything not right, any lack or limitation, could be seen as a manifestation of evil. To talk of the kingdom of God means speaking about God being active to save. So if the present situation is understood to be in the grip of evil, if it is oppressed and bound by diabolic forces, then to speak about the coming of God's reign means asserting that the stranglehold of evil is being broken because God is transforming the present. The kingdom of evil and calamity is being pushed back, its strength is being overcome, all that is ungodly is being reversed, and gracious space is being offered to people.

Some Christians have tended to think of salvation in a limited way, as something that happens within their souls, something that has little to do with the body, with history, or with the quality of life around them. It is something that really only happens in the next life. Jesus could not make such divisions. Salvation was about overcoming limitations and faults, binding up the bruised, the broken, and the maimed, and making everything whole again. When God saves, he touches the whole person, body, soul, mind, heart, and strength. It is against this kind of background that Jesus proclaims that this God-given transformation is beginning to take place in him through him. 'The blind see, the lame walk ...' He is convinced that the in-breaking of the kingdom is already happening in the hiddenness, anonymity, and ordinariness of his own ministry. The reign of God is manifesting itself by realising the signs of the times of salvation prophesied by Isaiah. It is saving, releasing, restoring, and making whole. It is in the light of this conviction that we must try to understand the significance of Jesus' miracles and exorcisms and healings.

What can be said here is necessarily brief and incomplete. This is not an easy area for us because we often approach the miracle stories with ready-made definitions of miracles gleaned from the catechism or apologetics. If we think of miracles as events that contravene or contradict the laws of nature or as proofs, we must realise that these categories are completely foreign to the Bible where God is seen as creating, sustaining, and constantly renewing the world. Everything comes from the wondrous graciousness of God: the creation of the world, the delivery from Egypt, safe delivery in childbirth, deliverance from 'terror of the night, the arrow that flies by day, the pestilence that stalks in darkness, the destruction that wastes at noonday' (Ps 91). What we call miracles, the Bible sees as happenings that provoke our wonder, praise, and thanksgiving because through these signs we come to recognise the graciousness and mercy and power of God. Likewise the healing, exorcism, and miracle stories in the gospels speak to us about compassion of Jesus, about his doing nothing but good for people, about his deliverance of the unfortunate from suffering and distress.

To those who have faith, these actions speak of a gracious God who, through Jesus, is showing his unconditional care for his children in their distress and his desire to save them. To others, they speak of the presence of the antichrist, who, through the power of Beelzebub, the prince of darkness, is able to perform these 'wonders' (Mt 12:27). In the gospels we find that while friends and opponents alike accept that Jesus exorcises, heals, works miracles, they differ radically in their interpretation of these events. Does this indicate that he is 'from God' or that he is 'from the Evil One'?

Why is there such divergence and contest among those who acknowledge that he does signs and 'acts of power' (Mk 6:2; Acts 2:22)? What is it that makes people opt for the absurdity of Satan divided against Satan rather than acknowledge that God is active? The miracle stories of Moses or Elijah were re-told lovingly. It was acknowledged that 'the sons' of the Pharisees (Mt 12:27; Lk 11:19) cast out demons. Some rabbis and other extraordinary people were remembered as having remarkable healing powers. So why is there such an unprecedentedly sharp reaction to Jesus and his healing work?

It is obvious from the gospels that Jesus was remembered as an exorcist, a miracle worker, and a healer of many kinds of illness. We find these references in the earliest strata of the tradition about Jesus. The context of some of the exorcisms and miracle stories –

their taking place on the Sabbath, giving rise to the charge of sorcery, being explained in terms of 'the kingdom divided against itself' (Mt 12:24-27) – point to definite authenticity. We remember the case where Jesus has cured a dumb man and, although the people marvel, some say that he did it through the power of Beelzebub. Jesus points to the stupidity of this argument and asks, 'If your sons cast out demons and you attribute this to God, why exclude it in my case?' He goes on to say, 'But if it is by the finger of God I cast out demons, then the kingdom of God has come upon you' (Lk 11:20; Mt 12:28).

What is important here is the concentration, the depth of interpretation. The kingdom is not inaugurated every time a demented person is healed but only when Jesus (or his disciples in his name) does so by the 'finger of God.' This is not a random occurrence but is the beginning of the binding of the power of evil, looked forward to as heralding the end time. If it is happening now, in anticipation of the end time, it means that God's reign is already active among them. So too, the curing of a leper is not simply a matter of the healing of a skin disease; it means that God's kingdom as salvation is asserting itself, through Jesus, against the kingdom of evil. The multiplication of loaves or the Cana story are not just about the working of rare wonders. They proclaim that God's salvation is active in Jesus and will overcome all that is incomplete and niggardly, all that lacks superabundance and gratuity. The calming of the storm means that God, through Jesus, is overcoming disorders and chaos in nature (which were believed to come from evil forces) and is restoring peace and prefiguring the final re-establishment of all things. The raising of the dead proclaims that no area of life or death is outside God's transforming power, which invades the realm of the dead and overcomes the last enemy, death.

An exorcism is not simply about the healing of a demented person; it is the beginning of the binding of evil and the restoration of God's order. So we see that Jesus' message about the saving nearness of God's reign would be incomplete without his miracles and exorcisms. Glad tidings cannot be verbal only; they must make a difference in the way people live. The healings and exorcisms proclaim forcefully to those who have faith in the God of Jesus that this God is acting now, is doing battle with evil, is healing and restoring and reconciling. The miracles and exorcisms are enfleshments of his reign.

This king is against all evil and suffering. He wishes his children to have life and have it to the full. But he alone can overcome the weakness at the very heart of creaturehood and Jesus is convinced that he will do it. He is beginning to act already through the ministry of Jesus and he will bring it to completion. This goodness will succeed and it will finally overcome all evil. God's reign is dawning and it brings 'shalom.' It brings harmony and peace and liberation from all kinds of bondage for it breaks the grip of evil.

All of this is brought home to us very forcefully in the story of the Gerasene demoniac (Mk 5:1-20).[4] We are told that Jesus leaves the land of the Jews behind and crosses through darkness and storm into the pagan land of the Gerasenes. He crosses the threshold into another world and immediately he is met by a man who 'lives' in the abode of the dead. The man has been cast out by the community who have also attempted to bind him. He is excluded from their community and their communication. His cries are inarticulate, his despair is unbearable, his self-punishing violence suicidal. He is a total outsider. No one talks to him, loves him, or will even stay with him to be loved. He is enslaved, not only by the demon forces within him, but also by the community who bound him in his illness and then attempted to bind him in chains. He is one of the living dead excluded from those who live the 'right' kind of life because his behaviour does not conform to their standards. He is in exile, cut off and despised, consigned to hopelessness and nothingness. And Jesus crosses over. He is here, as always, to be with all those who are rejected by the civil or religious communities, even if, as in this case, they are not Jewish. He comes to bind all evil and unbind those who were bound.

Initially, the meeting looks like a setting for single combat. But evil has very many forms and very many names that do not always reveal its real nature. When challenged by Jesus, its name, its reality, is surrendered. 'My name is legion.' Before evil can be exorcised it must be named for what it really is. 'This is what I am.' Evil is never confined or singular. A brief question and address follow. Then, despite their final desperate attempts at self-preservation, at the sovereign command of Jesus, the evil spirits come out of the man and go into the swine and into the sea. The man 'whom no one had the strength to subdue' (Mk 5:4) is found by the Gerasenes, seated, clothed, and in his right mind.

What had been wrong is put right, disorder is reversed, and perfect order begins to be restored. The demons have returned to the abyss, the man has been restored to himself. He had come to himself and is healed, is at peace, has had his dignity restored, and can be a member of the human community once more. He has been brought from a state of death to the state of life.

But the people react against this. It is too costly. It upsets categories and crosses boundaries. If the insane become sane, what about the sane? Opposition to Jesus mounts again but this time he does not resist this human rejection and leaves their country.

But the healed man has come to recognise Jesus as the one who offers a way out of the past and into new life, the one through whom the goodness that opposes evil is mediated and he asks to be allowed to follow Jesus as a disciple. But now that this man can communicate again, Jesus sends him back among those who excommunicated him and made him a non-person. He is to proclaim to them 'How much the Lord has done for you and how he has had mercy on you' (19).

This man had been rejected and despised, turned into a stranger, a non-neighbour, an embodiment of evil by people who were afraid to risk love. Because they loved themselves so much, they set limits and thresholds and defined the world in their terms. But Jesus crosses over and gently, but firmly, confronts this old world with a love that does not discriminate. He treats the man as a human, as someone to be with, someone to love and be loved by. He re-establishes communication, re-integrates him into life, treats him as a brother. There is a radical reversal and restoration.

But that is not all. We are asked to see ourselves in the characters of this narrative. The respectable people cannot see themselves in this demoniac although he is in fact the abandoned, institutionalised embodiment of their judgment, condemnation, and exclusion. They are not overjoyed at the restoration of this unfortunate man to life. Instead, they choose death for him over life. Are their own daily lives, which they defend at all costs, also a choice for death? Will they allow the healing of the demoniac to affect their destiny? Will they make a break with the past?

Here then we meet many of the themes that we find in the narratives of miracles and exorcisms. Jesus is at hand, ready to step in and save those who are not free. He will not be prevented by religious, social, or legal considerations. Jesus is against all evil. He leads the fight to liberate others, confronting it head on. When he acts, those 'outside are drawn in' – people pass from violence to calm, from hate to love, from being 'beside themselves' to coming to themselves, from incomprehension to truth, from opposition to discipleship. Others may harden their hearts. His coming foretells the beginning of the end of evil. Jesus and evil cannot co-exist. As the kingdom of God approaches, it pronounces sentence against all alienating power, a sentence which will eventually be carried out. But it is beginning already; it is making its presence felt. In its name Jesus cries and continues to cry: 'Unclean spirit, depart from this man.'

We must read each of these stories carefully as biblical stories, paying special attention to the way the gospel writers use them and the meaning they wish to convey to us. They are not trying to tell us that they constitute a rupture in the laws of nature or that they 'prove' the divinity of Jesus. In fact, Jesus gladly admits that others besides himself cast out demons (Mt 12:27; Lk 11:19). He does not prevent a non-disciple from exorcising in his name and tells his disciples to do exactly what he is doing. 'Heal the sick, raise the dead, cleanse lepers, cast out demons' (Mt 10:8).

The kind of response to miracles that would have pleased Jesus is found on the lips of those who witnessed the raising of the widow's son and 'glorified God,' saying 'a great prophet has arisen among us and God has shown his care for his people' (Lk 7:16).

This question about the 'great prophet' brings us to the nub of the extremes of reaction to Jesus' actions. The eschatological prophet was expected to perform certain works (Is 26:19, 43:8, 61:1-3). Jesus seems to be doing these 'works,' so is he the eschatological prophet? That he could be is questionable to many, because these works done by Jesus are the very embodiment of his preaching, which they find intolerable. Yet, there is still doubt. Is he from the Evil One? If not, they would like him to overcome the ambiguity and the scandal for them with a single God-sized, legitimising sign they will recognise and find acceptable. They are looking for incontestable proof.

The Pharisees came and began to argue with him, seeking from him a sign from heaven to test him, and he sighed deeply in his spirit, and said, 'Why does this generation seek a sign? Truly I say to you, no sign shall be given to this generation' (Mk 8:11-12; see Mt 12:38).

He refuses to underwrite their belief that God should endorse his ministry as eschatological prophet. 'Unless you see signs and wonders you will not believe' (Jn 4:48). He is not concerned with proving something but with responding compassionately to people's distress in the name of God's benevolence. To attempt to do what they demand is to yield to the temptation to use power to establish himself, to prove his identity conclusively. It is to believe that the kingdom is about demonstrations of power rather than communion of mind and heart and new ways of being human together. This was part of the testing story and here they 'test' him again. Jesus refused once again to rely on the weakness of power.

One does not need a change of heart to understand power. But one does need a change of heart to understand the strength of weakness, sustained only by God. This is what Jesus is ultimately seeking. He announces the kingdom in weakness and in the renouncement of all displays of power. He is trying to wean people away from the power-God-idol so as to reveal the true face of this father-king. He is therefore willing to endure the waiting and the hoping for the emergence of God's definitive future. What is already happening is so clearly good that Jesus is certain that this is the beginning of the kingdom/reign of God. The presence of the blessings show those who have eyes to see that God's reign is making itself present. The end is not yet, but the jubilee year of God's salvation is now.

His opponents say: 'If this were the eschatological prophet you would expect more than a few doubtful exorcisms (which other people can do anyway) and a few strange happenings among the outcasts and down-and-outs who gullibly describe them as the works of the final prophet. If Jesus claims that the kingdom is present then let him give us a sign commensurate with that claim.' His opponents ask for a sign that will give them absolute proof of who he is. They seek a single stunningly dramatic sign commensurate with his claim. The problem is that they expect God to act from above, not realising that such a God is a God of their own construction. They have forgotten about the immanent God who is hidden, concealed, but active in the pain, suffering, and ambiguity of the passion history of Israel and in the individuals who had hope even in the apparent absence of God. But Jesus knows this God only and so the hints and the guesses are enough for him. He will not try to manipulate God nor force his hand. For then he would be no God.

Jesus, and those who accept him, are happy to allow God's future to emerge gently, hiddenly, and always in a surprising way. Thus, no sign is given, for God is not like that. Jesus wishes only to point to the true God, not to prove something about himself. *Abba* is the source of what is done through Jesus. These are not his own needs, his own deeds, or his own authority. He must not be used to draw attention to himself. He must always point beyond to *Abba*. Jesus proclaims that this God-given transformation is beginning to take place. What is happening may be slight and appear to be of little significance compared to the brute weight of human suffering that affects his contemporaries, but it is its significance, its symbolic value, that is important.

To Jesus, what is happening is promise. It is seed that will grow, the first fruits of a harvest. It is a symbol of the total salvation that is not yet but which is possible and which can now be confidently expected because it has already begun in Jesus' message and ministry. This is what is preserved for us in the intensely joyful reply to John. It is happening already! But only those who have eyes to see, who understand the kind of God that *Abba* is, who have faith in him, can understand the true significance of what is really taking place – that this is the inbreak/outbreak of the kingdom of God.

But it is possible to take offence at Jesus, and not merely at what he says, because he is not talking about the presence of the kingdom 'somewhere or other.' If it were as vague as that, it would cause no problem. He is talking about its presence in himself and through himself and its coming upon those around him. And the question is not simply, 'Do you mean to tell us that the kingdom is present?' but 'Do you *dare* to suggest that this is the shape of the kingdom? Could it have anything to do with you and your odd ways, your disconcerting preaching, your strange lifestyle, surrounded as you are by your rabble of outcasts and sinners? You yourself lead an irreligious life, careless about the traditions for which the martyrs shed their blood, you are part of our history of suffering. Yet you say that God's reign is manifest in *this*! That the poorest person we know is the shape of the king-dom of God!'

So they take offence at Jesus because of the contrast, the shortfall, the chasm between what he claims to be taking place the in-breaking of the kingdom – and the poverty-stricken and impotent message and ministry in which it is supposed to be tak-ing place. As far as his opponents are concerned, the irreligious character of his way of life and that of his disreputable followers and ignorant disciples prove the case against him.

So they reject all of the surprising things he does. To accept them as the shape of the kingdom would demand conversion, would require them to see with Jesus' eyes. It is not possible to deny that he does these works but they say that Beelzebub, not God, is their source. They reject the miracles for they are the ex-pressions of his compassion, inseparable fro,m his very self.

This helps us to understand that there is nothing absolutely compelling about Jesus' miracles (see debate in Jn 9:16, 10:19-21). It is only those who approach the miracles of Jesus in faith who can accept them or begin to appreciate their kingdom significance. In the context of the healing miracle stories we hear the word 'faith' very frequently: 'such faith,' 'lack of faith,' 'little faith,' 'your faith has saved you.' 'All things are possible,' Jesus says, 'to him who believes.' Immediately the father of the child cried out and said, 'I believe, help my unbelief' (Mk 9:23-24). 'If you have faith as a grain of mustard seed, you will say to this moun-tain, "move hence to yonder place," and it will move, and noth-ing will be impossible to you' (Mt 17:20).

His miracles always take place in a faith context. They are always a challenge and they summon people to answer the quest-ion: Who is this man who does these things? And they are free to decide; miracles cannot force faith upon people. The reactions of the people at that time were acceptance, rejection, or indiffer-ence. The story of the ten lepers (Lk 17:11-19) tells us that all were healed of their leprosy but the heart of only one was healed and changed. Jesus' miracles are never automatic nor magical. He refused to perform any legitimising signs (Mt 12:38ff). There are no independent displays of power. In fact, Jesus never init-iates this kind of activity and he responds only to people who trust in him.

Even from the foregoing it seems clear that 'faith' is not

being used here in exactly the same sense as we would use it today. It is not yet full-blown faith in God or in Jesus as unique Son of God. But it is a deep unwavering trust that he is God's final prophet messenger to Israel and that through his sheer goodness to people they are in touch with God's unconditional care for their good and are willing to allow it to change their lives. In that sense we should see these miracles and exorcisms as invitations to unconditional faith in God as Jesus represents him. But miracles can only invite; they cannot of themselves produce faith.

These works of Jesus speak to the hopes of humankind, of what could happen if people ceased trying to control God and each other, ceased desiring and responded to the love of a God whom they allow to be father. They speak of the hopes God has for the world, of what could be, of the end of fatalism. He wishes to give hope to those who are hopeless by human reckoning and a future to those who are futureless in the eyes of 'the wise and the prudent.'

Lastly, miracles call forth a love in people to match the originality, the newness, the extravagance of what God is doing for them through Jesus. They are invited to change, to restructure their lives, to forget themselves, and begin to be in solidarity with people in a new way. They are called on to imitate what Jesus has done, to enter gently into the pain and grief of others, to hold the frenzied and the fearful, to weep with those who weep. The powerlessness of those in need is to be matched by their own. In this way they will be put in touch with the love that heals.

In talking about Jesus' miracles, we tend to look for the dramatic and concentrate on the unusual and forget about the really profound miracles where nothing 'extraordinary' happened. It is in the conversion of sinners and all the apostles, in the response of Zacchaeus and Mary Magdalen that we see the final purpose of the miracles being achieved, although we do not call them miracles. Seamus Heaney has a line in a poem[5] in which a Protestant neighbour speaks about land being 'as poor as Lazarus' (Lk 16:20). We tend to forget this Lazarus and remember the other in John 11 because he was the subject of a miracle.

Finally, we should note two healing miracles which take place in remarkable faith contexts: the meeting with the centurion

(Mt 8:5) and the Syro-Phoenician woman (Mt 15:22). These incidents are important too for our understanding of Jesus himself and how his mission is clarified by encountering different situations. We must notice his initial reluctance and his vision of his mission as confined to Israel. But when he is face to face with both of these people, he recognises faith in response to himself as prophet messenger outside the boundaries of Israel, and sees that he must respond to it. It is hardly too much to say that Jesus was changed by this encounter. What explanation would we have had for the healings and miracles of Jesus: acceptance, rejection, or indifference?

7. COMMUNITAS

No one remains on his own as a disciple.
Bonhoeffer

In the previous chapter we looked at some of the striking characteristics of 'what Jesus did and taught.' This was what his enemies reacted against; this was what those whom he calls are asked to accept. Yet this Jesus was a sign of contradiction (Lk 2:34). He did not conform, he was critical of the religion of his contemporaries, he opposed legalism, he ignored the threshold between the sacred and the secular, he brought liturgy out into life, he unmasked much of what was masquerading as good in political and religious structures, and he opposed everything that diminished or threatened life or contributed to death. How could disciples accept all this? How can they dream of daring to embody it?

First, we must say they can only do it together. In Judaism the people are always called as a people to be a people. It would also be inconceivable that a disciple of Jesus could remain alone. But how does he wish his disciples to be together as a group and as a people? In the kind of church communities and religious communities that we have today?

We must remember that Jesus was in fact deeply critical of the church and the religious communities of his day and we have no guarantee that he might not also be critical of some of our institutions. We may not simply presume that everything we have today is what Jesus desired for his followers.

If we take seriously 'what Jesus did and taught,' we might begin to wonder how we might describe the kind of life together, the relatedness envisaged by Jesus for his followers. To use the word 'community' may be misleading for it may beg the very questions and paper over the very difficulties that should be acknowledged (rather like talking about 'the two communities' in Northern Ireland). If we need new words, how are we to speak of the implications of the message and ministry of Jesus for his disciples' life together? Are there any experiences analogous to what he proposed? If there are, they will hardly be found in the comfortable ordinariness of our day-to-day lives. Perhaps if we looked at situations where people are stretched, or transcend themselves, or are together in a new way, we might gain some insight into what Jesus had in mind. And remembering the hint given to us by the parables, we need not always look for such instances in religious contexts but can look to our own experience.

We have all known or heard of occasions when former disputes and antagonisms and divisions were brushed aside and people came together unselfishly to face the threat of death or natural disaster or imprisonment or war. It is easy to recall stories of extraordinary generosity and selflessness, self-forgetfulness, and risking of life for the sake of others. There seems to be no calculation, no cold, rational decisions but a spontaneous response to the needs of others. Within our own experience we may be able to point to occasions when old wounds were healed, when factions and frictions were laid aside, when priorities were put right, when new bonds were created, when people gave of themselves and did not count the cost. Or we may remember the spontaneous support given by neighbours and friends to those coping with illness or death (an Irish wake is a good example); or we recall the remarkable way that people can be together on pilgrimage and the transformation that can take place at such a time; or we remember occasions when we were recipients of, or witnesses to, the 'widow's mite' or the sharing of poverty rather than riches or the 'theology of the second mile.'

Even these few examples show the extraordinary things that can happen when one's response to a situation is determined by the *reeds* of the people in that situation. However, rather than continue listing such experiences, we might try to acknowledge some of their common characteristics and take our quest a stage further by using the categories of *liminality* and *communitas*. These are rather unusual words but it is important to grasp their meanings, for they may help us to draw together much of what has emerged so far about the message and ministry of Jesus. Let us try to unravel their meanings.

We know that we are all to a greater or lesser extent shaped by society, by culture, by religion. Our identity is shaped by these institutions and systems and the roles and responsibilities, the statuses and relationships they assign to us. A combination of all of these make up what we call the structures of society. Anthropologists, who study the structuring of society, pay special attention to the rites of initiation into what are inaccurately described as 'primitive' societies. In their studies, they point to three distinct but linked stages in the 'rites of passage' or of initiation into adult society.

1. There is a separation from the structures of group or social role or lifestyle previously taken for granted.

2. There follows a lengthy period of transition and testing when the initiates are on the boundary, on the *limen* or threshold, when they are 'betwixt and between what has been and what will be.' This is called the *liminal* stage.

3. Finally, there are the rituals to mark the incorporation into their new lifestyle or group or social role of those who have fulfilled the rites of initiation.

The second stage, the liminal, is the most important. Liminal existence is marked by the absence of the familiar, by separation from all cozy supports, and by the dissolution of all pretensions. The structures that had previously defined life are left behind. They are simply no longer there. This asceticism, this stripping away of the old, the familiar, and the taken-for-granted structured existence, challenges one to use one's resources (they are all one has) to take a stand, to create a new world of meaning. The liminal period is marked by pilgrimage, especially the journey inward. It is a time of deeper, more disturbing thoughts, of exposure to new values, of insight into the life of things, of seeing and living by a new vision. To inhabit this world is to be 'on the threshold,' to live 'betwixt and between' the structures, and therefore to see into the relativity of things. Furthermore, because of the pressures of what they are experiencing, liminal persons spontaneously begin to relate to each other in a most profound, direct, and personal way. A comradeship, a lasting companionship that does not recognise rank or status or sexual distinction, springs up among them. *Communitas* is the name given by Victor Turner[1] to this kind of spontaneous, other-directed relationship, characteristic of the liminal stage. It's an unusual word but we need it because it cannot be translated simply as community. It is not just about community; it is not about structures and systems and institutions; it is not about people living together for some purpose; it is about something far more important, people living *for* each other.

Of course, this development can take place even when a person is not in contact with any formal rites of passage. It happens because, despite all attempts to structure society or religion and legislate for the details, there is always a dimension of life that does not fall within the structures but lies between them or 'on the margins.' And thankfully there have always been women and men of insight and generosity who responded to this dimension, if only for a time. But there are some who constantly remain in touch with this dimension of existence that cannot be fitted into conventions. It is, literally, anomalous. It is they especially who see through the pretensions of structured society and bravely live by an alternative vision. Of course, because this insight threatens comfortable stability they are forced to pay the price for living it.

The history of Israel contains many examples of such liminality and communitas. Abram, for the sake of his vision, goes into exile from an existing Mesopotamian culture and begins his liminal pilgrimage. Moses, who had been 'instructed in all the learning of the Egyptians' stands outside it all and goes instead into God's future because of his moment of burning insight. In Exodus the whole people have left the old structures behind; they are in a liminal state that generates spontaneous communitas among them. In their celebrations we notice that the pilgrim symbols of the charismatic leader – the tent, the shared meal, the covenant commitment, the common story, and the single hope – are dominant.

But these Exodus symbols are difficult to maintain when they move from a nomadic to a settled way of life, from a liminal state to structured, institutional life. In fact, they are replaced by very different realities: the king, the palace, the Temple and its cycle of sacrifices and festivals, and the detailed laws for the preservation of social harmony. But people of insight, prophets, stand opposed to all this and rail against the decadence and formalism of Israel's life. They call the people back to a way of life that is characterised by liminality and communitas. But again and again institution and structure re-assert themselves until the Exile ushers in a new liminal stage. And so the pattern is repeated until the last of the Hebrew prophets, Jesus of Nazareth, appears.

It seems valid to interpret what we have heard of Jesus so far using these categories of liminality and communitas. (Their strangeness should alert us to the difference in what he was doing.) What he says is in line with the high points of Israel's vision: He embodies its genetic moments, but this Jesus stands outside its present structure. His own experience of God does not fit into the conventions and expectations of Judaism. Jesus uses language in a new way to enable his hearers to catch a glimpse of the absolutely radical reality that he calls the kingdom/reign of God which is 'not known because not looked for.' He tries to share his own liminal vision with others. Through his counter-proverbs and threshold stories, he calls them to take the risk and cross the threshold into the liminal world that he inhabits, a world of paradox and mystery that is the antithesis of their everyday world. It is only by letting go of all pretensions, achievements, and familiarities, by risking everything that is cherished, that one can really enter this world. It is offered as a challenge, a test of courage and conviction. The liminal period, as we saw, is a time of testing and ordeal. The ministry of Jesus is likewise characterised by testing, and so too will be the life of the disciples.

His revolutionary and shocking prayer to God, *Abba*, is the depth cry of a liminal person to the one who alone knows and sustains him. This God whom he addresses in the warm familiar tones of *Abba* is the source of all. This name, *Abba*, learned in the trust of childhood, in the first flush of success and in the lonely places of failure and prayer, is the code word of Jesus. It is the utterance of the absolute mystery of his life. It is the summary of his message and way of life, the very reason for his liminal state. In his conviction about the prodigal fatherliness of this gracious God, Jesus offers hope to the hopeless and a future to the futureless. He longs to extend his insight to all, to rich and poor, to the elite and the exiled, the masters and the marginals. This is his preaching of the reign of God in word and action. He proclaims the good news of God's kingdom as a new possibility, a final chance for humankind to live differently because they have come to know God as *Abba*. The voice of this kingdom becomes credible when the one who proclaims God's rightness stands in scandalising solidarity with the marginals of religious society even to the point of opposition to the law.

There is absolute consistency between what he is and says and does. The kingdom becomes enfleshed in the miracles and exorcisms of Jesus as *Abba* lavishes his prodigal love on the little and the lost. It takes the shape of all-inclusive bread-breaking and of a new freedom to do good for all kinds of people, but especially the downtrodden, the defenceless, and the hopeless cases. Jesus does not offer aid or handouts to them, he is not condescending, nor does he treat them as recipients. Instead, he sees each person as someone to be with, friend, companion, someone for whom he struggles, with whom he suffers, about whose well-being he rejoices. He translates his message into a practical way of life in solidarity with the outcasts of society, in service to the despised, the derided, the broken, and the lost. He is the one who hungers and thirsts for justice, for the right kind of world, and preaches it as 'good news.' He makes it concrete through a whole range of activities and celebrates it in a rich variety of ways. Jesus is involved in the struggle to bring God to people and people to God and to each other.

But it is a liminal struggle. It involves subverting the known, secure world and crossing into the radically new world offered by Jesus where God truly reigns. This does not mean that Jesus ignores the world around him or that he wishes to create a Utopia. The kingdom's beginnings are about *this* world, transformed and made new. Jesus is convinced that this can and must happen if the disaster that people are bringing upon themselves is to be averted. The catastrophe is not coming because God in his anger arranged it. If it comes it will be because people will not accept that they must love one another, since they are all quite simply children of the same *Abba*, who is impassioned with each and every one of them. Jesus passionately desires that his hearers would accept this new vision of his. This is what he consistently preaches and lives. His own liminal lifestyle is the model of all that he proposes. He is the one who cherishes all, who holds all he has, and is, in open hands. He is without any of the defensive barriers that we set up and hide behind, defences that make people timid and fearful in giving and in receiving. He knows how quickly the human heart spots defects in people, how it reacts to non-likeness, and how soon this turns to antagonism, rejection, and hate. He knows how easily people become suspicious, judgmental, threatened, walled in by prejudice and fear, how easily they form sectarian groups.

But he also knows that people can love, be unselfish, be accepting and forgiving. So, in his contact with people, we see that he is vulnerable, open, uncautious, unafraid. He lets people in, makes place for them in his own life and gives them the courage to accept themselves and lose their guilt. He opens up communication and builds up solidarity between those previously opposed to each other. The kingdom he speaks of happens where there is communion between people and between people and God. To this end he breaks down class barriers, welcomes prostitutes, talks with heretics and pagans, and brings tax collectors and Zealots together among the Twelve.

In his person, his liminal actions, his threshold stories, Jesus himself is the very incarnation of the kingdom. He is its living parable and so that same shock effect characterises all his words and actions. Outrage and scandal are the standard reactions to the liminal words and actions of Jesus. This, he says 'is the time of final salvation.' It is being offered now in and through his fragile, question-marked conduct and words. There are no God-big signs, no incontrovertible proofs, just the weakness, the ambiguity, and the challenge of a life lived in opposition to the prevailing religious certainties. Expectations, prejudices, and above all the familiarity of the old ways and set patterns, are dead set against him.

This is the liminal world of the kingdom of God and it is into this world that Jesus invites his disciples. He calls on them to cross the threshold and enter into communitas with him and with each other where they will experience the sustained and sustaining freedom necessary for discipleship. Already they have heard Jesus proclaim and seen him reveal God's infinite forgiving love toward everyone. In this way they encountered, through his own person, the mystery of *Abba*'s boundless generosity. They had been beggars before God but now, through this meeting with Jesus, they see into the mystery of God's fatherly love and they realise that they are children for the first time. They realise that they can now say '*Abba*' like a child of the household. They realise just how hopeful their apparent hopelessness is.

They are called on to accept, to decide. But Jesus' hope is that there should be only one response to such a revelation of the prodigal generosity of God, one response to the realisation that one is truly a child and not an outcast. That response is a complete change of heart, a total transformation, and a new life that is lived as a response to the father's love. The only thing asked of the prodigal son is that he rejoice in his father and Jesus expects his disciples to live lives of quiet rejoicing in their *Abba*.

And so, for Jesus, *metanoia*, or repentance, does not mean going back guiltily to the beginning, mulling over the past, beating their breasts, and mournfully recounting their transgressions for the rest of their lives. It means taking God at his word and his love and moving toward his future in the security of the Father's arms. If women and men respond freely like this, then they may be invited to join in communitas with Jesus.

The gospels tell us that very many people make contact with Jesus, are helped or healed by him, are near him, follow him in crowds. However, we also hear about the Twelve and a larger group of disciples. These are women and men, who, while they sometimes falter in their following of Jesus, stay with him, nevertheless. They are his constant companions; they are committed to him and experience communitas with him. They are not pressured or cajoled into joining. In prophetic style Jesus 'calls' them and 'appoints' them to be 'with him' (Mk 3:14), 'to follow' (Mt 8:22), or to 'go after him.' This is a most radical call to be with Jesus, the eschatological prophet of God's rule. It is absolutely final. It is a matter of life or death and every other obligation, however binding, is subordinate to it. 'Leave the dead to bury their own dead' (Mt 8:22; Lk 9:60). Commitment to Jesus in his dedicated service to the kingdom demands a total change of heart and life in order to be. The cost of discipleship is spelled out starkly.

> And he called to him the multitude with his disciples, and said to them, 'If any man would come after me, let him deny himself and take up his cross and follow me. For whoever would save his life will lose it; and whoever loses his life for my sake and the gospel's will save it. For what does it profit a man to gain the whole world and forfeit his life? For what can a man give in return for his life? For whoever is ashamed of me and of my words in this adulterous and sinful generation, of him will the Son of Man also be ashamed' (Mk 8:34-38).

> 'Do you think that I have come to bring peace on earth? I have not come to bring peace, but a sword. For I have come to set a man against his father, and a daughter against her mother, and a daughter-in-law against her mother-in-law and a man's foes will be those of his own household. He who loves father or mother more than me is not worthy of

me; and he who loves son or daughter more than me is not worthy of me; and he who does not take his cross and follow me is not worthy of me. He who finds his life will lose it, and he who loses his life for my sake will find it' (Mt 10:34-39).

There can be no half-measures and no procrastination. Conversion is to be total. Everything, no matter how cherished in the old order, must be surrendered by those who wish to be with Jesus, to learn from him and to be prepared to imitate him in all things. It is not simply a gathering together of the like-minded. To be in communitas with Jesus means that they are to live for the kingdom and if necessary die for it.

This kind of discipleship goes beyond anything found hitherto in master-disciple relationships in Israel. In fact, it declares that the old ideas about following the Law or God are insufficient. Traditionally, converts to Judaism were asked to leave home and family and to sell their property and give it to the poor in order to follow Israel's God. Now Jesus is making the same demands on those who wish to be his disciples. Salvation for them is now mediated through their relationship to Jesus as the final prophet who announces and makes God's reign present. Being his disciple means giving oneself in service to Jesus' message, being an imitator of him, being a co-worker with him, and being 'sent out to preach and have authority to cast out demons' (Mk 3:14-15). In being with Jesus, disciples are to experience the contagion, be infected by the lived conviction that is his. Like Jesus, they must be willing to give up all available presents and attainable futures for the new future to which *Abba* is calling them all.

What he is searching for is people who will really accept that God is the God of creation who lovingly created the world so that he might coax from his creatures the free response of love to his creative love. Jesus seeks disciples who know that Yahweh is the God of tender, covenant love, passionately dedicated to justice for his beloved Israel, who is ceaselessly active but hidden in her passion history. He is then a God of love, mercy, compassion, and justice.

But all Jews believed this for these are the convictions by which they lived, or so it was said. But did they really? This is what Jesus is preaching, yet it is being rejected by many who dedicated themselves to the study of the Bible and Israel's traditions. They say they cannot reconcile what they discover there with what Jesus is saying and doing. He is proclaiming that God is the God of love and that this love is the only force at the real heart of creation and human life, that this God acts like a Father-king, who can only love his children and who desires only what is best for each and every one of them. He is gentle, compassionate, forgiving, and against all evil and, through Jesus, he heals, makes whole, reconciles. He is pleading with humankind to accept that they are always loved unconditionally and are asked only to love unconditionally in return. Yet consistently they refuse.

To maintain that the world is founded on an abyss of unconditional love is incredible. To accept that there is love and only love is the most terrifying truth of all. To know, to trust, to hope in the weakness of love alone seems madness when the whole world of experience and everyday life is structured on other assumptions. To have faith in the weakness of love is to be absolutely vulnerable to the egotism, the desire for control, for power, for glory, for riches, for domination, for revenge that the world believes in.

Jesus knows this yet he hopes sufficiently in God and his creatures to ask his disciples to begin to live the alternative he proposes. He declares that God is love and, in complete obedience, he gives himself to *Abba* for the sake of all his 'little ones.' He allows this Father to live and love through him as the medium of his communication. Jesus is free precisely because he loves. This is what he lives and it is to this that he calls disciples. They are asked to live out the conviction that *Abba* is living and loving through them in their contact with their fellows. To live by, from, off love alone is the terror and the reward of discipleship. As he calls them to this way of life, their desire, their attachment, their centre is always elsewhere. That is why they need constantly to be converted, to be 'with Jesus,' to learn from him. They must be de-centred and re-centred. They must experience exodus and passover, death and life, constantly. What Jesus is seeking is co-workers who will share his vision, who will build with him a new world aligned with the only real centre that can save, the creator God of love, compassion, and justice. He is not talking about minor modifications of existing structures and institutions; he wants to establish the foundations of a new world. To ask for this is to ask for the most profound change imaginable in people's faith. It means being in a constant state of liminality!

Unless groups of people begin to live the difference that such an understanding, such an ideal, could make to human life it will be no more than a beautiful utopian dream. Jesus cannot be satisfied just because a few people are healed, because some of the 'poor' feel freer, because a little of the injustice in the nation is overcome. He wants people to be together in such a way that there will be no discrimination between the children of the one *Abba*, no sectarianism, no indifference to the suffering of others, no fatalism in the face of the flawed structures and institutions of religion and government. He is searching, not for ways of making what exists less unjust, but rather for a God-given new beginning where there will be an end to all injustice, hunger, and oppression. Only justice that goes to the root of all injustice does not enslave people.

In this new way of being together, that Jesus proposes, people will be free for they will be liberated by God himself (Lk 6:20-22; Mt 5:3-12) and rely completely on his love for them. Among disciples who take God at his word and at his love, no ambition or rivalry will be found and God will make himself present to them (Mt 5:8). They will have his *shalom* within them and they will work for God's peace and reconciliation among all (Mt 5:9). Their hunger and their thirst will be for the justice, the righteousness, the rightness that God desires among all his children.

To be committed to this pursuit of justice means setting their faces against the values of the systems within which they now live. Jesus insists on this, even if it means rejection and persecution, for in no other way can the new beginning take place. He sees that the hunger for God's love that is created at the centre of human hearts, the desire for fulfilment with God, has distorted itself into hunger for prestige, for power, for prosperity. These are the pathologies of the heart yet society is structured and centred on these anti-values and counter-fulfilments: fear rather than love, control rather than acceptance, oppression rather than freedom. It is these hungers which generate rivalry and discrimination, violence and revenge, greed and injustice.

These hungers are the counterfeit gods, the idols of the human heart. They destroy human beings because they leave no room for God or others in their lives. Clearly, then, it is not enough simply to keep them in check, and so Jesus asks for the conscious rejection of these idols, a free renunciation of these false values, and a break with the systems they produce. The disciples are asked to stand liminal to them so that communitas may replace them. It is not possible to imagine a more extreme demand, but this is what Jesus asks of his disciples. The vision of God as the Father, who treats all equally and has no favourites, 'who makes his sun rise on the evil and on the good, and sends rain on the just and on the unjust' (Mt 5:45) commands it. How can there be place for God in their lives, how can they say he is their Abba, if they are anxious about 'life itself, what you shall eat or what you shall drink, or about your body, what you shall put on' (Mt 6:25-33)?

Rather, they must live out the conviction that *Abba*'s love alone creates and sustains all life, 'the lilies of the field and the birds of the air,' he knows what all his children need even before they ask for it. 'He is a God of the living and it is his will that none of his children perish.' He cares absolutely for everything that he has loved into existence. If two sparrows are sold for a penny and this Father is present to their living and their dying, why should disciples be anxious? After all, he adds, with wry humour, 'You are worth many sparrows!' How can non-disciples come to believe that God is as Jesus says he is, if his presence is not discernible in disciples' lives, if its effects cannot be seen? So when he sends out his disciples to extend his mission, to communicate to others what they experienced with Jesus himself, he says:

> Go on your way; behold I send you out as lambs in the midst of wolves. Carry no purse, no bag, no sandals; and salute no one on the road ... remain in the same house eating and drinking what they set before you ... heal the sick and say to them, 'The kingdom of God has come near to you' (Lk 10:3-9).

The poorest of the poor would not undertake a journey in such an absolutely destitute state. The disciples are to undertake it out of service to the kingdom and in absolute confidence in the benificence of God, with whom what is impossible by human reckoning becomes possible.

Disciples and the Pathologies of the Human Heart

1. *Possessions:* Jesus wishes his disciples to renounce the hunger for the false value of possessions and riches. If they put their trust in possessions and riches to give them security, what faith have they in God who is the ultimate source of what they hoard and the only one who can enrich? If they amass riches, it is done at the cost of imposing poverty on others who have an equal right as sisters and brothers. The name of the poor is written on their possessions, so Jesus expects his followers to leave everything. 'Go sell what you have and give to the poor ... and come follow me'; 'Lo, we have left everything and followed you' (Mk 10:21, 28-30). Jesus sees this as the only way of breaking with the old system that breeds so much suffering and diminishment.

A disciple cannot have a divided heart. 'No one can serve two masters for either he will hate the one and love the other or he will be devoted to the one and despise the other. You cannot serve God and Mammon' (Mt 6:24). It is a choice between gods, between the old world and the new. You cannot break new ground, plough a new furrow straight, if you constantly look over your shoulder and hanker after the past. Jesus shocked and astonished his disciples by saying bluntly:

How hard it will be for those who have riches to enter the kingdom of God! And the disciples were amazed at his words. But Jesus said to them again, 'Children, how hard it is for those who trust in riches to enter the kingdom of God. It is easier for a camel to go through the eye of a needle than for a rich man to enter the kingdom of God.' And they were exceedingly astonished and said to him, 'Then who can be saved?' Jesus looked at them and said, 'With men it is impossible, but not with God; for all things are possible with God' (Mk 10:23-27).

The power of possessions to blind the eyes to the dire need of others and harden the heart against compassion is vividly brought home to us in the story of the rich man and Lazarus (Lk 16:19-31). No doubt the rich man's useless excuse would be the same as that of the people in the Great Judgment (Mt 25:31-46): 'I did not know. I never noticed'; 'Lord, when did we see you hungry or thirsty or a stranger or naked or sick or in prison, and did not minister to you? ... Truly I say to you, as you did it not to one of the least of these, you did it not to me' (Mt 25:44-46). Disciples are warned not to lay up treasures on earth: 'Where your treasure is, there will your heart be also' (Mt 6:21). He wants them to realise that they are temporary caretakers of what are ultimately God's good gifts and they must be ready with open hands to give them over to others. 'From him who takes away your cloak, do not withhold your coat as well ... and of him who takes away your goods, do not ask them again' (Lk 6:29-30).

Teachings like this about possessions and the need to reject Mammon drew upon him the derision of the Pharisees who were lovers of money and they scoffed at him. But he said to them, 'You are those who justify yourselves before others, but God knows your hearts; for what is exalted among others is an abomination in the sight of God' (Lk 16:14-15).

Not, of course, that Jesus canonises destitution or hunger or material poverty for its own sake. It is his desire to say no to all forms of evil, suffering, and poverty. We are told, in fact, that Jesus did not recommend austerities (Mt 11:18-19) or impose fasting on his disciples (Mt 9:14-15). Yet he and his disciples are never in need: 'When I sent you out with no purse or bag or sandals did you lack anything?' They said, 'Nothing' (Lk 22:35). And he even releases them from the Sabbath law when they are hungry (Mt 12:1-8). Even his audience and the bystanders are cared for extravagantly. Jesus acts as host in the stories of the multiplication of the loaves and the fishes for the multitude, taking the bread, blessing it, breaking it, and handing it around. His bread-breaking with close disciples and with 'tax collectors and sinners' and with wider groupings lest they go hungry is indelibly imprinted on their memories. It betokens the superabundance of the kingdom.

> Now John's disciples and the Pharisees were fasting and people came and said [to Jesus], 'Why do John's disciples and the disciples of the Pharisees fast, but your disciples do not fast?' And Jesus said to them, 'Can the wedding guests fast while the bridegroom is with them? As long as they have the bridegroom with them, they cannot fast. No one sews a piece of unshrunk cloth on an old garment; if he does, the patch tears away from it, the new from the old, and a worse tear is made. And no one puts new wine into old wineskins, and the wine is lost, and so are the skins, but new wine is for fresh skins' (Mk 2:18-19, 21-22).

Jesus is not arbitrarily releasing his disciples from fasting. Rather, his disciples are so enthralled by his sustaining and transforming presence, so gladdened by his good news about the new presence of God's merciful salvation, that their hearts overflow, they must rejoice and celebrate, they simply cannot fast and mourn. Indeed, as Schillebeeckx remarks, being sad in the company of Jesus is 'an existential impossibility.'[2] The freedom and the rejoicing in the Father's care that characterises the attitude of Jesus and his disciples to life and creation is what annoys those who do not share it. But Jesus' reply is simply: If you are renewed and forgiven you cannot but rejoice in your enthrallment with this gift.

Again and again we hear of incidents that radiate joy. In John's gospel Jesus' signs begin at Cana with an extravagant merry-making miracle, as if to highlight the festive character of his entire ministry. People must rejoice. And this note of joy runs through all that Jesus has to say. The harvest time has come, the new wine and the bread of life are offered already. They must rejoice now. Joy must be unconfined, for the Father is in-gathering the poor and the little ones into the festive banquet of the last times. His peace is definitively offered. The wedding feast has begun, the banquet is prepared. The happy gathering of friends is in session. The treasure has been found. Unexpectedly high wages have been doled out. What was lost has been restored and the dead have been raised to life.

So how could people be gloomy? How could they even fast? Pure gift, with no right to reward, must be answered by pure joy. Once they had come to this vision, to this moment of recognition, once they had decided, it reversed everything, even pain and sorrow (Mt 5:3-4). They now had the absolute assurance that 'All shall be well and all manner of thing shall be well.'[3] And so everything is now seen to have been worth the risk, because nothing is ever lost to a God who looks after sparrows and counts the very hairs of our heads. They now know the value of the pearl, so the sacrifice involved in giving up everything to possess it appears to be of no account. It appears to have been a joyful undertaking from the very beginning.

Because they have now been forgiven, because they have been brought from death to life, God lays claim to their entire life. And that claim alone frees them for it realigns them, brings *shalom,* allows them to be what they are, to be restored to themselves, to be children of *Abba.* There is no calculating now. There is no discrimination among people, no bargaining or huckstering with God. They themselves have received without calculation and with utter generosity. So they must give without counting the cost, without hesitation, not once but every day and every moment of every day. They do not ask 'Who is my neighbour?' They ask, 'To whom can I be a neighbour?' Their only defence against an enemy is to love. They forgive every offence against them because *Abba* has forgiven them everything. Their response must be one of simple joy because at last they have been found, they have come to themselves and so they must help others to allow themselves to be found. Jesus declares in deed and word that God's forgiveness is freely available to sinners. Paradoxically this does not encourage laxity, but makes the most stringent demands. They must give themselves totally. They must match the graciousness of what has been given to them by the graciousness of their response. The kingdom is pure gift. It is offered to those who have no right to reward. *Abba's* love is infinite and undeserved and the realisation of this has 'charmed back the luxury of a child's soul' (*P. Kavanagh, Advent*).

Those who have come to his vision, those who recognise that this is how things are, must simply live out what they are – *Abba's* children. They are told to be prodigal as their heavenly father is prodigal, compassionate as he is compassionate. He gives himself totally, they must give themselves totally. Their response to the people they meet must be modelled on God's loving initiative toward them. And they need no further directions. 'Be merciful, even as your heavenly father is merciful.'

2. Prestige:[4] If Jesus was adamant about freeing his disciples from the seduction of prosperity and riches, he is no less insistent on their being relieved from the destructive effects of the hunger for prestige. (Indeed these three insatiable hungers, for prosperity, prestige, and power, are always interlaced.) The fact that the disciples renounce the desire for riches does not guarantee that they have thereby renounced the desire for control, the desire to lord it over others, to be looked up to, to be an 'important person.'

Prestige was the most important issue in the oriental world and to lose prestige was to lose life itself. Status then was dependent on considerations like ancestry or role or authority or virtue or, like today, it might be 'bought by riches.' It did and still does exercise a peculiar fascination for human beings and preoccupation with prestige and esteem can take over and control life. In liminality and communitas, we saw that all status and rank is forfeited, liminals become de-classed and roles and differentiations become unimportant for them. We notice that Jesus lives like this and asks for such an approach from his disciples.

He enters into solidarity with those who are without prestige or status, even the blind, the lame, the insane. He de-classes himself and willingly forfeits even his own ritual purity in the process. The esteem of people counts for nothing to him. 'Teacher we know that you are true and care for no man; for you do not regard the position of men' (Mk 12:14). He sharply criticised the hypocrisy of those who do 'holy' things in order to impress and elicit admiration, who 'practice piety before men in order to be seen by them; for then you will have no reward from your Father' (Mt 6:1-6,16-18) or who 'do all their deeds to be seen by men' (Mt 23:5ff, indeed the entire chapter). To want to have 'a name' for holiness and for the prestige it brought in the eyes of the impressionable, to 'love the place of honour at feasts and the best seats in the synagogues and salutations in the market squares and being called rabbi' (Mt 23:6-7) is anathema to Jesus.

The disciples are not immune to this cancer but when Jesus notices it he intervenes quickly to destroy it. The disciples came to Jesus, saying:

'Who is the greatest in the kingdom of heaven?' And calling to him a child, he put him in the midst of them and said, 'Truly, I say to you, unless you turn and become like children, you will never enter the kingdom of heaven' (Mt 18:1-4).

In response to their quest for 'greatness' and group prestige he proposes the littleness of a child. In the society of that time a child had no legal or religious status, so Jesus is saying that their being together must be characterised by this kind of absence of status. They will have to accept that to choose to be in solidarity with the marginals of society means having to forego any possibility of ever being looked up to. They will never be prestigious. 'Blessed are you when men hate you, and when they exclude you and revile you and cast out your name as evil ...' (Lk 6:22).

In this sense too we must understand the contrasting of the 'babes' who receive God's revelation with the 'wise and intelligent' who cannot receive it (Mt 11:25), or his statement about the greatest among disciples being 'last of all and servant of all' (Mk 9:35).

We noted earlier that sexual differentiation becomes less important in communitas. This is seen in a remarkable way among the disciples gathered around Jesus. That he had women among his disciples, that he loved them (Jn 11:5) and accepted their love was scandalous to his contemporaries. None of the four major movements within Judaism would allow a woman to join them and rabbis and scribes would never accept a woman as a disciple. Women were regarded as the 'lowest of the low' in that society; men even gave thanks in their morning prayers that they had not been born as women. Jesus treats women as equals, they are his 'sisters and mother' (Mt 3:35). They travel with him on his journey, they 'followed him, and ministered to him; and also many other women who came up with him to Jerusalem' (Mk 15:41). (Unlike some of his male disciples, they remain faithful during the crisis of his passion and women play a vital role in the empty tomb and appearance narratives.) His acceptance of women and his attitude toward them is beautifully illustrated in the story of the woman in the house of the Pharisee:

> One of the Pharisees asked him to eat with him, and he went into the Pharisee's house, and sat at table. And behold, a woman of the city, who was a sinner, when she learned that he was sitting at table in the Pharisee's house, brought an alabaster flask of ointment, and standing at his feet, weeping, she began to wet his feet, and anointed them with the ointment. Now when the Pharisee who had invited him saw it, he said to himself, 'If this man were a prophet, he would have known who and what sort of woman this is who is touching him, for she is a sinner.' And Jesus answering said to him, 'Simon, I have something to say to you.' And he answered, 'What is it, Teacher?'
>
> 'A certain creditor had two debtors; one owed five hundred denarii, and the other fifty. When they could not pay, he forgave them both. Now which of them will love him more?' Simon answered, 'The one, I suppose, to whom he forgave more,' and he said to him, 'You have judged rightly.' Then turning toward the woman he said to Simon, 'Do you

see this woman? I entered your house, you gave me no water for my feet, but she has wet my feet with her tears and wiped them with her hair. You gave me no kiss, but from the time I came in she has not ceased to kiss my feet. You did not anoint my head with oil, but she has anointed my feet with ointment. Therefore I tell you, her sins, which are many, are forgiven, for she loved much; but he who is forgiven little, loves little.' And he said to her, 'Your sins are forgiven.' Then those who were at table with him began to say among themselves, 'Who is this, who even forgives sins?' And he said to the woman, 'Your faith has saved you; go in peace' (Lk 7:36-50; see Jn 4:4-42).

All human beings, irrespective of the value given them by society, are treated as children of the one *Abba* by Jesus. The new concept of solidarity within the communitas formed around him derives from the new vision of the relationship with God ...'who is my mother and who are my brothers? Whoever does the will of my father is my brother and sister and mother' (Mk 3:3435). This solidarity is not given but is a duty to be worked at. But it can be achieved by those who have found the right relationship with the Father and who experience his presence as the one who constantly sustains and invites them to renewed humanity. It is precisely this conviction that brings them all into a liminal state. It can happen among women and men who realise that they are all poor specimens of the humanity that God desires, but who are willing now to change and to live off this inexhaustible source of love.

3. Power: Finally the disciples are to renounce the hunger for power. The kingdom Jesus speaks of is not given to the strong but to the weak, to those who mourn, those without resources, those cast out and wounded or broken by the power structures (Lk 6:20-22; Mt 5:3-11). He says to them: 'It is your Father's good pleasure to give you the kingdom' (Lk 12:32).

Discipleship of Jesus is about dedication to this kingdom. Those called are to serve it in obedience, evoke its presence in others by discovering only the strength of weakness and refusing the weakness of power. Love is its origin, its goal, and its only strategy. So it cannot be about wielding power or controlling or dominating. Rather, it is about liberating the hearts of others by love and for love. As communitas, the group of disciples are to live for others and to die rather than meet violence with violence.

> You have heard that it was said to the men of old, 'You shall not kill; and whoever kills shall be liable to judgment.' But I say to you that everyone who is angry with his brother shall be liable to judgment, whoever insults his brother shall be liable to the council, and whoever says, 'You fool!' shall be liable to the hell of fire (Mk 5:21-22).

> You have heard that it was said, 'An eye for an eye and a tooth for a tooth.' But I say to you, do not resist one who is evil. But if any one strikes you on the right cheek, turn to him the other also; and if any one would sue you and take your coat, let him have your cloak as well; and if any one forces you to go one mile, go with him two miles. Give to him who begs from you, and do not refuse him who would borrow from you.

> You have heard that it was said, 'You shall love your neighbour and hate your enemy.' But I say to you, love your enemies and pray for those who persecute you, so that you may be sons of your Father who is in heaven; for he makes his sun rise on the evil and on the good, and sends rain on the just and on the unjust. For if you love those who love you, what reward have you? Do not even the tax collectors do the same? And if you salute only your brethren, what more are you doing than others? Do not even the gentiles do the same? (Mk 5:38-47).

If God is truly their *Abba*, they must live and act differently. They must realise that the will to power breeds conflict, jealousy, hatred, violence, and revenge. It destroys both the oppressed and the oppressor. Disciples are to live in conscious opposition to the tyranny of power.

The disciples are not to jostle for personal advantage or grasp for power, to seek privileged positions, or desire,

> 'to sit one at your right hand and one at your left, in your glory '(Mk 10:37). 'You know that those who are supposed to rule over the gentiles lord it over them, and their great men exercise authority over them. But it shall not be so among you; but whoever would be great among you must

be your servant and whoever would be first among you must be slave of all. For the Son of Man also came not to be served but to serve and to give his life as a ransom for many' (Mk 10:42-45).

The energy that would go into serving power structures is to be released for service to others, even to the point of giving their lives. Authority here means service and nothing else. Jesus consistently maintains in his preaching that the real enemy is not the other but the egotistic self. So they are to love those whom they had regarded as enemies and overcome the enemy within by being totally available to others in service as Jesus is. This is a constant, crucifying struggle. 'If any one would come after me, let him deny himself and take up his cross and follow me' (Mt 16:24).

Furthermore, Jesus even warns them against accepting titles and honours that would feed the lust for power.

But you are not to be called rabbi for you have only one teacher, and you are all brethren ... Neither be called masters, for you have only one master ... He who is greatest among you shall be your servant; whoever exalts himself will be humbled and whoever humbles himself will be exalted (Mt 23:8, 10-12).

Nor are they to feed this hunger in others by offering flattering titles of respect to them. 'And call no man your father (extended as a courtesy to some venerable person) on earth. For you have one Father, who is in heaven' (Mt 23:9).

It is not surprising, then, that Jesus vehemently opposes those who pervert the authority they have as interpreters of the law and use it as power to oppress the little ones. 'You load men with burdens hard to bear and you yourselves do not touch the burdens with one of your fingers' (Lk 11:46) or 'You shut the kingdom of heaven against men; for you neither enter yourselves, nor allow those who would enter to go in' (Mt 23:13). He attacks the legalism which tithes herbs and neglects the weightier matters of the law-'justice and the love of God' (Lk 11:42).He is angry with those who use their God-given intelligence to make distinctions so that the rich will inherit the earth and the poor will only have their poverty (Mt 23:16-22).

This use of the law, and 'the fence around the law,' to separate precept from life and its experience makes religion into an unbearable burden for the little ones and is criticised and opposed by Jesus. This brought him into sharp conflict with the authorities and the establishment. Some of the things he said and positions he adopted on the question of the law, while close to positions adopted by Hellenistic Jews, must have seemed like the work of the antichrist to some of the strict Jews.

Yet, Jesus does not at all wish to reject the law. Far from it, he wishes to restore its God-given purpose – to enable people to do good.[5] Greek-speaking Jews had been looking forward to the final prophet who would be a true teacher of the true law, freeing it from human accretions. Jesus is presented to us as restoring the law to its original purpose, namely, the freedom to do good. And this is Jesus' whole purpose too, to communicate to people God's concern for them so that, being assured of his unconditional love and allowing it to suffuse their lives, they may be freed to do good. So when Jesus exercises this ministry and is opposed by people armed with a negative interpretation of the law ('It is not lawful to do such and such on this day or in these circumstances'), he opposes them vigorously. He refuses to allow the law to be used to bind people.

> Again he entered the synagogue, and a man was there who had a withered hand. And they watched him, to see whether he would heal him on the Sabbath, so that they might accuse him. And he said to the man who had the withered hand, 'Come here.' And he said to them, 'Is it lawful on the Sabbath to do good or to do harm, to save life or to kill?' But they were silent. And he looked around at them with anger, grieved at their hardness of heart, and said to the man, 'Stretch out your hand.' He stretched it out, and his hand was restored. The Pharisees went out, and immediately held counsel with the Herodians against him, how to destroy him. (See the confrontation in Mk 3:1-6; Lk 13:10-17; 14:1-6.)

Again, it was to free the little ones that Jesus set himself against the heartless casuistry of his day. He was convinced that they must be free to exercise their God-given freedom and responsibility as children of *Abba* and so he proposes what his opponents would have regarded as an ethic of marginality for them. Out of conviction he 'breaks' the Sabbath to help the little ones and says, 'The Sabbath was made for man, not man for the Sabbath' (Mk 2:27).

This saying did indeed exist among the Hellenistic Jewish communities, but on the lips of Jesus, when linked to his whole message and way of life, it must have sounded like the cry of the antichrist to his legalistic opponents. In the gospels, we do not find Jesus castigating those who broke the Sabbath but he railed against those who prided themselves in keeping it. The same is true about adultery and cheating. He recognises sin as sin but, unlike the authorities, offers exodus, a way out, a new beginning. For Jesus 'keeping' the commandments is not negative, but supremely positive.

It was concern too for these little ones that made him oppose current interpretations of the law. He breaks through the network of laws, of religious and moral tradition ('the fence') and reaches for the human heart, freeing it by binding it more closely to *Abba*. Jesus even submits passages in Scripture to criticism, for example, on the question of regulations on cleanliness in Mk 7:14-23, which was tantamount to questioning the authority of Moses. He also does this in his statements about not resisting evil, for he goes far beyond the Old Testament moderating law about 'an eye for an eye and a tooth for a tooth' (Lk 6:29-30; Mt 5:39-42). He even enjoins love for one's enemies and a blessing on those who curse you (Lk 6:27-28), which must have sounded like madness to many of his contemporaries.

Or notice how, in the Sermon on the Mount (Mk 5:21-48), he differentiates his teaching from that given 'to the men of old.' The 'do not' of the commandments becomes the 'not even' of Jesus. It is not that you do not kill, you do not even have a thought about violence. It is not just that you do not commit adultery, but you do not cast a lustful glance at man or woman. He knows that 'to love the Lord your God with all your heart and with all your soul and with all your strength and with all your mind and your neighbour as yourself' (Lk 10:27) is the essence of the law but for Jesus it means *whole* heart and *whole* soul. Nothing must be allowed to distract from this. Your whole yes must be yes and your whole no, no.

We ask who is this man who claims this supreme authority and makes these unconditional demands? We are listening to an unparalleled claim to authority that shocked the scribes and

Pharisees and was understood by them as a revolutionary attack upon the law and the tradition of the elders. It gained for Jesus the accusation of being a false prophet. And we should remember that apostasy from the law was taken as a sign of the last times (Dan 7:20, 23; 1 Macc 1:44-49).

It is obvious then that Jesus is not concerned only with the small group of close disciples, nor can they be concerned only with themselves or with feeding upon the group itself. Jesus is concerned, above all, to prevent barriers being put up or boundaries set in position. They must not allow themselves to become a clique of like-with-like or cut themselves off from others or allow old prejudices and fears to shut anyone out. The ingathering that Jesus is concerned with must be their concern too. They must incarnate it. There are to be no outsiders, no boundaries, no divisiveness, no defensiveness. The focus for action is simply wherever there are people, especially those in need. The thrust of their life together is primarily toward relatedness to the kingdom and each other. Within this relatedness there is ample room for vibrant relationships.

In all this, Jesus seems to be saying that they must quite simply respond to the gift of the present. They must understand the decisiveness of the present for the future. Disciples must allow themselves to be amazed by the radical and gracious newness of every moment, to be aware of the everlasting significance of each heartbeat, to be intensely committed to what is passing, to be dedicated to what is provisional and see present appearance as already the arrival of the future.

If they fail to see things in this way, he says, they are in flight from God's call. They are losing themselves and rejecting the future which is offered by God, because, instead of simply helping it to unfold, they are creating an alternative future doomed to failure (a description of sin). Above all, their lives together and with others must be characterised by love and compassion and forgiveness.

A disciple has to live in absolute generosity, in a willingness to forgive ceaselessly, with a love which embraces everyone (even enemies) and with a compassion that is moved by incomplete, suffering humanity. This is the ideal of absolute love and it is proposed to everyone. Jesus maintains that any lesser standard is a refusal of the God he proclaims.

Everything he says and does is based on the conviction that

the source of love, named by him as *Abba*, wishes to love through us. So to refuse undertakings that call for heroism is, in fact, to underestimate God's love and to set limits to it. Only the person who lives on God's love itself can be the channel of that love toward the other. 'Give me a lover and he will understand,' St Augustine wrote.

Because disciples know themselves to be loved in this way, they know that they are accepted and forgiven by their compassionate Father, that they are precious in his sight. They are imperfect, sinful, self-centred, blind, yet they are loved and called to greatness. This is what forgiveness is – it is realistic and idealistic, at one and the same time. In the story of the prodigal, the father sees both sons as they are *and* as they could become. He knows what they have done so far; he is aware of their shortcomings, but he does not punish, he does not judge, he does not demand, he does not force them to be what they cannot yet be. He accepts, he loves. But he also knows what they can become and, without pressure, he gently but passionately hopes for their total happiness. He loves them far more than they can love themselves at that moment and in love he longs for them to accept their sonship.

To accept gently, and without probing the raw wounds of those who are 'coming to themselves' and to hold open for them the fantastic new future that can be theirs, is to forgive. This is what *Abba* does, this is what Jesus does, this is what disciples are called to do. Everything has been forgiven them, they have been called out of death into life so they are to live that forgiveness now, always. 'How often shall my brother sin against me and I forgive him? As many as seven times?' Jesus said to him, 'I do not say to you seven times, but seventy times seven' (Mt 18:21-22). Their being together is to be characterised, above all, by forgiveness and that forgiveness must be inexhaustible.

Disciples are to pray to *Abba*: 'Forgive us our debts as we also have forgiven our debtors,' and Jesus adds 'For if you forgive men their trespasses your heavenly Father will forgive you' (Mt 6:12,14), 'Forgive and you shall be forgiven' (Lk 6:37). They are to be with others in such a way that they will experience acceptance and forgiveness and be transformed. Despite all their faults and weaknesses, they are to refuse to shut them out, to build walls, to allow wounds to fester. Instead they are to hope for them in the name of God's reign. This is what they themselves experienced through being with Jesus and it must extend outwards. Only those who come to themselves, who acknowledge their pain, their hurt, and their sin, yet rejoice in the Father's love, can be compassionate toward others and so be mediators of his forgiveness.

This call of God always takes the shape of those at hand. The sacrament of the sister and brother is what is basic. In acting like this, their only motive is gratitude for God's graciousness and so they do not worry about reward because 'Your father who sees what is done in secret will reward you' (Mt 6:6). To think of reward or to calculate merit is to sin 'like Lucifer by this anticipation.'[6] They are to cast all their cares on *Abba* and yet they are warned to count the cost of discipleship. And indeed to the outsider this lived discipleship appears to make radical and brutal demands. Disciples are to take up their cross and to follow the way of Jesus. They are, in effect, being asked to live the last days now, called to live the future in the present. They are called to be faithful in the least things, and they are called to pour themselves out to death if necessary for the poor and the little ones.

But the secret is that they are not doing this by themselves. Like Jesus, they are never alone … 'the Father is always with me' (Jn 16:32). So to the children and babes who can call God *Abba*, all of this is simply 'his good pleasure.' It is just natural to want to please a father in everything, no matter what the cost. In all of this they are called on to imitate Jesus who exists to gather together the one family of God. And he has the capacity to stir up perpetual disquiet even in this new *communitas*. They can never say, 'This is enough.' 'When you have done all that is commanded you, say, 'We are unworthy servants; we have only done what was our duty' (Lk 17:10). What he asks for is single-mindedness and consistency. These are to be the hallmarks of his followers if they are to take up the challenge of the kingdom. He makes extreme demands on his disciples. They are to leave family, leave everything and follow him, 'go the way of the kingdom.' He knows what he is asking but he asks it all the same, and he wants people to be aware of the demands.

Implicit in all of this is the claim that response to him, here and now, determines one's stance toward God for the future. 'The call of God goes out in the call of Jesus.'[7] 'Whoever receives me receives him who sent me ... He who denies me, I will deny him before the Son of Man.' Those who stand in judgment on Jesus are now passing judgment on themselves by their reaction to him.

The petty questions of the day about politics, about Rome, about theological disputes between the schools, theories about the mystery of evil, God's providence, were all put to Jesus. But we must notice that in each case he refuses to be drawn into the distractions of the debate and he always brings them back to thinking about God. Equivalently he is saying that their mentality is all wrong. If only they had some insight into *Abba*'s love for all women and men, then their whole frame of reference would be so different that they would see how relative these questions were. If they believed with their whole heart that God is *Abba*, then all of these things would find their own level and his joy would be theirs. Because Jesus spoke like this they dismissed his teaching as irrelevant to the burning issues of their day.

In fact he was giving the only real answer to the questions that no one wanted to ask. The vision Jesus proposes and lives, the answers about *Abba* and his Fatherly love, could give them the hope and confidence necessary to live life and live it to the full. It gives the serenity to accept the incomprehensible, to accept even suffering, evil, and death, not in a fatalistic way but in the transforming knowledge that everything comes from Abba, the creator God. By being accepted in this way they are transformed.

They realise that *Abba*'s prodigal care for them makes a mockery of their concerns and worries about themselves. Disciples must pray constantly but without anxiety. 'In praying do not heap up empty phrases as the Gentiles do for they think that they will be heard for their many words. Do not be like them, for your father knows what you need before you ask him' (Mt 6:7-8). Those who are anxious (Mt 6:25) about tomorrow lose the joy of living today to the full, toward God and the neighbour who needs them. Of course, things will happen to them, evils will befall them but if they can call, like a child, on *Abba*, the Father who cares, the one who always listens will take them by the hand through these rough passages into deeper communion with himself. St Augustine summed it up by saying, 'Leave the past to his mercy, the present to his love, and the future to his providence.'

If, then, this is what discipleship means, would we have been called to it by Jesus? If this is what it entails, would we have remained faithful to such a call? Does our preferred model of discipleship really correspond to what Jesus had in mind for his followers?

8. GOING UP TO JERUSALEM

Love is the unfamiliar name
Behind the hands that wove
The intolerable shirt of flame
which human power cannot remove.
T. S. Eliot

Sometimes, in a flight of fancy, we imagine that if we had the privilege of meeting the historical Jesus, our difficulties with faith in him would vanish. We would believe unwaveringly. Yet, it is far from clear that we would have accepted without question what Jesus did and said. Perhaps we would not have accepted it at all. The questions in the minds of his contemporaries would have been in our minds too. Ultimately, they and we would have to decide about the most basic question of all: Is he a man of God, a prophet doing the work of God, or is he from the Evil One doing the work of the antichrist? The people of his own time took up dramatically opposed positions on these questions, interpreting what they experienced in the presence of Jesus in profoundly different ways. It is important for us to remember this, because some writings about the 'quest for the historical Jesus' may give the impression that an un-interpreted Jesus of history exists somewhere and can be recovered if only we use the right approach and methods.

It is clear that an un-interpreted Jesus never existed. Each of his contemporaries decided about him when they heard of his reputation or came into contact with him. They tried to define him and label him. So we begin to realise that it was not then, and is not now, possible to enclose the mystery of his person within a single category or describe him by using a single, neat formula. Some may have compared his teaching with that of the Pharisees, concerned as they were with the sanctification of all life; some may have regarded him as being an unconventional rabbi or teacher; some of the ideas of apocalyptic writings may have been recalled by his language.

But the differences far outweigh the similarities, for he mixes with people whom the Pharisees and rabbis avoided; he was 'careless' about the religious duties, which they observed in minute detail, and he called people (including women) to be his followers, and not just to learn and practice the Torah. Others may have asked themselves whether he might not be the Teacher of Righteousness, spoken of by the Essenes, but again he is in basic disagreement with their separatist, elitist code. No doubt too, some saw his potential as a nationalistic leader but his talk of turning the other cheek and his mixing with pagans was treasonable to them.

Jesus does not align himself with any of the movements or groupings in that society. What he says or does calls them in question and threatens their self-regarding piety and their fanaticism. So, if we must use a category that will disclose something of his historical appearance, it will have to be that of prophet. 'Is Jesus of Nazareth a prophet like John or like one of the prophets of old?' (Mk 6:15, 8:27ff; Lk 7:39, 24:19) would have been a question many of his contemporaries would have had to ask.

Many people accepted him as a prophet, as a man sent from God. Those who did not stayed within the category if only to condemn him as a false prophet. Much of Jesus' teaching and activity would have been understood as belonging to the prophetic tradition. He presents himself as a man with a mission, sent by God and acting in his name. Also, he seems to have been willing to accept the title of prophet (unlike other titles) and probably referred to himself in this way in sayings about a 'prophet like Jonah,' about 'no prophet being accepted in his own country' or 'dying outside Jerusalem.' We have seen that he claimed prophetic authority, claimed to possess the Spirit of God and to cast out demons by the finger/Spirit of God.

Yet Jesus is not just another prophet in a long line of prophets. Unlike the prophets of old, he does not speak of 'the word of the Lord coming' to him. He understands himself to be, and asks to be accepted as, the eschatological Spirit-possessing prophet. He is God's final messenger bringing the last offer of salvation and asking for a total change of heart so that God's hopes for the world may be realised.

Yet it is precisely here that conflict and opposition arise. Some people do accept him as the great prophet calling the people to *metanoia* so that they may follow the true law. Others maintain that he is the antichrist opposing the law of God (Dan 7:19, 25) and leading the people astray. While Jesus still carries on his ministry, each position can be plausibly maintained showing the ambivalence that was really there in his words and actions.

We have seen that Jesus took the initiative, sought out and

gathered to himself the poor and the outcast, the wounded and
the sinners. He offers a new vision of the relationship between
God and humanity and invites humankind to move in a new
direction. He actually seeks to change people's faith as he calls
them to God, as he understands him. The reign of this God, Jesus
says, is manifesting itself through what happens when he acts
and speaks. Yet he and his followers live within this world,
marked as it is by sin and suffering and death. Where is the co-
relation between what he proclaims (God's reign) and the experience of suffering? There is no obvious basis for his hopes and his
promises. To convince us, he offers only his actions and his
words.

To preach the kingdom in weakness and freedom may be
understood as entrusting oneself to God, who will vindicate this
trust at his own good pleasure, but it might also be understood
as being based on an illusion. For there is nothing self-
authenticating or self-certifying about what he says. It is proclaimed in powerlessness and vulnerability. Still he is adamant
that God's reign is not to be limited to any time or place or group
or project. He opposes all those who w ʃ· to limit the kingdom,
to make it coincide with their vision, or to exclude anyone from
it. He is critical of the attitudes of the dominant groups, the pract-
ices linked with the Temple, formalism in religion, the 'fence
around the law.' He declares that God's presence is everywhere,
that he is to be worshipped in Spirit and in truth, that extrinsic-
ism in ritual is harmful, that there is nothing outside a person
which going into them makes them unclean (Mk 7:15). He himself lives with the ritually unclean, forfeiting his own ritual purity
through his solidarity with outcasts and sinners.

Jesus is struggling to liberate the consciousness of all, to implant a new imagination in them, to propose a radical new alternative to them. This alternative is seen as exciting or dangerous,
depending on which side you take. It either offers freedom or
strikes at the very foundations of your faith. The ambiguity of
what he says and does constantly re-asserts itself. He can declare, 'And blessed is he who takes no offence at me' (Lk 7:23).
And people *are* offended and outraged by his conduct and preaching. To them, Jesus seems to be deeply irreligious, godless,
opposed to all the values upon which everything of significance
to them was built.

Positions polarise and harden. Conclusions urge themselves

upon them. He is an 'imposter' (Mt 27:63); 'He is leading the people astray' (Jn 7:12); he is 'of the Evil One'; 'in league with Satan' (Mt 12:24ff); he 'blasphemes against God' (Mk 14:64); he is the antichrist. All that is included under the motif of testing is relevant here. (See pp 71-81). Jesus knows that he is engaging in a provocative lifestyle and ministry that is at variance with the consecrated traditions and that he must explain and defend his approach. He does not close his critics out.

He takes their difficulties, their objections, and their accusations seriously and tries to explain his position to them. He tries to liberate them from the assumptions, the prejudices, and the distortions that hold them captive. He tries to convince them that he must act as he does because the one God is *Abba* to all. It is difficult to liberate the oppressed, but it is even more difficult to liberate the oppressors. But Jesus tries. He does not impose himself, he does not browbeat. All are free to accept or reject what he says; they are free even as they conspire against him. But conflict and opposition continue; his radical positions on the law, on formalism, his solidarity with the poor, the sinners, and the unclean are irreconcilable with the official positions of the dutiful.

Some scholars try to limit this opposition to Jesus to the final part of his ministry and say that the earlier 'Galilean springtime' was much more peaceful and successful. It is probably more accurate to say (as Mark's gospel makes clear) that, from the beginning, Jesus experienced a mixture of success and failure, of popularity and hostility (Mk 2:1-3:6). We hear of opposition from the scribes and Pharisees, of the indifference of clan and country (Mk 6:4), of rejection by whole groups of people, even disciples (Jn 6:66), of entire towns turning against him (Lk 10:13-15). Yet, given this opposition and rejection, it would be difficult to conclude from what we have seen so far that, from the outset, Jesus expected that his death in Jerusalem would be the climax of his life's work.

Jesus confined his mission to Israel and seemed convinced that, if she were converted, then she could expect that the kingdom would arrive when the nations flocked into Israel (Mt 8:11). (We also find this hope in the Old Testament.) So events and circumstances must have brought about a turning point that led to Jesus' decision to set his face for Jerusalem 'from that time onwards' (Mt 16:21). Because of the nature of the gospel material, it is difficult to discover the precise reason for this decision. It seems reasonable though to link it with his growing sense of the failure of his ministry which we have just acknowledged. His sending of disciples to share in and spread his ministry of the good news, to take the final offer of God's graciousness 'to every town and place' (Lk 10:1) probably intensified that sense of failure, for it does not seem to have been as successful as they thought. And from then on Jesus keeps them away from the crowd, a separation that becomes more complete after the incidents following the feeding of the multitude. It too ended in misunderstanding. From then on, Jesus seems to concentrate more on the Twelve and he faces toward Jerusalem.

This 'toward Jerusalem' motif is stylised in the gospels, but all four of them see it as crucial (Mk 8:31, and parallels, Jn 6:66-70). Mark gives us a fascinating mood description of it when he says, 'They were on the road going up to Jerusalem and Jesus was walking ahead of them and they were amazed, and those who followed were afraid' (Mk 10:32). It is an extraordinarily powerful picture of grim, conscious determination on the part of Jesus and trance-like awe and fear and fascination on the part of the disciples. That is what Jesus' call to discipleship means: to be with him, to go after him. And yet he is always ahead, always preparing the way, and he takes them with him toward a new and unexpected and, at times, frightening future.

In going to Jerusalem the possibility of a violent death became more acute for Jesus. We know how the gospels understood this journey to Jerusalem, but, without psychologising or indulging in speculation, can we gather something of how Jesus himself would have understood this journey and its possible outcome? Going to Jerusalem heightened the probability that he would be put to death there and this must raise the question: How did Jesus relate this probability to his life as a whole, to his preaching of the kingdom, and to the consummation of the kingdom?

Our first impulse might be to turn to the passion predictions in Mk 8:31, 9:12, 31,10:33-34, 45 and say: 'That is how he understood it.' Jesus, the Son of Man, was going up to die in Jerusalem and he would rise on the third day. However, as we well know, these predictions show a deliberate pattern. They are interlaced with post-Easter christology and they contain precise details that are best explained as having been influenced after the event by the actual details of the passion itself. The overwhelming majority of exigetes accept that in their present form they date from the post-Easter period but that they do have a basis in the earthly life of Jesus.[1]

Perhaps, as some Scripture scholars suggest, the predictions are derived from only one original saying of Jesus (but they argue about the exact wording of it), and maybe it took the enigmatic form: 'God will deliver up the man to men.' However, in addition to these texts we also find less clearly defined references to oncoming suffering and possible death. First of all, throughout the gospels, alongside statements about the great joy that the kingdom brings, we find an emphasis on the opposition, tribulation, and suffering that may be experienced by those who are dedicated to this kingdom. If the kingdom involves a revolution in the present structures, it will draw forth opposition and Jesus seems to expect a time of distress, a final test. Disciples are warned to be alert, to remain with him, to be ready 'to take up their cross and follow him.' Now, if we add to that his whole outlook, which expected strength from weakness and victory from defeat and life through death, we can see the kind of mental approach that Jesus would have brought to this whole question about his future and his destiny.

Secondly, we find brief, indirect remarks about the 'bridegroom being taken away' (Mk 2:20), about 'drinking the cup' and 'undergoing a baptism' (Mk 10:38-39; Lk 12:49-50), about 'anointing' him for death (Mk 14:8), about a son put to death (Mt 21:37-39), about bringing division rather than peace (Lk 12:51). Many scholars would regard these as deriving from the post-Easter Church though some would argue that they could credibly come from the pre-Easter situation. But even if they could be shown to derive from Jesus himself we do not have to postulate some kind of divine inspiration in order to explain them. Lesser men could have known as much. Jesus was far too clear-sighted, too sensitive to people's reactions, to be unaware of the risks he faced. Bluntly, Jesus could not act as he did or say what he said about religion, piety, liturgy, politics, and business, in the highly volatile situation of that time and expect no opposition (Lk 12:51-53; Jn 5:18). 'If they hate me they will hate you ... whoever loses his life will save it.' 'The Jews were seeking to stone you.' 'Let us also go that we may die with him.' He himself prays and tells his disciples to pray in the *Abba* prayer: 'Do not let us fail in the time of the testing ordeal.'

We have seen too that he had to reckon with the possibility of being denounced as a false prophet or a sorcerer in league with Satan and, if the charge were carried, he could face death by choking or stoning. Yet he continues the same ministry, 'going about doing good' (Acts 10:38), undeterred, although he knew he was on a collision course with the powerful people of the establishment. To go up to Jerusalem in such circumstances was to come within the grip of people who opposed him and were capable of destroying him. He knew that John the Baptiser's violent death was the outcome of his fearless criticism of those in power and this must have left Jesus in no doubt as to where his own much more radical message and uncompromisingly critical stance might lead him.

After hearing the news of John's death, Jesus went off to 'a lonely place' (Mt 14:13) doubtless to pray, to interpret this new and frightening event, and to prepare positively for whatever might now happen to him. The writing was on the wall, the old pattern was re-emerging: Israel was once again killing the prophets. Yet when he was told that Herod (who had the *jus gladii*) was trying to kill him, he says, 'Go and tell that fox that I continue to carry out my mission' (Lk 13:32). Even if he did not have the example of John's tragic death before his eyes, he who understood himself to be the last of the prophets, the eschatological prophet, knew how Israel had treated other prophets (see Mt 23:29-39; Mk 12:1-9). Again this requires no special gift or inspiration. Lesser people could have read the signs of the times and come to the same conclusion. Even his disciples, not otherwise noted for their insight, saw the possibility, however much they may have wanted to ignore it.

> Supreme realist that he was, Jesus must have seen, combined before him, his opponents' rejection of him, their power to destroy him, Israel's endless resistance to God's messengers, and the absolute imperative of his own unique mission.[2]

So he must either continue to proclaim the kingdom in the face of all opposition and failure and accept the consequences of this, even death itself if necessary, or else he must abandon his mission.

As the possibility of death hardens into probability, the choice of accepting almost inevitable death or abandonment of his mission must have crystallised at some stage and his faith in *Abba* would not allow him to retreat nor to meet evil with evil. All that remains open to him is the way of a hopeful and transforming acceptance of the future, even if it involves suffering and death. So death by stoning (the Sanhedrin), the sword (Herod), or crucifixion (the Romans) were possibilities that he must have contemplated and attempted to relate to his ministry of preaching the kingdom of God.

How can suffering and death be integrated into preaching about the reign of a God who is against all evil and promotes only the good? Can such a God countenance the death of the one who dedicates himself to proclaiming his utterly gracious reign? How could Jesus integrate his own suffering and death into his total surrender to God and yet reconcile it with the urgency of his preaching? If he dies, it will be as a consequence of his preaching the kingdom, but will his death not be the negation of his whole life's work? What does God's beneficent reign mean if the one who proclaims it can be put to death *because* he proclaims it? What will happen to the little group of disciples that he had called, instructed, and protected? Will death call everything in question, negate everything? Or will *Abba* intervene and establish the kingdom in its final form before he suffers? Will his death be significant for the coming of the kingdom? Will Abba vindicate him even in death?

Of course, these questions will seem futile to anyone who believes that the will of God was an open book for Jesus, a directive that was immediately and clearly available. But Jesus is not acting out a part in a well-rehearsed drama whose outcome is clear. We must not wrest him from the human situation where the future is unknowable and where people recoil from the prospect of suffering and violent death. Instead, we must try to see the priorities proposed to us in the Scriptures. Jesus carries out his ministry in the name of *Abba* and if, because of doing this, he must suffer and be rejected in death, he will accept even that rather than belie the mission he has undertaken. This is what the New Testament means when it insists that Jesus accepted suffering and death freely. This is a far cry from imagining (as some people do) that Jesus did certain things in order to be put to death, which would be tantamount to suicide.

So, with the strength of faith, Jesus goes forward to face the future entrusting himself in hope to *Abba*, after prayer and agonising. No doubt this fundamental but terrifying decision was ratified again and again in the varying circumstances as they arose right up to the last moment. How else do we explain his prayer in the garden? Again, if we are to take his prayer seriously, while reckoning with death as a real possibility, he hoped that *Abba* might inaugurate the kingdom in some other way, without his having to face the horror of death. We tend to forget this, because Jesus actually died, but in the prayer in the garden, as we shall see, he is still asking about another way. Yet Jesus does not seek to avoid opposition nor does he try to hasten the 'hour of crisis,' nor will he ignore the present task: 'Behold I cast out demons and perform cures today and tomorrow and the third day I finish my course, nevertheless I must go on my way today and tomorrow' (Lk 13:32). Bultmann says this text is 'in the strict sense a piece of biographical material.'

His prayer in the lonely places gave him the strength and courage to be prepared to fail according to the criteria of human success, as did his table fellowship with his disciples and sinners. As the ultimate implications of his solidarity with the little ones became clearer, perhaps his table fellowship with them took on more and more the character of an interpretation of what was happening. They would have had the structure of memorial, remembering and celebrating God's saving action in history. His own primordial and continuous experience of God as *Abba* would have enabled him to explore the darkness and difficulties of the future in the confidence that *Abba* would be with him, come what may. Perhaps, too, his prayer at table with them emphasised the themes of service and self-sacrificing love. These themes are present explicitly in his last meal with them, but perhaps they were not entirely lacking at earlier meals, at least from the time when he decided to go to Jerusalem.

After acknowledging the rejection of his mission by Chorazin, Bethsaida, and Capernaum, Jesus prays, 'I thank you, Father, Lord of heaven and earth, that you have hidden these things from the wise and understanding and revealed them to babes: yes, Father, for such was your gracious will' (Mt 11:25-26). Perhaps his prayer at table in the face of failure and suffering was eucharistic, thankful, like this. If it were, he would have been reading his present experience of opposition and questioning as part of *Abba*'s loving but unsearchable ways, as part of his mysterious but trustworthy plan to which Jesus had completely entrusted himself. So he could continue the awesome task of living a life totally from *Abba* and for others even in the face of death. Jesus believed the kingdom would come through witness, service, and suffering and maintains that the disciples' service and suffering are inextricably bound up with his own. They, of course, do not want to hear anything about suffering, either his or theirs (Mk 8:32-33, 10:35-40), so he must try to prepare them for the time when they 'strike the shepherd and the sheep are scattered' (Mk 14:27) and warns them that 'Whoever loses his life will save it' (Mk 8:35).

When we inquire more closely about how Jesus interpreted his death, we find it difficult to untangle post-Easter from pre-Easter material. There are sayings in the gospels that give a positive interpretation to Jesus' death and are credible as authentic words of Jesus. But if this is how Jesus interpreted his coming death, why were the disciples so surprised and shattered by it? More importantly, how is it that some proclamations of Jesusas risen are found after Easter that do not offer a salvific interpretation of his death? We must be aware of these questions and work with the material in hand as best we can.

In the gospel passages which contain no explicit post-Easter theology, Jesus interprets his death as 'losing one's life to save it,' as faithfulness unto death, above all in terms of the master image of service. There is nothing haphazard about what is going to happen. His approach to the future is not fatalistic. God and his reign are involved in what will happen to him. The radical confidence is expressed that even if the worst should happen, then out of evil and suffering, out of darkness and death, out of what appears to be pointless failure, God as *Abba* can bring forth his own designs in sovereign freedom. The future can be left in his hands in the unwavering conviction that *Abba* would vindicate his ministry even in failure, even in death itself. God will not be gainsaid: 'it has to be.' This is part of God's all-wise, all-loving, but inscrutable ways.

The theme of 'the suffering righteous one' who is nevertheless vindicated by God was present to the consciousness of Israel at that time. Perhaps Jesus used it to interpret his own situation.

Perhaps he also drew on the hope of resurrection of the dead (Mt 22:23-33) or used the traditional phrase 'on the third day' to speak of the final triumph of the kingdom or the vindication of his message.

This is the kind of approach that comes across to us in these passages. Luke 13:31-35 ('I cast out demons' ... quoted earlier) concludes, 'For it cannot be that a prophet should perish away from Jerusalem.' His mission is not exhausted by the healings and exorcisms found in his ministry so far; there is a final God-sustained 'given' yet to take place in Jerusalem. He seems to imply that the definitive fulfilment of God's reign will take place through that event.

This is further confirmed by sayings about losing one's life to save it (Mk 8:35), about coming 'not to be served but to serve, and to give his life as a ransom for many' (Mk 10:45), and most clearly in 'Truly, I say to you, I shall not drink again of the fruit of the vine until that day when I drink it new in the kingdom of God' (Mk 14:25). We will return to these texts in the context of Jesus' last meal.

In Jerusalem

So Jesus enters Jerusalem, in the company of a group of people who have come with him from Galilee or joined him on the way. If we look, for example, at the way Luke presents this journey the incidents that happen, the opposition he encounters, the rejects, the outcasts, the lost ones he gathers to himself, the stories he tells – we can get an overview of the kind of people who accompanied him. Such a motley group would not be very welcome to the holy people, in the holy city. We realise that, while this is a journey into danger and suffering, it is undertaken so that the oppressed, the little ones, may be liberated. It is, then, an exodus, a journey into life. But what is the cost for Jesus?

When we think of the events immediately preceding the arrest, trial, and death of Jesus, the cleansing of the Temple and the Last Supper readily come to mind. This is how Mark describes the 'cleansing' of the Temple:

> And they came to Jerusalem. And he entered the temple and began to drive out those who sold and those who bought in the Temple, and he overturned the tables of the money changers and the seats of those who sold pigeons;

and he would not allow anyone to carry anything through the temple (Mk 11:15-16).

The synoptics relate this incident as if it took place some days before his arrest and as if it sparked off the final violence against him. Reading these accounts we might imagine Jesus standing on the Mount of Olives looking across the Kedron valley at the colossal Temple complex and deciding to challenge it for the last time.

At first sight, this approach appears to explain many things. But when we look at the accounts of his trial and the passion narratives as a whole we realise that there is no explicit mention of this event. This is strange if it is supposed to have been the immediate cause of his arrest. Furthermore, when we turn to John's gospel, we discover that this episode is placed at the beginning and not at the end of Jesus' ministry. So we reach an impasse. In the face of this, some scholars[3] have suggested that the cleansing of the Temple was not associated with the final entry into Jerusalem and so they tend to place the event earlier rather than later in his ministry. When Jesus acts like this in the Temple courtyard (not within the Temple), he is simply continuing his ministry as eschatological prophet, calling the whole people to *metanoia* and pointing to the chasm between 'theory and practice in Judaism ... the gap between orthodoxy and orthopraxis .... It is not the Temple (or cult) that is under attack but the Temple praxis.'[4] 'My house shall be called a house of prayer for all the nations, but you have made it a den of robbers' (Mk 11:17).

Such an action would have been very significant at any stage in view of the religious, political, and symbolic significance of the Temple. In itself it is an ambiguous action and could be interpreted in many ways. Among the Sadducees and the Sanhedrin it would have given rise to fierce suspicion and opposition and they would regard anyone who acted like this as being a subversive. Others might have regarded him as a hero, a prophet liberating the people from the malpractice of those who surrounded the Temple. Or perhaps some Zealots began to look to him as a potential leader. So although it seems better to locate the Temple affair earlier in the ministry of Jesus, we must realise that the way it was interpreted by various groups was bound to influence their reaction to Jesus from that time onwards. This prophetic act led to a polarisation of attitudes. It seems to have caused political anxiety, brought Jesus popularity and notoriety, and perhaps linked him to Messianism.

Such reactions would throw light on the opposition of the authorities to Jesus and explain why he was under frequent surveillance and why he went away from the crowds and wandered outside the borders of Israel (Mk 7:24, 31, 10:1). We notice too that all gospels link it to the question of the authority of Jesus, for such an action would provoke serious questions about him. Also, although the cleansing of the Temple is not mentioned at the trial of Jesus, confused versions of a saying about the Temple are included in the evidence against him (Mt 14:58-59, 26:60ff), perhaps reflecting the rumours that spread about him after this incident.

So, while we may not think of the cleansing of the Temple as taking place immediately before Jesus' arrest, we should remember how very significant it must have been and that it was ultimately a decisive factor leading to his arrest and death. What he did in dramatic fashion at the Temple he simply continues to do unrepentantly in other ways all through his ministry. Plans for his extermination would have been made between the parties most likely to be incensed by this action at the Temple, the Sadducees, the Herodians, and the Pharisees. 'The Pharisees went out and immediately held council with the Herodians against him, how to destroy him' (Mk 3:6; see 14:1-2; Jn 11:47-52). Jesus finally stood trial before the Sanhedrin, the great council that numbered the chief priest, Sadducees, and Pharisees among its members. They would certainly have remembered this incident.

Whether we believe that Jesus cleared the Temple during the first months or last days of his ministry, we are certain that he was in Jerusalem for the last time just before the Passover feast, which in itself is truly amazing and astonishing. The Jewish law demanded that false prophets be put to death at the time of Passover so the pilgrims would see it and be dissuaded from following them. Now Jesus knew he was being denounced as a false prophet. Indeed, all the accusations against him of being in league with Satan (Mt 12:24), of blaspheming God (Mk 2:7), of being a rebellious son (Mt 11:19), a false prophet (Mk 14:65), of not condemning his disciples who broke the Sabbath, and of deliberately breaking it himself (Mk 2:24-28) were punishable by death.[5]

Even though he knew that he was being denounced as a false prophet and that false prophets had to be put to death in Jerusalem at Passover time, and even though he understood Israel's history as involving suffering and at times martyrdom for the messengers of God, yet here he is at Passover time in Jerusalem, the place that is always 'killing the prophets and stoning those who are sent to you' (Lk 13:34). Despite the hardening of attitudes and actual rejection of him, he has come to Jerusalem and has done nothing to escape violent death. He is risking his life and the only explanation is that he understands himself as still continuing his eschatological mission, that he risks death because he wants to gather the people to himself 'as a hen gathers her brood under her wings' (Lk 13:34). It is this compulsion to speak about God and his salvation that made Jesus ignore all threats and face even death itself.

The Last Supper

This brings us to the Last Supper. A detailed treatment of this belongs to the study of the New Testament and eucharistic theology. We can only say a few words about it here in an attempt to see what it meant for Jesus himself.

The meaning and significance of this meal should not be discussed without linking it to the other meals taken with Jesus. It is the last in a chain of very significant table fellowships with him. These earlier meals translated his whole message and way of life into concrete actions. They are his solidarity with and his service to others, distilled into the actions of serving at table and eating and drinking together. Jesus was concerned with gathering together the reconciled, new communitas of Israel, with establishing a solidarity with them that does not acknowledge status or rank or division. To this Jesus dedicates himself; it is his service to their humanity and it becomes palpable when they all sit at table together. In order to establish and maintain this solidarity, whose basis is common humanity, he is willing to give himself to them, pour himself out in self-forgetfulness for them. He is utterly compassionate toward them and seeks to rid them of all that diminishes their lives. He denies himself for them and is more than willing to suffer with them and for them.

As we have seen, he meets with opposition and hatred and if he continues with this ministry he will be put to death as a subversive agitator who wishes to overturn things. But to withdraw is to refuse to continue to believe what he has always proclaimed, that this is how God's reign manifests its humble beginnings. Jesus passionately believes this, so he continues with his ministry of service even when it becomes clear that violence and certain death will follow. Jesus is not only willing to live a life of service to and solidarity with *Abba*'s little ones who suffer, he is willing to suffer for them and, if necessary, to lay down his life for them. This is his absolute dedication to the kingdom that is theirs.

The kingdom is the only absolute. The love of this *Abba* and king is more than love of father or mother or spouse or friend; it is more than life or death itself. To give, and not be prepared to give everything, is to declare that fear is finally stronger than love. To be willing to die for others, for the life of others, is paradoxically to proclaim the absolute value of life and love. 'The one who saves his life will lose it; the one who loses his life will save it' (Mk 8:35; Mt 10:39; Lk 14:26; Jn 12:25). And Jesus has truly come 'not to be served but to serve, and to give his life as a ransom for many' (Mk 10:45). Sayings about solidarity and service are also found in Mark 8:35, 37, 10:39, and Matthew 18:5, 25:40, 45, in sayings about the master who serves at table (Lk 12:37), and above all in the Last Supper narratives.

At Table

In a situation of intense expectation, and with an awesome sense of finality, Jesus as host gathers his disciples for a last fellowship (Passover?) meal. His whole ministry so far and all that it could become is compressed into the stylised, ritual gestures and pregnant blessing prayers of this final meal. The life of Jesus and all that it meant is present in symbolic density. This meal interprets everything he has done and been for others but it also requires to be interpreted by his whole life and destiny.

We are given a key in Luke's account: 'For which is the greater, one who sits at table or one who serves? Is it not the one who sits at table? But I am among you as one who serves' (Lk 22:27; see Lk 12:37). Jesus not only shares this last meal with his disciples, he is actually the servant of his disciples at table. In John 13:1-20 we are told that Jesus washes their feet before they sit at table. These acts of service are the intensive summation of his whole ministry, his pro-existence. It is service to others out of love that has brought Jesus to this hour; this is what finds expression now; this is what will bring him to his death. His death, which faces him as a direct consequence of his life of service, will itself be freely accepted by him as an act of loving service on behalf 'of many,' i.e., for all.

In Judaism it was accepted that:

> Any death has the power to atone if it is bound up with repentance ... The death of a righteous man ... was to the advantage of others ... yet greater atoning power was attributed to the death of a witness to the faith ... it brings God's wrath upon Israel to a standstill and is a substitute, a cleansing, and a means of atonement for Israel.[6]

This must have been present to the intentions of Jesus, but he offers his life and his death, not just for Israel, but for all. In life and in death his approach is one of service in love and, as always, it is all-inclusive.

Furthermore, at this meal Jesus declares: 'I shall not drink again of the fruit of the vine until that day when I drink it new in the kingdom of God' (Mk 14:25 or ...'until the kingdom of God comes' (Lk 22:18). As Jesus sees things now, only his death stands between this meal and the final realisation of God's kingdom. This cup, then, is literally the last cup of earthly fellowship, yet

> Jesus offers with it the prospect of fellowship renewed in the kingdom of God. The renewed fellowship-at-table or offer of salvation by Jesus to the disciples, in the face of approaching death, still makes perfect sense to Jesus; he has come to proper terms with his death, which he evidently does not feel to be an absurd miscarriage of his mission. Jesus stands open to God's future for man and, on the other hand, his whole life is a service to people, a service of love ... unconditional obedience to God's will, revealed in the decalogue and in various situations of man's life, persisted in to the point of death, do indeed evince Jesus' fidelity to his message, which keeps open God's future, gives God the final word, and makes Jesus persevere in loving service to people, as a manifestation of God's own benevolence toward them. In other words, the coming of God's rule remains linked to fellowship with Jesus of Nazareth. One can

hardly eliminate from these New Testament reports, as a historical suggestion on Jesus' part, the suggestion that fellowship with Jesus is stronger than death. He is not just passively allowing death to overcome him but has actively integrated it into his total mission, in other words, that he understands and is undergoing his death as a final and extreme service to the cause of God as the cause of men, and that he has communicated this self-understanding to his intimate disciples under the veiled sign of extending to them the fellowship-at-table shared with his friends.[7]

The bread and cup sayings spell out the implications of this conviction. They draw on the exodus and covenant experiences and typologies. Exodus involved liberation from slavery and the gathering of these liberated slaves into communitas. The covenant established a new relationship between these liberated slaves and one Yahweh, their God, who had liberated them. So now the words, accompanying the distribution of the bread and the cup, speak of a new exodus into a new freedom and a new covenant between Abba and all people which is to be established through death 'in my blood.' 'This is my body (given) for you ... This is my blood of the covenant which is shed for all.' The body is not just what is contained within the skin; it signifies the personal. It is the medium of communication, that which is at the centre of a web of relationships. The blood is not simply that which courses through the veins; it stands for the individual as living and sustained by God. If he is pouring out 'his blood' it means he is pouring out his very soul on their behalf. If his 'body is given' it means he is willing to give up this medium of communication and the possibility of living human life and relationships as they now exist. He is willing to give his body, pour out his blood for the sake of a deeper communication and communion between himself and 'all,' and between them and the God who sustains all and lives through all.

The narratives tell us that Jesus is not simply gathering reconciled disciples or even Israel, but all humanity. He is presented in a representative role which fulfils and surpasses the role of the servant in Isaiah 53. The new exodus people, whose relationship to God is ratified through this new covenant, will encompass all peoples. The disciples being served by the master at table are given a privileged anticipatory share in the blessings that will come from his offering. They are to be the foundation members of this new people.

Jesus had offered *Abba*'s forgiveness to those with whom he shared a meal during his lifetime. He offered salvation concretely. It happened where he was. But at this last meal he relates that forgiveness directly to his own body which will be given and to his blood which will be poured out. Forgiveness no longer comes from God in a general way, through the mediation of his presence and his word, but it is concretely and indissolubly linked to what will be done to his body, and so to his own self-sacrificing, vicarious death.

And just as they had shared the forgiveness he had offered during his ministry by sharing in his meals, so now they are given a share in the salvation that will be achieved through his death, by sharing the elements of this last meal. Jesus had always proclaimed that God's kingdom was breaking in, that God was communicating himself as inexhaustible, forgiving love in the ambiguity and weakness of his own ministry. Now he proclaims that, through the final weakness of his imminent death, in the crushed space of his broken body, in the misery of his blood poured out, God's supreme, forgiving self-communication will take place! The kingdom will be definitively established through his death. Another circle has been broken. Jesus de-centres even the religious meal that lies at the heart of Israel's life and worship. The bread and wine could not have had this meaning for Jews before now. What had previously referred to and celebrated events in the life of a nation, now refer to and celebrate the life history of this person Jesus.

His death is not to be seen as an accident or a tragedy, but as a self-offering freely made in the faith-full hope that, through this solidarity with the little ones, even to the point of death, *Abba* will achieve what he wills for them. And so Jesus has come to terms with the prospect of death. He has succeeded in integrating it into his overall mission of service, into the consistency of his life and his hopes. Into and against the absurd nothingness of death and into the heart of its dark mystery, Jesus utters the name of *Abba* as the God of hope, the God whose love is stronger than death.

In speaking of his death as a covenant, the Last Supper narratives see it not just as a human act Jesus will perform or undergo (though of course it is that), but as an act in and through which God himself is acting, inaugurating a covenant. ('I have given you as a covenant to the people,' Is 42:61.) The answering love, faith, and hope of Jesus make it possible. As John puts it, he was laying down his life as a supreme proof of love. But the poignant contrast between what Jesus is doing and the others' reaction to it is painfully brought home to us in the Last Supper and passion narratives. The context is one of betrayal, denial, and infidelity to Passover solidarity. Jesus goes forth from the supper room to experience his agony, betrayal, arrest, trial, and execution.

In Gethsemane, the Place of the Olive Press

'Comforter, where, where is your comforting?' wrote Hopkins. We have been examining what the Scriptures tell us about Jesus' understanding of the suffering and death he would have to undergo if he continued on 'his way.' What emerges is his absolute conviction that even his death, should it occur, would be integral to God's offer of salvation. Of course, even as we say these things in such a schematic way, without going into the more difficult details, we may have the disturbing impression that we have made it all too neat, that each stage has somehow been rehearsed beforehand, that it was acted out with rather detailed fore-knowledge. If we have this impression it is right to be disturbed by it. Our approach must attempt to do justice to the complexity of the Scriptural data, which defies neat oversimplification, and we must remain true to the integral humanity of Jesus himself. We must hold onto our conviction that his relationship to *Abba* did not give him detailed stage directions. Jesus is not acting out a part in a drama whose script and movements he knew perfectly well and whose outcome is guaranteed and foreseeable.

His life is about a call to give himself with total obedience to all that *Abba* asks of him. This call is not heard like a voice speaking in his ear but is communicated to him from the varied circumstances and situations of life. Jesus was confident that *Abba* would be with him in the consistency of his own life. He did not have some kind of divine fore-knowledge but, rather, hope in a real future and the future as it is, is unknowable. Jesus read the emergence of the future in the present and reacted to it with utter consistency and single-mindedness, while recognising that there were other interpretations possible. If we need a final proof of all this, we have only to turn to the gospel accounts of the agony in the garden and take his mortal terror in the face of suffering seriously, and try to grasp its implications. When we try to do this, we realise that so far we have only considered part of the Scriptural data and what has been said must be qualified by what is revealed to us about the garden and through the cross.

The garden episode clearly made a deep impression on the tradition. We must then cherish these accounts and ponder them. (See Mk 14:32-42; Mt 26:36-46; Lk 22:39-46; Heb 5:7; Jn 12:27). In Mark's version we are told that Jesus first said to his disciples: 'You will all fall away (14:27); you will all lose your faith.' Peter protests his fidelity unto death: 'Even if they all fall away, I will not' (29). Then we read:

And they went to a place called Gethsemane; and he said to his disciples, 'Sit here, while I pray.' And he took with him Peter and James and John and began to be greatly distressed and troubled. And he said to them, 'My soul is very sorrowful, even to death; remain here, and watch.' And going a little farther, he fell on the ground and prayed that, if it were possible, the hour might pass from him. And he said, '*Abba*, Father, all things are possible to thee; remove this cup from me; yet not what I will, but what thou wilt.' And he came and found them sleeping and he said to Peter, 'Simon, are you asleep? Could you not watch one hour? Watch and pray that you may not enter into temptation; the spirit indeed is willing, but the flesh is weak.' And again he went away and prayed, saying the same words. And again he came and found them sleeping, for their eyes were very heavy; and they did not know what to answer him. And he came the third time, and said to them, 'Are you still sleeping and taking your rest? It is enough; the hour has come; the son of man is betrayed into the hands of sinners. Rise, let us be going; see, my betrayer is at hand' (Mk 14:32-42).

One striking feature of his prayer is its repetition. Matthew says he repeated his prayer three times and Mark sees his prayer progressing through three moments. Luke confirms the repetition in general terms: 'He prayed more earnestly.' His prayer to

Abba here is the prayer of one who has always found strength and direction in prayer and who is searching for the same strength and courage in a situation of intense distress and crisis. Mark tells us of Jesus' struggle through prayer to accept the Father's will.

We should also note that there is nothing noble or heroic about this prayer. It is not the reaction of a stoic sage who faces death without fear and without hope. His suffering, like his life, is unspectacular and unimpressive. It is simply the prayer of someone, like ourselves, who recoils in anguished horror from the prospect of pain and suffering and death. This recoil, this shrinking away from pain, has repercussions on all levels of the personality. Mark says (the others soften its impact): 'Horror and dismay came over him.' These are powerful words that convey the traumatic intensity of this experience to us. Shuddering horror, brutalising terror, and unbearable suffering came over him and he said to them: 'The sorrow in my heart is so great it almost crushes me.' Sorrow and fear and terror threaten to destroy him.

Nothing allows us to enter so fully into the mystery of the true and full humanity of Jesus as this scene in the garden. Yet despite the fear and the trembling and sheer terror expressed in these words, it is not a prayer for escape. Jesus could have escaped at any stage. He need never have begun or continued on this path of opposition to those who could destroy him. He might have remained in Galilee. He could have returned to its relative safety even now. However, he lived and preached without compulsion and he freely and willingly came to Jerusalem. He had said that whoever saved his life would lose it and he remains true to these words.

It is not then a prayer of escape; it is a prayer in which he still freely and willingly accepts his God-given mission of service. He is still absolutely faithful in his dedication to bringing about the kingdom. But it is a prayer in which he is literally agonising over the last possibilities. While death seems inevitable now and while he has understood it to be the privileged moment of God's definitive act, 'he kept praying' that it might take place in some other way. The horror and ambiguity of the situation force him to cry out from the depths of his soul and to plead that, if the kingdom can come in some other way besides the way that now inexorably looms before him, then let him see this even at this last moment and let it come in that way. So it is not a prayer simply to avoid something, it is a prayer for vision and for ultimate acceptance and the strength to carry it through.

Perhaps we could paraphrase it:

Abba, my Father, I have been faithful to you in everything. My only wish is to follow your will, to do your truth as I have discovered it. Zeal for your kingdom, for your future, for your poor has brought me to this hour and I accept it totally. I have seen the way of suffering and death harden into inevitability. I have accepted even that and I have interpreted it as part of your unsearchable but all-wise and all-loving ways. Remembering the faith of the prophets and martyrs of Israel before me, knowing the language of the servant songs, and believing that strength can come only from weakness, I have seen that my death could be the seed from which new and more abundant life would come. Knowing that your kingdom and your lordship come only in lowliness and obscurity, I believe that my death could be a work of service through which you would establish the new covenant of service. I can see that this final act of mine could be the decisive event in the ingathering of your lost daughters and sons from all nations.

I believe that, through all this, you will be with me to save me even in death, according to the hopes of my people and your good pleasure and, in this way, you will achieve the final fulfilment of the kingdom that I so eagerly desire. Yet this way of suffering and death seems to call my whole ministry and my proclamation of your graciousness into question. Will the poor continue to be exploited? Will the sick waste away? Will hearts continue to be hardened and eyes blinded? Are the hopes kindled by you through me to be negated? Death places all my words and actions, in your name and in the hope of confirmation from you, in jeopardy and it looms before me now with an immediacy that brutalises and crushes me.

Is this the only way, *Abba*? Have I read your will aright, my Father? Is this the only way in which the kingdom can come? Is it not possible for it to come in some other way that is not yet clear to me? Will you at last establish your kingdom *before* I suffer? Can it come in some other way besides this terrifying way of suffering and death? If there is another possibility, please let me see it even now and please let it be by that other way ... But it is *your* kingdom, and whatever way your kingdom is to come, welcome be your will, not mine. Now as always. Thy kingdom come.

If this is what it means, then we may have here a privileged insight into the prayer and the questioning and real agony with which Jesus must have faced various crises in his ministry. It would have involved a discovery of God's will through an intense and yet diffident sensitivity to new persons, events, and insights as they emerged. In his ministry Jesus has been concerned to communicate love, not power. Even when he who goes around doing good is about to be subjected to the final onslaught of evil, he still relies only on the weakness of love. He does not ask God to use his power or might on his behalf, even if reliance on the strength of weakness will lead to death at the hands of the strong and powerful. This is the only way of breaking with the law that meets violence with violence. Jesus rests content with the foolishness of God. He wants only to know that this is truly the father's will for him. We learn that it is.

Jesus has once again integrated suffering and death into his overall vision. He has recovered his confidence and composure. He is prepared for what follows, but the disciples are completely unprepared. 'Rise, let us be going,' he says and he goes forward to endure Judas' kiss, his arrest, and trial. The final test begins.

The tangled circumstances of his trial, the accusations and charges brought against him, the nature of the collusion between the Sanhedrin and the Romans need not concern us here. It does seem that Jesus was finally rejected by the Sanhedrin because he remained silent before Israel's supreme court, thereby refusing to recognise its right to call him to account for what he is saying or doing in the name of God's kingdom.[8] This was a truly remarkable stance to adopt. Because of this final contempt for their authority, they decide to hand him over to the Romans. Pilate was a cruel administrator and had a paranoid fear of anything or anyone who might be even remotely threatening to him (Lk 13:1). Perhaps he was already interested in Jesus who gathered crowds, exercised leadership, and had a following and so was a disturber of the peace. If not, it would not have been difficult to convince him that Jesus was a threat. In a world that did not separate religion from politics, it would not have been difficult to retell Jesus' message so that its inherent political significance would be highlighted as dangerous to the administration.

On trial before Pilate, Jesus again refused to answer the charges and remained silent. 'But he gave him no answer, not even to a single charge' (Mt 27:14). So Jesus of Nazareth was finally put on a cross, to be crucified by the Romans as a political rebel against their rule in Judea, a disturber of the *Pax Romana*, under the mocking title 'King of the Jews.' He was crucified as a state criminal, a messianic pretender indistinguishable, so far as the Romans were concerned, from Barabbas (Mk 15:6-15) or from the other two men of violence who were crucified with him on that day.

The Death of Jesus

As disciples, we are asked to recall and to relive the last days of Jesus' ministry, his suffering and his death, because it is only by first of all reliving these events that we can really go on to appreciate what Easter means. We are asked to ponder all these things in our hearts. But they are, or should be, disturbing memories because they call all our neat little schemes into question. However, we must allow them to disturb and dis-ease us if we are to follow the path of discipleship.

It has always been traditional to meditate on the passion of Christ, on the pain caused by his wounds, on the cruelty of his executioners. We have all done this and no doubt it has helped us greatly. 'Compassionate your saviour thus cruelly treated.' But we should ask ourselves: Have we ever really tried to come to grips with the inner pain, the inner significance of the cross of Jesus? Do we not tend to stay at the external level and to picture what happened from the outside? This may lead us to pity Jesus and perhaps become angry with those who caused his suffering, and in this way exonerate ourselves. But even as we picture the scene to ourselves, we know that all will be well, that it is going to turn out right in the end. In that way, we may even have removed the scandal of his death. We may even have made the passion of Jesus of Nazareth cozy for ourselves.

It is possible to neutralise its effect if we do not allow it to call our discipleship into question. We can think about his passion and meditate on it, yet shy away from accepting the full implications of the suffering and death of Jesus. In a rush of fervour, outraged by his suffering we may foolishly want to try to save him from death. That is a foolish thought indeed. Only the God and Father of Jesus could do that, and the Father did not save Jesus from suffering and death. Perhaps, then, in wanting to save Jesus from death, we are really trying to save ourselves, to cushion ourselves against the real significance of his death. We know deep down that if we took it seriously it would upset all our cherished notions of Jesus Christ, of God, of human beings, especially of ourselves. However, if we want to be his disciples, we must not hide the reality of his cross from ourselves because, after all, we say that we are struggling to take it up every day and to follow him. But this familiarity dulls our understanding of what is involved. It makes it difficult for us to keep alive the significance of the cross in our lived discipleship.

The cross of Jesus Christ is not merely about a few hours of intense and brutal pain. It is that, but above all it is the mystery which is a 'stumbling block to the Jews and a folly to the gentiles, but to those who are called ... the power of God and the wisdom of God' (1 Cor 1:23). The cross of Jesus Christ speaks to us of the mystery of God's total involvement with humanity, with our human history, with the depths of the human situation as we know it. So it is wrong to try to save Jesus from this, because it is foolish to try to reduce the mystery to what we think it should or should not be. This is God's mystery, not ours.

In theology and spirituality today, many people are struggling to say something worthwhile about the real significance of the cross. It is as if we are only beginning. But we must say this much: If Jesus Christ has not truly and really lived our life and died our death, then there is no salvation for us in our life or in our death. It is as serious as that. Therefore the life and the death must be real.

But this way of looking at his death may make extreme demands on us. That should not surprise us because, after all, his disciples who had been with him from the beginning were probed and questioned and baffled and scandalised by the tragic events of the first Good Friday. They were forced to endure the pain of the failure, the powerlessness, uselessness, the despair, the abandonment of his suffering and death. In the face of his death these disciples broke down. They fled from him (Mk

14:50). They ceased to go after him. It would be a mistake to think of ourselves as better than they. Rather, as disciples, we must really try to take our place with them at a distance from the cross and to see it as they saw it. This would mean that we try to allow ourselves, for once, really to experience with them the shock, the offence, the scandal, the outrage of his suffering and death. Let us refuse to diminish the experience or search for the easy answers that destroy the mystery because they remove the scandal.

Above all we must try to ask about the *theological* significance of what happened, theological in the sense of: 'What has it to say about God?' In this way we must look at the inner pain of the cross of Jesus, to view it theologically by relating it to the God and the Father of Jesus of Nazareth. This has never been a popular approach because the implications of such a death seen in this way are shattering. They are too disturbing to allow us to remain comfortable. Yet they are the test of the orthodoxy of our faith, for here we touch the final revelation of the mystery of God's involvement with us.

We cannot simply pass over the death of Jesus to the joy and glory of Easter. We must try to pass through the death and endure his suffering and his death as disciples. If we have a Good Friday that is not costly, we will not appreciate Easter for what it is. Only by facing up to the death of Jesus can we really begin to appreciate Easter as the new creation. This is far from easy.

When we listen to the accounts of the passion, we inevitably read back into them what we know about Easter and the divinity of Jesus Christ. Of course, this is how they were written, from the stand-point of Easter-faith. But Easter had not taken place as the historical disciples watched his death agony. Nor did they understand its significance. They had to endure the death of Jesus as his disciples.

If we wish to enter into their pain, it would be better for us not to rely on foregone conclusions. We should try to move fearfully with the disciples into the unknown. Maybe we should try to hear Mark's passion narrative only, as if there were no other. Can we hear it in the context of what we have discovered about Jesus and discipleship so far? Is it possible as we listen to try to leave aside what we know about Easter from elsewhere? At least let us not reduce the mystery of the passion to the dimensions of a passion play, where everything is known and rehearsed and predictable in advance. Whoever Jesus is, he is not the chief actor in a passion play, who simply looks uncomfortable for a while but who knows that all will be over soon and life will return to normal. And we must be involved. It is not about the Jews, it is about us. And as Jesus dies, we must finally let our discipleship be called into question.

A Meditation[9]

As a first stage, we will try to appreciate the significance of the death of Jesus as experienced by disciples. We ask: Who is this man Jesus whom they have nailed to the cross? As a disciple I must answer: He is my master and I have learned to love him. I have accepted his call 'to come and see.' I have followed him. I have heard him preach in parables about God's indescribable love for sinners like myself. I have heard him proclaim that those who stand as open-handed beggars before God are already loved and forgiven. I have seen him heal people. I have seen him make them whole by pouring himself out into their broken and deranged lives. He made intolerable, crucifying demands on us, his disciples, yet was profoundly sympathetic to us in our failures. He spent his time with outcasts and sinners, with the broken and the wounded, with the marginals and the poor. He said that those who possess nothing will attain everything, that the weak are the true strong ones, that the sinners are chosen, and that the last are first. He gathered us all into table fellowship with himself, to celebrate and mediate the unconditional gracious love and forgiveness of God. We knew Jesus to be someone who cherished all equally, possessed nothing, held all in open hands.

He was without any defences or barriers; he was powerless and vulnerable, used only the feeblest of means. He entrusted himself completely to God and devoted himself to the poor and the sinners. He was not anxious, not cautious; he entered into solidarity with people, restored their self-respect and responsibility. He lived in crucifying solidarity with, and availability to, others so that every-one's life was transformed. Among the twelve, he held together Zealots and tax collectors and fishermen. His own security was founded on his own awareness of being unreservedly loved by God, whom he called by the intimate name of *Abba*, my Father.

The fact that this Jesus is now being nailed to this cross is a direct consequence of the life he lived among us and with us. Those who wished to hold on to their prestige and privilege and power could only desire to rid themselves of this man whose dangerous, challenging, provocative, and healing freedom stood in searing judgment on their own pathetic, self-centred, captive lives. It was because of his gracious offer of true liberating salvation, because of his uncompromising love of and care for the powerless, that he was rejected by the powerful. Their rejection of Jesus' message and his way of life meant that they had to reject him as a person because his existence, his word, and his mission merged completely. So they could not simply reject his message, they had to destroy him. He is rejected by inhuman people because of his love for those they had dehumanised. To be scourged and torn asunder, to be edged out of the world and onto the cross is the fearful price of remaining open to God in this world of ours.

This is a world alienated from God, a world where human beings oppress human beings. To attempt to be consistent in one's involvement with God and humankind can only lead to suffering. The upright attempt to hold two things in tension is always the shape of the cross. He always told us that, but we did not want to hear it and we cannot bear it now. His crucifixion cannot be understood in isolation from his life and ministry. That life and that ministry cannot be understood without that for which he lived, the kingdom of God, nor without the one for whom he lived, his Father, *Abba*.[10]

And it is here that the most painful, most agonising questions arise for us, his disciples. Jesus had always lived out of a childlike trust and confidence in *Abba*. He staked his life and hopes on the future that *Abba* was to bring about. He lived his Father's promises. His ministry was structured toward the future. He consecrated the unknown to God. He always spoke of the *coming* of God's kingdom. He expected final salvation. He caused scandal because of the discrepancy, the shortfall between what he said and did and the promise implied in these words and actions. He never gave his opponents the conclusive sign they demanded, because it was not available. It could only come from the future. He spoke and acted in a way that looked only to a future authentication. The Father, he believed, would confirm what he said and did in his name. And now, how can we as disciples continue to hope for just such a future legitimation of his ministry when he is hanging on the cross faced with imminent death which, by human reckoning, is the negation of the future?

And there is nothing edifying about Jesus' death. (In Mark's account of the crucifixion there are no apt quotations from Scripture, no prayers, no confident utterances, just a pathetic cry of abandonment.) If he had been attacked and killed when he cleared out those who were ignoring what the Temple really stood for, he would have been remembered as a prophet and martyr. But now what we witness is a numbing, squalid, tragic, grotesque, secular affair. [11]

How are we to continue to hope in this man and his promise? Can we continue to believe in his God and Father, dreadful and blasphemous as that question may be? How can we listen to him say: 'My God, my God, why have you forsaken me?' How can we look at him dying on the cross and know that, according to the Scriptures, a 'hanged man who hangs on a tree is accursed by God' (Deut 21:23). It was in the name of his Father, *Abba*, that Jesus did and said all the scandalous things that have brought him to the cross. All the questions raised by him in people's minds turned on the one basic question: Was he from God or was he from the Evil One? Is his *Abba* God the true God and, if he is, what does that imply for the concept of God held and taught by the scribes and Pharisees? Or is he a false God and, if he is, then Jesus is an idolater and a heretic and a blasphemer and we as disciples are condemned with him, for in accepting Jesus we have accepted *Abba*, the God of Jesus.

The scribes and Pharisees will not accept the God that Jesus preaches as their God, and, in the name of their God, they condemn Jesus for being faithful to his God. And so it becomes a contest over Gods, a question of the God we believe in. The God of Jesus and the God of the scribes and Pharisees are in conflict. Jesus is put on the cross in the name of their God and his God does not intervene to save him. If Jesus were any of the things that his ministry implied, if he has this special relationship to *Abba*, then *Abba* will not let him die but will intervene to save Jesus and vindicate himself. These are not just our thoughts, they are there clearly in the taunts being flung by the crowd at the dying Jesus. 'If you are the Son of God, come down from the cross'; 'He saved others; he cannot save himself'; 'Let the Christ the King of Israel come down now from the cross that we may believe'; 'He trusts in God, let God deliver him now *if* he desires him.' These questions are not simply there in the minds of his enemies, they are there in our minds too, as disciples.

Jesus had never preached himself. He had always pointed away from himself and toward *Abba*. On the cross he is literally dying from his love and faithfulness to *Abba* and he still points in the same direction. But now, to those of us who look at him, he appears to be pointing only toward the darkness and nothingness of death. Seldom has anything begun with greater promise than his ministry. Is it all to be negated in death? Jesus claimed to bring others to God but God does not come to him now. So is he to die a death of abandonment by God as the supreme mockery of his claims and of his whole way of life? Jesus had been rejected by the Jews as a blasphemer. He had been rejected by the Romans as a rebel. Is he now being rejected by his God and Father, because since he is dying on the cross, he is dying as one accursed by God? The Jews and Romans might have been mistaken, but God could not be mistaken ... or was Jesus mistaken about God?

These questions torture us, his disciples. Jesus had not lived a private person. His preaching, his ministry, his very life are one. He *is* his proclamation and, if he dies, will his conviction about God's reign not be put to death with him? What will become of his proclamation about the God who cares for all and will eternally bless all those who entrust themselves to him? Will death not contradict and shatter such dreams? It is this that makes Jesus' experience of death unique.

Two men of violence die with him, but their cause will go on. It will be strengthened by their death. Jesus does not have a cause in this sense, so what he lived and embodied will die with him. It will become literally incredible, non-sense in the face of his death. Our discipleship is threatened with death as well. If Jesus dies, if death is the end, the God of established religion will be seen to have triumphed and Jesus will have lived and died in vain. For the sake of God Jesus has lived and is now dying. Is he to be forsaken by this God? Is he to die as the God-forsaken one? In the eyes of his enemies and followers he will die in that way. He will die as the God-forsaken one if God does not intervene to save him. Just as he had experienced unique fellowship with

Abba in life, had identified himself with God's cause, had felt assured that God identified himself with him and with his words,
had proclaimed his immediate and gracious loving presence in
all moments of life, so now on the cross, precisely because of this
experience, we his disciples understand his death as the unique
abandonment by *Abba*.

We are forced to this understanding. To know that God
should be close at hand and yet to see Jesus abandoned and
about to die as one rejected and spurned is unbearable. Jesus has
given himself over completely to *Abba*, he even goes to the cross
out of love for *Abba*. Has *Abba* in return handed him over to the
nothingness of death and given him up to its dark mystery? It is
all of this that wrings the cry of God-forsakenness from Jesus in
his death agony: 'My God, my God, why have you forsaken me?'

What is it like for us, as disciples, to hear Jesus utter this
cry? We know that is the opening verse of a Psalm, but while the
psalmist was addressing the God of Israel's covenant in these
words, on the lips of Jesus it is not simply addressed to the God
of the covenant; it is much more intimate than that. On his lips it
becomes a tormented, agonised cry to *Abba*. And as we listen we
hear the whole content of his message and ministry uttered in
this cry as question: *Abba*, why have you allowed this? Why have
you abandoned me? We hear it not just as a prayer addressed to
God, but it is the totality of Jesus, as defenceless cry and question
addressed to the one who seems to have forsaken him, the one
whom he has always called by the name *Abba*. In this pathetic
cry of utter helplessness, everything about Jesus is uttered as
question. His whole understanding of God as *Abba* is at stake,
his whole message and way of life are called into quest-ion. This
cry is a call for God to reveal his faithfulness and justice. The
fatherliness of God and the deity of *Abba* are in question in this
prayer. God himself is called into question.

It is possible to see it in legal terms. Jesus has been rejected
as a blasphemer, a false prophet proposing a false doctrine of
God, because of his words and actions in the name of *Abba*. If
Abba is allowing him to die as a blasphemer, is he not thereby
sustaining the charge against him and declaring that those who
put Jesus on the cross are right and that they, and not Jesus, have
understood God? We cannot avoid asking this question. Jesus is
called into question and with him the deity of Abba is called into
question. Why does *Abba*, if he is God, let such an obviously just

and innocent man die? Where is his justice? Why does he allow evil to triumph? What does his reign mean? Is he powerless or has Jesus misunderstood him? If Jesus dies, then *Abba*, if he is not the true God, will die with him.

The question finally becomes: Is there a God at all? And so the cry '*Abba*, why have you abandoned me?' becomes 'Why have you abandoned yourself?' There is no answer now from the cross, only the dumb animality of death. 'The Word within a word unable to speak a word swaddled with darkness.'[12] And so Jesus dies.[13] And everything he has said and done dies with him, it disappears. Jesus the questioner about people and God, Jesus the questioner of people in the name of God, is finally and totally called into question by people in the name of God. And so Jesus, the question, the enigma, the promise, has found his answer: apparently in the nothingness of absurd death. For he dies as one apparently rejected by his God and Father, dies as the God-forsaken one.

To the Romans it was the end of another routine execution of a trouble-maker. For the Jewish leaders, immediately responsible for his death, it was the moment of supreme triumph. He had finally been silenced. Their understanding of God had won the day. They had been vindicated. They had been shown to have been right and he had been proven to be what they always said he was, a blasphemer, a false prophet, an anti-christ.

And all of us, his closest male disciples, fled from the crucified Jesus (Mk 14:50). Not one of us even waited to bury him. But then what else could you do except flee from one who was so visibly rejected? We were caught off-guard and shattered and demoralised by the abject failure of such a contemptible death. And it was so public there was no possibility of explaining it away or toning down its horror and its significance. From the religious point of view, the whole life and message of Jesus have been completely discredited by the crucifixion. He has failed us, his followers, not only at this final moment but, because this moment cannot be separated from his whole message and ministry, his whole life is now seen to have been a movement of messianic hopes that are shattered and permanently destroyed.

One of us said later, 'We had been hoping that he was the one to restore the kingdom to Israel' (Lk 24:21). It caught the mood of resigned hopelessness that existed among us, his disciples, after the crucifixion of Jesus as an outcast and as one rejected by people and God. He had disappointed all the hopes we had placed in him. A dead leader is a dead leader and everyone knows that a messiah does not die. The messiah will certainly not be crucified as a blasphemer. Our acceptance of Jesus, belief in the God he preached, our discipleship, our hopes for the future have been broken on his cross. It is all unreal now, like a bad dream. We felt justified in running away.

We were right to flee because they might have turned on us next and one such death is more than enough. Some of us even began to say that we should have known better from the start, that it was doomed to failure, it was too Utopian, that he went too far, was too uncautious, and the rest of us nodded. But the gnawing emptiness of loss was there too. The one who had given us so much was now dead and we had failed him in his time of need. The memory of rash words such as 'Let us all go and die with him,' 'I will never disown you,' stung and cut deeply.

> After the torchlight red on sweaty faces
> After the frosty silence in the gardens
> After the agony in stony places
> The shouting and the crying
> Prison and palace and reverberation
>   of thunder of spring over distant mountains
> He who was living is now dead.
> We who were living are now dying
> With a little patience.[14]

9. A USELESS PASSION?

*The communication of the dead
is tongued with fire
beyond the language of the living*
T. S. Eliot

Christology is concerned with relating Jesus of Nazareth to God and to humanity in life and in death and in glory. We are heirs to a tradition that proclaims the uniqueness of that relationship. In struggling to follow the way of disciples we have been asking: Who is Jesus of Nazareth? We have been reacting to what he said and did. We have been wondering, with his contemporaries, about whether or not he should be related to God in a special way, even a unique way. To disciples, the foundations for such a relationship appeared to be there in his message and ministry taken as a *whole* (not relying solely on any single hint or indication we may have unearthed). It seemed plausible to relate Jesus of Nazareth to God in a very special way from the portrait of him that we have discovered. 'And the authenticity of this portrait was urged on us by the variety and contrariety of lines that converge into the representation of someone unlike anyone else, and yet someone who is obviously our brother and fellow man.'[1]

But the apparent foundation for relating Jesus of Nazareth to God seemed to have been destroyed by his death. This is the last threshold. We cannot simply relate Jesus to God as if this presented no problem. It does not seem adequate to say, as Bultmann and others do, that when they had fled the disciples re-assessed the meaning of the life and death of Jesus in a new way, that they got a new insight into what he meant and therefore, 'He rose into their faith' or 'into the kerygma' or that 'his cause goes on' or that 'he was too great to die.' Moltmann[2] makes some very telling points against those who argue against Easter in this way and diminish its reality. He maintains 'The cross makes every Jesuology and every christology impossible' because, since he died as he did, his ministry and his message and his cause are thoroughly discredited. His preaching and teaching are inseparable from his person and this person has been put to death as a blasphemer. So if any of his teaching were to survive his shameful and sinful death it would have to contain its own truth. But then it would no longer be the expression of the uniqueness of Jesus nor of what he died for.

If, for example, disciples now talked about the teaching of Jesus, they would have to explain that the man who taught emphatically, 'But *I* say to you,' was of course condemned by experts on the law for saying it, so what is implied in it is thereby contradicted. Would his teaching not now seem like 'words of a dead Jesus to the universe'? Of course, they might argue that he was willing to die for his teaching. 'Yes, but the fanatics we will always have with us ...' They would also have to say that they found his chosen solidarity with the oppressed and outcasts, his forgiving of sin and offer of salvation thoroughly embarrassing now. It would be rather absurd to try to speak of the forgiveness of sin in the name of a dead man who was put to death as a sinner and a blasphemer! How could they call anyone to faith in this dead man or to the God of this dead man who allowed him to die? And they could hardly dare to mention hope in his name when as disciples they fled because of the apparent hopelessness of his death.

As Moltmann puts it provocatively:

He, who proclaimed that the kingdom of God was near, died abandoned by God. He, who anticipated the future of God in miracles and in casting out demons, died helpless on the cross. He, who revealed the righteousness of God with an authority greater than Moses, died according to the provision of the law as a blasphemer. He who spread the love of God in his fellowship with the poor and the sinners, met his end between two criminals on the cross.[3]

If it all ends with the cross, there is no gospel, no faith, no christology, no church, no worship.

Our search for an implicit christology in the words and actions of Jesus breaks down in the face of the scandal and folly of the cross. Any attempted christology that implies that, after his death, his disciples simply gained a new insight into what Jesus was about, has not only failed to take Easter seriously but has failed, above all, to take the cross seriously. Only an approach to Jesus of Nazareth that treats the cross with deadly seriousness and shows how it has been overcome could claim to be a credible christology. 'Without the cross there is no christology nor is there any feature in christology which can escape justifying itself by the cross.'[4] Some christologies today do not always justify themselves in the face of the absurdity and scandal of the cross. But we will be aware of these inadequacies only when we have attempted to see what the inner pain of that cross meant for disciples.

Let us listen to what these disciples are saying now. They are found sometime later, some yards from where that cross stood, preaching about the crucified Jesus in a way that spoke of the overcoming of his death to the very people who had put him to death, at the risk of meeting the same fate themselves. This is an amazing turnabout. If true, it seems to provide a genuine basis for relating Jesus, who died on the cross, to God and therefore we must inquire about it. It immediately gives us two limit points: (1) The disciples' shattering experience of the death of Jesus and (2) their proclamation about this Jesus as being 'no longer held by death.' (see Acts 2:24). So we will have to postulate that 'something or other' must have taken place between these two points, that some as yet unknown event or experience must have interposed itself between their panic-stricken flight and this fearless preaching, between the breakdown of discipleship and its re-creation. And the disciples said that something *did* interpose itself. They expanded on this by saying that they had been converted because God had not allowed Jesus to be held by death.

The question is, What did they mean by this statement? To really hear what they said through these narratives it is not enough merely to read them carefully; we must first try to listen to what *they* heard in the whole of their history and tradition. In the story of the rich man and the poor man Lazarus, the rich man in torment asks that Lazarus be sent to warn his brothers but he is told: 'If they do not hear Moses and the prophets, neither will they be convinced if someone should rise from the dead' (Lk 16:31).

If we are to try to grasp what the disciples meant by 'not being held by death,' we too must listen to what 'Moses and the prophets' have to tell us. We will have to try to become attuned to the Old Testament. Jewish disciples, in the face of this radical newness, naturally had recourse to this source in their attempt to say who Jesus of Nazareth really was. They had to tell the story of Jesus by re-telling the story of Israel. But they tell the stories in such a way that transforming contact is made with the experiences, the hopes, the fears of their own contemporaries. They will have to tell the story of Jesus in such a way as to speak to fellow Israelites *but also*, if they claim he is of universal interest, to every woman and every man no matter what their previous religious background may have been. So in order to appreciate what they say we must look not only at the Bible but also at human experience.

To begin with, experience does not mean that we are relegating the Bible to second place. In fact, when we turn to the Bible and wonder about its origins, its preoccupations, its structures, its answers, we are immediately brought face to face with the experiences, questions, and hopes not only of the Jewish people but of humankind everywhere. These experiences and questions and hopes may help us to appreciate what the Bible is saying to us about God's involvement in human history. We may be able to recognise ourselves, our lives, our real questions and problems in what it says to us about God and his Christ.

Moments of Glad Grace

In the mediocrity of our lives some moments stand out from all others and continue to haunt us long after they have passed. There are such moments in the lives of all.[5] It seems that they are archetypal in human experience. They may occur seldom or often in a person's life but they cannot be programmed in advance or commanded. We must await their arrival, for they come to us obliquely, gently, and graciously. They are given and can only be accepted as a gift. They are elusive and mysterious and dissolve like snowflakes on our hand if we try to analyse them. 'We had the experience and missed the meaning' (Eliot). They remain ineffable because of their profundity, so sages simply cherish them and even poets can do no more than offer 'hints and guesses' about these 'unattended moments, moments in and out of time,' moments when the world seems charged with mystery, when the 'dearest freshness deep down things' seems to disclose itself to us, moments when we have a palpable 'sense sublime of something far more deeply interfused,' when 'we see life steadily and see it whole,' when the 'luxury of a child's soul' lets us 'pray un-selfconsciously with overflowing speech' and we are honoured with 'arguments that cannot be proven' – if we may draw on the language that poets use to try to give expression to these moments.

Often these moments arise spontaneously out of our laughter or our tears. The joy, the sorrow, the pain we experience directly and can name, but somehow in the midst of all, and yet greater than all, there is something more. It is as if the fabric of things is rent, a split in the 'ordinary' occurs and for a moment we see into a whole world of integration and happiness or a frightening world of emptiness and nothingness.

Although such experiences lie too deep for words, it seems accurate to say that they have both positive and negative aspects. But strangely these polarities seem to shift even as we experience them. We might try to hint at this ambivalence by speaking of them as 'moments of glad grace'[6] that still confront us with the 'shock of non-being' (Tillich). They seem to be moments of profound depth and richness and superabundance, yet this perception can shift to reveal only emptiness and an absolute void. These moments seem to hold together 'time present and time past and time future,' potent, pregnant moments. Yet simultaneously 'the past is all deception and the future futureless' (Eliot). These can be moments when the unfeigned ecstatic rapture of being alive and the precious underserved character of every heartbeat is borne in on us. Yet at the same time we may be profoundly aware of the shock of non-being and the absolute fragility of existence.

Such moments, which arise spontaneously, are unforced and unforceable and are therefore gracious or gift-like. Through them people have been led to understand that they themselves, their very life, their health, everything they have and are, indeed everything that is, is given and is received as sheer, undeserved and precious gift. We realise that everything is given absolutely *gratis* or graciously or as a grace. This insight can leave people standing in awe, wonder, fascination, and thanksgiving before the mystery of life. It may draw them to recognise that the mystery is near at hand, that there is a source to everything.

However, because of its disclosure of the negative, it may lead to the opposite conclusion, unless the negative too can be opened up so as to enable them to become 'aware of the power of being through the shock of non-being.'[7] Both possibilities exist because we experience not only what is positive but also a deeply disturbing, dis-easing insight into the absolute fragility of all that exists. Why, as the philosophers ask, is there something rather than nothing? We know viscerally that all that we have perceived as gift, precisely because it is gift, can be snatched from us. What is so precious is absolutely fragile for we have no hold whatsoever on anything. Nothing is self-guaranteed, all that is need not be at all.

If we were to ask those who have had these negative insights what they desired most, they would probably say that they hoped for something or someone to make life secure. They longed to be safe or hoped to be saved but knew security could only be received as an unmerited gift. So we find that people spontaneously use what we recognise as the secular analogates of religious language. Indeed, what has really happened is that we have taken up these words and used them in a particular way to communicate religious meaning. Anyway, we note that when people speak in everyday language about hope or about 'being saved' they use the image of 'space' – secure space between themselves and whatever it is that threatens them.

The same language and the same dominant themes and patterns emerge when we move from this intuitive level to the more analytical approach of anthropologists and philosophers.[8] They tell us that we are free because we have a future, that we live insofar as we hope. (Hopelessness brings not only despair but death.) So we experience ourselves as incomplete, as unfinished, as being constantly in search of ourselves, as lured beyond everything we can achieve. We hunger for the new and the not-yet, we leave every achievement behind in the very moment of accomplishment. But our attitude to the future is ambivalent; we can only live in tension toward our own fulfilment, toward a future that need not exist. We are 'beings-toward-the future,' we are 'hope-ers.'

Hope is a fundamental structure of human life. But our hopes, our desires to realise our potential go far beyond any fulfilment possible in this world. So they ask: Are we justified in seeing ourselves as a question about the possibility of an absolute future where the desired fulfilment could take place? We cannot achieve this of ourselves and, should it happen at all, it could only come to us as pure, gracious gift.

Such thoughts are highlighted if we think of ourselves not

as individuals but as a *community* and if we hope in a future common to all of us. As community beings we are called on to hope not only for ourselves but for all people because our future is their future. Does this common hope hint at a call to an absolute future?

Such questions are further sharpened if we consider the dialectic between ourselves as 'hopers' and as 'beings-toward-death.' Death is both our inexorable destiny and a constant terror in our lives. Despite our preoccupation with the 'denial of death,' its inescapability tarnishes the glitter of ultimacy in all human plans and projects. We die like other creatures but we alone can 'rage against the dying of the light.'[9] Death is not only the basic question about human life – we *are* that question.

We cannot give ourselves life now, we cannot save ourselves from death, and we certainly cannot give ourselves renewed life beyond death. What then is the point of this-worldly hopes in the face of the total collapse of death? Must we not hope in the face of death by going beyond death? The wholeness, the integration, the 'salvation' we desire could only be achieved by reaching a destiny we can never reach on this side of death. If this destiny should await us, it is only because an absolute source of life loves and cares for us and is graciously willing to renew or transform our lives even in death.

These positive insights and questions about hope and the future must also be coupled with the negative insights that run through much twentieth-century literature and philosophy. The common theme of existentialism and the storyline of many novelists and poets is that we are not only finite and limited, not only in the process of developing or evolving and therefore unfinished, not only death-bound, but that we fail to be what we could be. We experience tensions and polarities in our existence but over and beyond all that there is 'a massive disorder in existence, a pathology that seems to extend all through existence ... and that stultifies it. The potentialities of existence are not actualised as they might be, but are lost or stunted or distorted.'[10]

While these authors might not speak of sin, they do speak of destructive, hostile forces in life, which hold people in situations of frustration, helplessness, estrangement, and alienation from self and reality. So they speak of human persons as fallible and flawed, culpable and lost. We even hear them speak in terms of stain and guilt and defilement. They speak of the culpable contradictions in life. (No one, however, has bettered St Paul: 'I do not understand my own actions ... For I do not do the good I want but the evil I do not want is what I do' (Rom 7:15, 19).

If that is how it is, if there is a universal solidarity in disorder among the race, then it is foolish to think that the help and healing we need could come from within the human community. Yet as individuals and as race we need such a remedy, such salvation, if we are to be what we could be. So once again we ask: Must we not continue to hope for help and support, for healing, wholeness, and totality that cannot come from ourselves but can come only as a gift or a grace from the future?

People have always had the kind of experience or 'experience with experiences' which we have been trying to outline, and they have always struggled with the questions that arise from such experiences. Does life have a meaning? Does it make sense? Is life 'a tale told by an idiot full of sound and fury signifying nothing'?[11] Can there be a focus in life at all? Is death the final negation of everything? Is humanity the great absurdity, a 'useless passion'? Is there anything or anyone to whom we can entrust ourselves? Can we have faith in the future? In various ways each person gives birth to the questions: Why am I? Who am I? Where have I come from? What am I to become? What does it mean for me to be human? What is the meaning and future destiny of my life? Can I be forgiven? Can I be whole again? Can I be liberated from guilt? Can there be meaning in suffering? Who will free me from injustice and oppression? What, if anything, is the meaning of my death? Faced with these experiences and questions we may try to trivialise them, to distract ourselves from them. But in doing so, are we not ignoring the ineluctable question that we *'are'*? These questions arise spontaneously to mock all such attempts at suppression. We cannot stoically accept the impotence and meaninglessness that threatens to overwhelm us.

Faced with the bewildering complexity of life, with the mysteries of death and suffering, we feel helpless, threatened by the chaos outside and within ourselves. If we are to lead a human life at all we need to push back this threat, to distance ourselves from all that encroaches upon us. We need to impose order on the confusion, to create cosmos out of chaos. If life is to be human we must attempt to make sense of it. We must be involved in questions about and, in an active quest for, meaning, wholeness, forgiveness, 'salvation' in the widest sense.

We need to adopt some position toward the mysterious horizon of life. So we ask, 'What does it take to make and keep life human?'[12] 'Is there anything ... which gives unity, depth, density, meaning, and value, which makes graceful freedom possible?'[13] We are searching for something that will integrate our past, our present, and our future, for we need both a memory and a hope, a sense of identity and a project for the future. We are looking for some way to grasp all the implications of our own life story.[14] How can we communicate with each other about the paradoxes of 'the dream-crossed twilight between birth and dying'?[15] How do we speak about fear, suffering, death, love, absolute hope? Not that we can ask or answer these questions on our own! These moments, these experiences –contingency, relativity, temporality, transience – these questions, these needs which people have always had and with which they have always wrestled, can be seen as the starting points of god-thought and god-talk.[16] They are genetic moments in the development of religious beliefs in gods or faith in God, the beginnings of acknowledging mystery, of addressing oneself to the ultimate, of being involved in worship.

We find that all the great world religions and philosophies are concerned with the agonising experiences, enigmas, and questions that humankind must always face. Each in its own way tries to give a consistent vision of reality, a hope for the future, and the promise of 'salvation.' Basically they ease us into a 'context' by allowing us to participate in the life, the traditions, 'the shared stories ... of a tribe, nation, cult, or church.' Our past, present, and future are bound together by the memories and hopes, the ritual and the stories that are basic to the life and identity of this group. They provide a coherent answer to the enigmas of life, to the mystery of life and death. They offer a vision of the world that can satisfy the soul. This is offered concretely through story and ritual. A complex of symbols and stories, metaphors and rituals is found at the heart of every meaning system and every religion.

Why exactly is a symbol system necessary? Why do symbols exist? Why are they necessary? These feelings, these fears, these anxieties that we have been trying to hint at are so profound, so all-pervasive, so incommunicable that only the complex, multivalent, broken language of symbol, metaphor, and ritual can cope with them successfully. Other approaches will tend to distort these experiences because they will try to fit them into patterns and pre-ordained molds. Symbols alone can illuminate and interpret these experiences without distorting them, for symbols can speak to us about the mysterious dimensions of life without diminishing them. Why? Because the symbols that have developed organically out of the depths of human consciousness and experience have a unique evocative power. They appeal to the whole person – feelings, emotions, imagination, intellect, and will – and not just to a part. Symbols do not speak to us as words do, they speak of that which lies too deep for words, of that which cannot be brought to speech. They speak of the heart of things and they speak to our hearts.

Paul Ricoeur says that symbols are not a dispensable extra bit, but, 'because there is evil there are symbols.'[17] In other words, the realities we have been referring to – finitude, creatureliness, incompleteness, contingency, bafflement, helplessness, the abrasive daily threat of non-being (all of which are evil in the broad sense) – are so formless, so elusive, so unidentifiable, so incommunicable that human beings must have symbols and stories if they are going to cope with them in any sense.

Symbols enable us to recognise evil as evil; that is their first function. But if symbols could do no more than that for us, they would simply bring us to despair. In fact, they enable us to do something vitally positive. They enable us to counter-pose a more powerful positive reading of our situation which tells us how evil can be overcome. In that way they give us hope for the future by pointing the way of our true destiny and enabling us to follow it.

We think of the cross (see Epilogue) where we see simultaneously the heights and the depths of which we are capable. What we take for granted as 'normal,' as the way things are, or 'what people are like,' is revealed for what it really is, *evil.* 'Good,' pious people like us, with zeal for God and his revelation, put Jesus of Nazareth on the cross. That is what we are really like. This is the revelation of our desperate need for salvation. At the same time, the utterly consistent dedication of the crucified

Jesus to *Abba* and the poor and the sinners points the true way for us and enables us to follow him.

Symbols light up, interpret, thematise, and unify our experience so that we can give order and meaning to and make sense of all that is of ultimate significance in our lives. Without symbols all of this would remain mute, painful, and unliveable. Symbols enable us to identify evil and to overcome it, to recognise good and to celebrate it. They enable us to be human.

Such contact with symbol and story is not confined to special occasions. What we discover in these symbol systems we also find within our own lives. Human beings are often described as symbol makers. Erickson[18] has advanced a theory of the interplay between symbol and ritual and the development of the human personality. He contends that the first patterns by which parent and infant initiate mutual communication are composed of recognition symbols and sense stimuli, the smile, the touch, the cuddling embrace. Here the whole mystery of distinctiveness and separateness is being coped with. We are being born into the symbolic order. He says that all personality development in the child subsequently depends upon the adequacy of these primordial experiences. Each later stage of growth builds on and incorporates the earlier stages. If these early stages do not give a sense of security and identity, problems are bound to develop later.

Erickson refers to the most distinctive elements of these communication patterns as 'numinous.' It is laying the foundation for the sense of the 'holy' or the 'sacred' to which they may be introduced in later life. With young adulthood, processes begin to come more fully into focus and they become symbolisers and ritualisers in their own right. They constantly engage in these quintessentially human activities. They come together to tell stories, engage in ritual, use symbols to try to communicate those experiences in life which are the richest, but also most incommunicable .

An example may help. A group of five people spend some time together. They share experiences, communicate their hopes and fears, tell stories, pray together. They part company, convinced that this was a significant experience, that it made a difference in their lives. When they go their separate ways their shared experience can no longer be mediated through sense perception, through being in the same place, through affective response, because the immediacy of circumstance, time, and place is gone. They are alone now, each distanced from contact with the other four people.

Yet so much remains: memories, feelings, hopes and plans, thoughts and reflections that keep returning. They are beginning once again to cope with the self and space and time and distance and loss, with personal presence in physical absence. The relatedness of me and the not-me, the now and the no-longer-now, the now and the not-yet are at stake. Visible realities that capture and evoke their time together become very important – a pressed flower picked at a definite place at a significant moment, a little stone, a written word, photographs. An interplay between memory, imagination, creativity, and visible realities allows them to make explicit the human meaning implicit in the complex of experiences that went to make up a weekend together. They are engaging in a process of symbolization, evoking, narrating, and re-telling the 'story' of the weekend until the pattern of words becomes more commensurate with the inner significance, the most profound meaning of that time together for each of them.

When they meet again they will retell the story as each of them has created it. They will not tell it in the same way nor highlight the same moments in it, for each person's story is about its meaning for that person. But each narration is valid and as they hear the others' stories they are all trying to share the difficulty of coping with what has been lost and what has been found and are creating a new reality together by discovering common symbols and language. Ritual action, play, dramatisation of events, eating and drinking together will also play a vital part in their being together, their being bonded to each other, their creation of a common world.

They have moved from the experience (Stage 1), through the use of symbol and narrative, into a common appreciation of the human significance of that experience (Stage 2). But even more may be happening. Perhaps when they were alone they were already saying to themselves, 'In that silence I became aware of mystery,' 'I really believe life has a meaning,' 'I came to accept that there is a source of all life that loves all life,' 'I felt I could really pray at that time.' Such statements are obviously not on the same level as statements about Stages 1 and 2. They are now naming realities that cannot be seen or located in time, 'not given or not fully given within perceptual experience.' They are speaking about something that is vitally important, about experience interpreted in a religious way, about the absolute source of their being together, about ultimate meaning (Stage 3).

In effect, they are saying that, for them at least, a Stage 2 interpretation is not adequate. There is a dialectic between the 'now' and the 'not merely-now,' there is 'more,' a 'depth,' a 'beyond' that must be acknowledged by making these faith statements. They are talking about the way they have been changed by struggling with the human significance of certain events (moving from 1 to 2) and how through the dynamism of that movement they have been brought to a new transcendent level. They are trying to say how they now understand faith, how it makes sense now to say 'I believe in God,' 'I believe in Jesus Christ,' 'God spoke,' (Stage 3). This level of experience and expression is open to ever deeper exploration and embodiment. But it is possible for them to make these statements only if they have come in contact with people, with a church group, who live the truth of these statements and so can offer them a living language of faith, a lively mediation of faith. We realise that such statements of radical conviction are dense abbreviations of a long and difficult process of conversion and need to be expanded so that what is compressed into them can be appreciated by others.

The Approach to the Human Predicament within Israel

When we consider Israel we find the same concerns, the same human quest for meaning, humanity, wholeness, solidarity, salvation, the same general framework emerging. But we must allow the uniqueness of Israel's approach to strike us. Perhaps this will become clearer if we remember the role of hope in the life of Israel. In the history of religion, this people brought to birth and kept alive a unique understanding of hope. Because of this the Bible can be understood as a library of books about hope. This is not self-evident at the level of explicit reference on the pages of Scripture, but thanks to recent research we can see that hope is the underlying reality in the Bible.[19] This is so because of the importance of the future in the eschatological religion of Israel. The reality of hope underpins every page of the Bible, even if it is rather sparing in its overt use of the word.

A casual perusal of the Bible might give the impression that

Israel discovered her God in times of prosperity and victory. However, it would be much nearer the truth to say that she discovered God and purified her understanding of him and of herself above all in suffering. Her history could be described as a passion-history in which she wrestled with the archetypal problems of finitude and failure, of lost opportunity and guilt, of evil and sin, of suffering and death.

The content of the images of 'salvation,' of happiness, of wholeness in Israel as elsewhere, are conditioned by the experience of the absence of salvation, and so are projected out of situations characterised by suffering and oppression. If we are in the dark, we long for light; if ill, we hope for health; if we are enslaved, the passion for liberation is dominant and the hope is for exodus, a way out; if we are in exile, salvation is homecoming; if death threatens, we hope to live. We know the hopes of Israel so we know her sufferings too.

It was in situations of suffering, threat, and exile that Israel became most acutely aware of the fragility, the transience of everything. In such situations she had her most profound insight into the precious quality of all that she had received from the sheer, unmerited graciousness of Yahweh, her God of love and mercy and justice. Israel was able to interpret even her suffering, exile, and defeat as being part of God's all-wise, if inscrutable plan. She could 'christen her wild worst best' and see God as 'father and fondler of heart thou hast wrung' (Hopkins).

Narration transformed her painful experiences. Through her symbols she could expose and name what was evil and negative in her experiences and counter-pose more powerful symbols of good that proclaimed God's constant presence in her history. In this way she could read her situation in a hopeful way.

We could not over-stress the transforming power of this narrative. 'Things as they are are changed on the blue guitar.'[20] Through her mystics and prophets and people of prayer (prayers), Israel was able to interpret her trials and sufferings as revealing her true position before God. She was able to see that even at such moments God was with her and that he was taking her, through her sufferings, to a deeper communion with himself. She knew he had done it before and was convinced that he would do it now and in the future, therefore she saw these present negative experiences opening out toward a new, brightening, beckoning future. This enabled her, in the course of her developing history of groping toward God, to continue to believe that despite appearances to the contrary, her God was personal, that he cared for her in a providential way and was passionately involved in all that happened to her. So she could believe that he held her in the hollow of his hand always, even in suffering, that he 'always listened to the cry of her distress' and that ultimately he was 'with her to save her.'

In this way she was able to find meaning in the midst of apparent meaninglessness. She discovered that the most powerful presence of God was to be found in his apparent absence, that his strength lay in her weakness. These were the genetic moments of breakthrough when he could be truly God and she could be truly herself. Again she knew that this strength and hope came, not from herself, but from Yahweh alone who 'loved her with an everlasting love' and this hope is seen to be his most precious gift because it raised her up and knit her together again when she was most broken and most torn (Hosea 6:1-2; Ez 16). So she can hope when 'hope had mourning on.'[21] Israel came to accept this pattern of dying and being raised in her history long before she ever came to formulate an explicit doctrine of the resurrection of the dead.

The faith of Israel is her hope. Her God is a loving God who has literally given her everything, is calling her to love in return and only if she does so can she be truly herself. We know that we cannot discover meaning in life unless we are convinced that we are constantly loved and are capable of loving in return. So too with Israel; she accepted Yahweh as her source of refuge, help, and salvation, as a loving, merciful, and just God who was in love with her and was asking her to receive herself back from him by giving herself to him. This is the essence of her faith as hope. So faith, hope, and love are inextricably linked and to speak of one is necessarily to speak of the others as well.

We see all this working itself out throughout the Old Testament. In the story of Abraham, 'the father of all believers,' whose life is the paradigm of Israel's faith, we are immediately in touch with the realities of call, promise, hope, and the future. Abraham leaves all securities of country and kin and father's house and awaits God's future as he lives by promises. It is hope that sustains the patriarchs in their wanderings. In the book of Exodus we are in touch with 'the dark side of hope' for here Israel's hopes are prayed out of the negativities of slavery and suffering. Yahweh hears this *de profundis* cry and grants them salvation by overcoming their oppression, giving them a way out of slavery and a way into freedom (Ex 3:7-8). All that confines and chokes life is overcome and space ('a good and broad land') for life is granted.

During their exodus pilgrimage they are following a God who is up ahead leading them toward the future he desires for them. But the people grow weary of questing for this future and long to return to the 'fleshpots,' the old securities of the past, or to rest content dancing around the static idols of the present. 'Let us choose a captain and go back to Egypt' (Num 14:4). However, through the mediation of her leaders Yahweh lures them out of these futureless longings and promises more than even posterity and land – 'I will be their God' (Ex 6:7) and they will be his people. And we hear the foundational story of exodus narrated again and again and again.

The covenant was understood to recapitulate the totality of her life and history – everything that happened previously took place to bring about the covenant. Thereafter every recall of covenant in story or ritual gathered up the unedited fragments of history and their daily stories into a coherent whole. It brought light into darkness and sorrow. It rekindled hope for the present and the future in the memory of the past. This gave them a new consciousness, a new imagination, a security in the present, and hope for the future. It enabled them to be more intensely aware of Yahweh's constant saving presence in life and to respond to it in heartfelt thanksgiving. He who delivered their ancestors from Egypt would deliver them too from the myriad captivities of their daily lives. God would be with them in the 'bits and pieces of everyday' (Kavanagh) just as surely as he had been with their forefathers on the first Passover night. Past, present, and future are always intertwined in their hopes and in their experience of salvation.

However, it proved difficult to keep hope for God's salvation, dedication to his future, commitment to his justice, alive when they had journeyed out of slavery and suffering and into the land where their liminal pilgrimage ended and they settled down. It was easy to think that the promises had been fulfilled, that no further pilgrimage was necessary, when they were content and complacent in the present. When nobody else in the world thought about history and religion as they did, it was easy to slip into the ways of their neighbours and into the endless cycle of fertility and eternal return.

It was difficult to be ceaselessly called to live up to the demands of monotheism, radical justice, and the insatiable straining toward the future. Israel failed and settled for false, futureless securities at variance with the real future to which God was calling her. The events of history (see chap. 2) challenge the people, and the prophets hammer the message home. They confront a people who luxuriate in the false securities of the present and who have given up faith and hope in the true God. Yahweh is the God of mercy and compassion, so such people are declared by the prophets to be worshippers of false gods because they deny the future to widows and orphans and subordinate the future of the oppressed, the weak, and the defenceless (with whom Yahweh always identifies) to their own selfish present. A pair of sandals (Amos 2:6) is the value tag they place on fellow human beings. The prophetic strategy is to destroy the basis for their illusory hopes so that the foundation of true hope may be laid bare. If Israel can be convinced of her radical sinfulness and realise that of herself she has no real life, no future, and no hope, then paradoxically she can have real hope for a true future!

In summary, we realise that Israel's hopes and expectations are constantly directed toward an on-coming salvation which is always new. Therefore it is not possible to give a definition of their hopes or of the content of 'future,' 'destiny,' 'salvation' in the Old Testament. These are not static realities but ever-expanding, ever-deepening dynamic concepts with a living history of their own. We must unfold rather than define, because the hoped-for destiny, the longed-for salvation, are constantly being surpassed. The shell of apparent ultimacy is broken open to reveal new depths, the promise is never fulfilled exactly as expected, the aura of finality is removed from every goal and every horizon so that the people are drawn inexorably onwards.

A childless nomad couple are promised posterity and secure possession of rich land; an exiled, enslaved people are liberated and taken to a safe secure space; a broken, hopeless, exiled people are promised a new exciting future. These are the highpoints of

Israel's experience of hope and salvation. In daily life the content given to concepts like hope, future, and salvation could be quite ordinary and materialistic – basically the antithesis of how things were at any given unpleasant moment. It could be about safety in danger, protection from evil, good crops or fertile flocks. But the foundational events remained central and so they enabled the people to interpret or read what was gradually emerging in the present as suffused by the same saving presence of this gracious God, and, therefore, as salvific.

This, however, is understood as provisional, as a prelude to ultimate salvation which God was even now bringing about in a partial way and would realise in its totality only in the eschatological future. Latent possibilities in Israel's relationship with Yahweh are always being uncovered. So she must not be seduced into accepting any present experience of salvation, any present realisation of hope, as ultimate. She must always remain restless and venture into the unknown with only the confidence that comes from God's past and present action to sustain her. So gradually, in the course of her passion history, the transitory hopes of kingship, prosperity, even the land are pried from her grasping fingers.

During and after the exile, Israel's hopes and understanding of salvation broaden and deepen. This movement coincides with a profound re-interpretation of history in the prophetic writing which retains the symbols of liberation, exodus, covenant, dramatically re-working them so that they no longer refer merely to the promise of the past but open up a hope for the future far outstripping anything previously experienced. A definitive messianic salvation is promised when all hopes for liberation, victory, and security will be fulfilled and the community of the end time will come into existence. This community will be ruled over by God's Messiah so all can live in harmony, safety, and peace.

At this time, too, it was seen more clearly that the *sin* of Israel, her infidelity to Yahweh's faithful love, was the greatest obstacle to her salvation, for it cut her off from her real future. Forgiveness and reconciliation and new beginnings are hoped for (see the Servant passages) and offered, and integrity, justice, and a consistent response are demanded from each individual. They are called on to be saved by being saviours.

In the Bible a cluster of words is used to speak of all this, to hint at what we translate as faithfulness, salvation, graciousness, compassion, and justice. The basic image under-pinning the notion of salvation is that of space; to provide a secure place, to be roomy, to be broad; it is opposed to all that is narrow, confining, or constricting, all that weakens or oppresses or enslaves. Weak, oppressed persons cannot achieve deliverance, salvation, liberation (except by becoming oppressors), so they are totally dependent on Yahweh. Hence, the stress on hope in this faithful, reliable God, on waiting for him in quiet confidence, of trust and surrender to him. Such notions are further enriched by concepts which evoke God's showing gracious favour to his people. He is understood as brooding lovingly over Israel, as being gentle to the fragile, defending the defenceless, and being merciful to the sinner. They are found in passages that speak of the steadfastness of God's covenant love for Israel which makes her loveable, or the visceral compassion of God for his creatures, of his faithful justice on their behalf which calls them to struggle for justice in his name.

The question of the hope, destiny, and salvation of the individual was bound to arise in Israel as in every other symbol system. It is reassuring to know that the quest for meaning and the hope of salvation will be fulfilled and the painful enigmas of history will be resolved in the future, that the new covenant and new exodus will come. But what about the pain, the anguish, the personal passion-history, the death of the individual?

The pattern of Israel's history is one of dying and being raised, for God, who sustains history, will bring it to fulfilment. The nation will be saved from death and if Yahweh hears the prayers of the individuals who cry to him, he will save them from death. But who will save them in and through death? It is good to know that they will live on in their children (Sir 30:4-6) and that, as long as Israel continues, their contribution to its life will not be forgotten. But they must still die their own very personal death and what if they have no future beyond death?

The limit question about death demands an answer. Death stands intransigently in judgment of all human hopes for salvation. Is there real life before death if there is not hope for life through death? Is there hope for salvation beyond death? If there is, we are here at the bedrock of human hope for no greater hope is possible than to have one's longing for an ultimate destiny fulfilled.

We see the beginnings of this questioning about the destiny of the individual especially in the post-exilic period. Echoes of it are heard in the psalms: 'Can one tell of God's steadfast love in death or of faithfulness in Sheol? Are thy wonders known in the darkness or thy saving help in the land of forgetfulness?' (Ps 88:11-12). The questioning continues through the books of Job, Ecclesiastes, and Sirach and pushes toward an answer. But before a final breakthrough could be made, traditional Sheol theology, with its dismal shade-like destiny for all the dead would have to be overcome. Such a prospect of a shadowy twilight existence offered cold comfort to anyone who hoped for *life* beyond death. It was at most a kind of negation of life where the just and the unjust are equally lost. Gradually this vision of Sheol was overcome and formative images in that struggle were like those we find in Hosea 6:1-2; Isaiah 26:19; Ezekiel 37:1-14, and the Servant in Isaiah 52-53.

The final breakthrough to hope for life through death took place during the disturbed and anguished period of her history in the daring and fantastic imagination of the apocalyptic writers. Their lurid imagery may be frightening for us, the dualism and determinism in their view of history may seem strange, but they give us a new insight into humankind and God. They inspired hope in their contemporaries who were being persecuted. In the face of the anguish of so many good and holy people, who were suffering because of their faith and hope in Yahweh, earthly reward (Wis 2:6-11) no longer seemed adequate. Despite their righteousness they are not being saved from death. The question was: Will they be sustained *in* death and saved through it and so enter into the fullness of life? These writers said yes and radically modified the old Sheol theology so as to make room for this vibrant new hope of life through and beyond death. This hope is found in many apocalyptic documents which draw on a whole range of models to express it – exaltation, vindication, eternal life, assumption, removal of spirits from sheol, resurrection of the body, etc. [22] In the book of Daniel eternal life is promised to the just who live through the days of the final tribulation under Antiochus Epiphanes. 'And many of those who sleep in the dust of the earth shall awake, some to everlasting life, and some to shame and everlasting contempt' (12:2) and the just will be elevated to join the angelic host. This is the first undisputed evidence for belief in resurrection in the Bible. Other traditions build on a wisdom story about a wise man who was persecuted but vindicated by God (Wisdom 2, 4, 5). In 2 Maccabees 7 it speaks of the physical 'resurrection of life' of all the just.

The range of models used to give expression to this hope is rich and varied and must be retained without trying to make these images coalesce into a single unified archetype. We must remember too that these models are based on metaphors which try to use ordinary language to achieve a 'spark across' into the unknown world of life beyond death. Resurrection of the dead is a metaphor used in discourse about this indescribable reality. The daily experience of falling asleep and being roused from sleep is used in this model (Is 26:19) to hint at what it might be like to fall asleep in death and be roused into new life by God. We run into trouble if we forget that we are dealing with metaphors to hint at the ineffable and hear them instead as literal descriptions. 'Through a chink too wide there comes in no wonder.'[23]

Here, then, on the threshold of her history, Israel confesses Yahweh as the one 'who gives life to the dead.' They have brought to its finest conclusion what is implied in the saying, 'I am the God of Abraham, Isaac, and Jacob, the God of the living and not of the dead.' The breakthrough has been made into a hope that the God, who graciously gives life and sustains it at all times, will sustain them through the final threshold of death and graciously renew life so that they may be with him and draw life from him forever. This is the ultimate hope, the greatest grace, the definitive destiny. So salvation is now used absolutely – one is saved in life and through death. God himself is salvation; gracious gift and giver are one.

10. READING THE EASTER NARRATIVES

Through a chink too wide
there comes in no wonder.
Patrick Kavanagh

Even this sketchily outlined background should help us to appreciate the Easter narratives. These narratives came into being in the first place because disciples brought two thousand years of Israel's tradition to bear on the mystery of Jesus of Nazareth. They use these centuries of tradition, concerned with handling images, concepts, metaphors, and symbols, in order to discover and express religious meaning in their new proclamation. So we must try to understand the old if we are to appreciate the new. 'But if there is no resurrection of the dead, then Christ has not been raised' (1 Cor 15:13) is St Paul's way of putting it.

The Easter narratives, using the core stories of Israel, were told and retold over a considerable period of time before being written down in the form in which we now find them. If we do not keep this constantly in mind, we are bound to be faced with needless difficulties. If we do not appreciate the nature of biblical narrative, we will hardly grasp what is being said in the Easter narratives. Indeed, in our struggle to come to grips with them everything we know about the influence of presupposition, pre-understanding, and prejudice on human understanding will be pointedly verified both in ourselves and in what we read. It is easy to be convinced that we already know what these narratives are saying before we approach them, because of our traditional faith in resurrection.

Because we assume that we *know* what Easter is, what resurrection means, who God is, how history is to be understood, we will simply hear these narratives as confirmation of what we already know and not as a proclamation of what is shatteringly new. We inevitably approach them with preconceived ideas and ready-made definitions. (This problem is not peculiar to approaching biblical narrative, but is simply the way we approach all human knowing.) If we could admit the extent to which we are held captive by our presuppositions and consequently be prepared to re-define our cherished notions of history, of the relationship between God and the world, of what is and is not possible in the light of these narratives, we might then be in a position to begin to hear what these narratives are really saying to us.

We would need to recall the relationship between experience and interpretation and how interpretation enables experience to become communicable through symbol and story. It would be especially helpful to understand how people narrate transforming experiences, give expression to genetic moments of profound insight, or communicate a radical breakthrough in religion or love or poetry or science. Human beings cannot express themselves without interpreting, or interpret without transforming. The interplay between the choice of a dominant image or model and its narration is always vitally important. The narration will always be in terms of the concepts that are historically available. We must constantly remember the limitations of language, even of religious language, that 'not everything has a name. Some things lead us into the realm beyond words ... for an instant you glimpse the Inaccessible ... and the soul cries out for it' (Solzhenitsyn).

In the struggle to speak about Easter we may find that mystery is there where language ceases, that we are 'lost between awe and wonder' (Tolkien), and that 'words after speech reach into silence' (Eliot). In that sense it is helpful to realise that the Easter narratives are much more the poetry of love, expressing the most liminal of experiences, rather than pedestrian literal descriptions. We need to be 'drawn by our delight' before we can appreciate them. 'Show me a lover and he will understand.'[1] In fact, this appeal to the analogy of interpersonal love is very helpful and we would do well to keep it in mind. People who love each other are absolutely convinced about the reality of their love. It brings about a radical transformation in life but it cannot be 'proven.' It can only be lived. Even those who live out its implications stammer in their attempts to articulate its meaning and significance, for it lies too deep for words. The discourse of disciples about the resurrection of Jesus has many of these characteristics.

The Narratives[2]

We have two limit points: (1) the death of Jesus and the scattering of the disciples, (2) the disciples' proclamation of this Jesus as not 'held' by death. To understand how the latter could follow the former we must ask certain questions: What happened to the disciples? Did something happen to the crucified Jesus? How did someone who died the kind of death he died become the focal point of good news? How could you proclaim anything about the crucified Nazarene? Our question, then, is not 'How did the proclaimer become proclaimed' (Bultmann), but how did the *crucified* proclaimer become proclaimed; how did he become anything? How could shattered, scattered disciples proclaim something new about this dead Jesus at the risk of meeting the same fate themselves? Why did the church come into existence and how did it continue to exist with Judaism? How are we to explain its genesis and its continued growth in the face of opposition?

Whatever it was that brought 'the followers of the way' of Jesus into existence and transformed that way into a world religion must have been extraordinarily strong and distinctive, otherwise they would have been re-absorbed easily into Judaism. What was this strong, transforming, distinct-ive experience or event that interposed itself between Jesus' death and the disciples' proclamation? The disciples said they now proclaimed Jesus as saviour because they had been converted and they had been converted because God 'did not allow him to be held by death' (see Acts 2:24.) This is the single Easter message we discover in all the accounts of Easter. Although the theologies found in these accounts are very varied and the inconsistencies and historical problems they contain are very puzzling, they are all seeking to give expression to the same basic Easter message: 'God has raised Jesus and he has appeared to Simon/me/us/them' (1 Cor 15:5-6; Lk 24:34; Acts 2:32;1 Cor 15:20, perhaps combining two traditions).

There is then *one* Easter message but *many* Easter stories. We will confine ourselves to examining the Easter message or kerygma. In the Easter kerygma (and in the Easter stories) there is no attempt to say how this overcoming of death took place. This is something that took place between the crucified Jesus and his God and Father and obviously there could be no eyewitness to such an event. It is only in the apocryphal writings, especially the gospel of Peter,[3] that attempts are made to describe the overcoming of Jesus' death. Unfortunately, visual representations of Easter have all too often drawn either on these apocryphal accounts or, more usually, on a literal reading of the Easter stories, and they have become embedded in the popular imagination and piety. Because of these influences, which combine with our own desire to reduce everything to the empirical level, it becomes difficult to think of Easter as being anything more than the simple resuscitation of a Jesus who is larger than life.

In contrast, the canonical accounts insist that the disciples are together again proclaiming Jesus as saviour because they have been transformed, converted to faith in his being no longer held by death. Their conversion, their totally changed hearts and lives are due, they say, to an antecedent transformation of the crucified Jesus by God. This Jesus is no longer held by death; he now lives the very life of God himself and he has graciously made himself present to them and enabled them to recognise him *as* transformed. What happened to the crucified Jesus is refracted to us through the narration of the experience of the disciples: 'He who had set me apart ... was pleased to reveal his son to me' (Gal 1:16). 'God ... has shone in our hearts to give the light of the knowledge of the glory of God in the face of Christ' (2 Cor 4:6).

Jesus had died by crucifixion but they claimed that he, who had not been overcome by death, had enabled them to encounter him in a new way after his death. The accounts speak of an initial 'doubt and fear' but the disciples arrive at an absolute certitude that this Jesus who had been known among them and had died on a cross had entered into radically transformed new life. [They are not speaking about some kind of 'Joe Hill' existence or 'Che lives' or 'His cause goes on' or 'He was too great to die,' nor is it any kind of *ET* revival.] Rather, they insist that Jesus, the one who was crucified, lives now by the very life of God himself. 'The death he died he died to sin once for all, but the life he lives he lives to God' (Rom 6:10). They are maintaining that Jesus has not come back from the dead, like Lazarus, but has gone on from death into the depths of the glory of God. If Jesus who had died has entered upon this utterly new life, and so can be present to them in an indescribably new way, it can only be because God has acted definitively or eschatologically in him and has not allowed him to be held in death.

Jesus had always left the future in God's hands. He had declared people to be blessed because God would overcome their hunger and mourning, would reward in his own time what was done in secret and so without reward now. He had hoped for the consummation of the kingdom at God's good pleasure, had declared against the Sadducees his conviction about God's ability to transform his creatures even in death. Now he himself, they say, has been held in the hollow of God's hand even in the realm of the dead and has been brought through death to life, into God's future. He is now at the very heart of the heart of God. Here disciples begin to stammer, 'for not everything has a name' and 'words strain and crack and sometimes break ...' and '... after speech reach into silence.'

This absolutely liminal experience, this ultimate threshold between history and mystery, this re-creation of new communitas among disciples cannot adequately be expressed in language. It is God's mystery. To say something is a mystery does not mean we must give up trying to understand it, but rather that it is infinitely intelligible and lures us toward an ever deeper acknowledgment and a ceaseless wrestling with life and language to express it. These disciples cannot define the indefinable or describe the indescribable simply in the language of everyday happenings. Symbols, metaphors, and models must be used to disclose something of the reality of this mystery, but even when they are stretched to breaking point the disciples still only strain after mystery.

They do not simply *state* what Easter means, they *incarnate* it. So it is not enough to examine what they say in the text; we must look especially to the transformation in their conduct and way of life. They may only be able to say in words, 'God did not allow Jesus to be held by death but raised him and made him appear ...' But if we wish to understand what they are really saying we have to listen to the flesh and blood language of their converted, transformed existence. Those to whom the crucified one (in whom God has acted) is present, experience his presence as self-authenticating, as laying hold of their entire lives, as possessing them now and for the future (hence, the love relationship analogy). So we have to try to hear what it was that brought Peter the Rock out of Simon the denier, or a crucified Paul out of a crucifying Saul, or the church of apostles and martyrs out of scattered disciples.

When the disciples attempted to put into words the transformation which took place in the crucified one, and which alone is responsible for their conversion and their re-assembling, they drew on various models which, as we have seen, developed within late Judaism to give expression to the people's most profound hopes. So we find a range of complementary models used by them to express their faith in Jesus as no longer held by death. The very variety of these models alerts us to the profundity of the mystery and we must try to acknowledge it as such. It is easy for us to slip into other ways of thinking.

This act of God on behalf of the crucified Jesus is best described as an eschatological act, not because this expression explains anything but because its strangeness may prevent us from thinking that here we are dealing with one act among other acts within our space and time and history. We are trying to come into contact with something that takes place beyond the fringes of human experience, that is metahistorical and yet is graciously refracted through human history. So while we cannot come into direct contact with it, we can examine its effects and its repercussions within history and it can transform us too. Its centre is beyond the threshold of our world, yet its effects reach into our world or, to use Dodd's[4] phrase, there is 'traffic between two worlds' here.

This makes it difficult for us to hear what the disciples are saying, for we tend to try to locate and describe this eschatological act in the unmodified terms of our everyday world. We leave no room for wonder or mystery. If we diminish these narratives in this way, we will end up hearing about a Lazarus-type return to this life or the resuscitation of a corpse and nothing more. Nothing further is possible within the limits of language that we have set for ourselves.

The Easter disciples struggled to overcome this difficulty for they wished to speak about the mystery of a new creation, a totally new order of existence, a passage into the glory of God. So the wrestling with language and meanings had to begin and continue. One dominant model emerged and holds pride of place within the New Testament's interpretation, and that is the model of resurrection. Paul maintains that if we do not accept the Jewish hope of resurrection, we will not be able to accept that Christ has been raised (1 Cor 15:16).

Yet even here we see how at times the root image of awakening is used (Mt 28:7; 1 Cor 15:4; Rom 10:9). At other times the image of rising is dominant (Acts 2:24; Lk 24:7). The disciples were aware of the inadequacy of this model and strove to offset its limitations. It is retained to give an opening into mystery, but its content is transformed so that it now speaks of the mystery of the crucified Jesus who has broken the bonds of death. We have continuity with late Old Testament thinking and hoping along-side a radical discontinuity, for they have to take account of the reality of the life, death, and new life of Jesus of Nazareth. In other words, they use what is best in their tradition but introduce char-acteristic modifications into even this most privileged model. The choice of model is very important. Out of many available models, resurrection of the dead is found to be most adequate in communicating the significance of God's action on behalf of the crucified Jesus. Yet even this is substantially qualified in order to take account of the uniqueness of that action. It will be helpful to look at the modifications we can discover in their proclamation.

1. *The first modification* introduced into this model makes it clear that they are not referring to the mere resuscitation or revi-val of a corpse or the return of a dead person to life. If the raising of Jesus is on the same level as that of the story of Lazarus (Jn 11) or of the widow's son (Lk 7:11-17) then we have no hope. Such a temporary return to the structures of life, a brief reprieve before falling back into death, could offer no hope to us in the face of the deadliness of death. 'If for this life only we have hoped in Christ, we are of all men most to be pitied' (1 Cor 15:19). But Paul is not talking about a return to the structures of this life when he says, 'We know that Christ being raised from the dead will never die again; death no longer has dominion over him. The death he died he died to sin, once for all, but the life he lives he lives to God' (Rom 6:9-10).

The raising of Jesus involves a radical newness, a most pro-found transformation. Jesus did not return to ordinary life but entered into transformed, new eschatological life. He will not die again. He lives now in the glory of God. Even in the Easter stories that come closest to a more physical description of Jesus as raised (especially in Luke and John), he is nevertheless presented as no longer confined to our time-space continuum. They do not recognise him; they doubt; he comes and goes suddenly even if the doors are shut. As Paul says, 'Flesh and blood cannot inherit the kingdom of God nor does the perishable inherit the imperishable' (l Cor 15:50).

All the narratives are proclaiming that the one who is raised is none other than Jesus of Nazareth who was crucified and buried but that in his being raised he is transformed by God. They are speaking about identity-in-transformation and both identity and transformation must be stressed simultaneously. To opt for identity only means that we may be reducing the new creation to nothing more than the revival of a corpse. To emphasise transformation only means being in danger of losing contact with the actual historical person, Jesus of Nazareth. We must hold both in creative tension. So we must not read, for example, the gospel stress on the identity and reality of the Risen One as literal physical description. Nor should we misunderstand the emphasis on transformation as if the risen one were simply some kind of ghostly apparition not essentially linked to the concrete life of the historical person Jesus of Nazareth.

2. *The second modification:* We saw that there was no universally accepted way within Judaism for speaking about the hope of life beyond death. Even those who spoke of their hopes in terms of 'resurrection of the dead' looked forward to a collective resurrection of the dead at the end of the age or the end of the world. There was no expectation of the eschatological resurrection of a single individual before the end time. Yet this is what is proclaimed in the New Testament. A movement has taken place from hoping for a future action of God on behalf of all (the elect) to proclaiming that this has already taken place, in anticipation, in the case of Jesus.

So they use the inherited model but qualify it, giving it a much more specific and definite content so as to speak about the raising of Jesus in all its uniqueness and convey a new revelation to us. Consistently throughout the New Testament we find that they speak of resurrection *from* the dead and not simply resurrection *of* the dead. The language and model are in line with those found in late Judaism but the new beginning of which they speak transcends these categories and demands a breakthrough. Yet, for those who had inherited these Jewish categories, to say that God has raised Jesus could only mean that the end time had already begun, that his being raised makes him 'the first fruits of those who have fallen asleep' and that the in-gathering of the collective resurrection is about to begin.

3. *The third modification* concerns the way in which the narratives link the raising of Jesus to the appearances. God does not simply act on behalf of the crucified Jesus and take him to himself into the heavenly realms out of contact with this world and its history. Rather, the narratives maintain that the one who is raised 'is made to appear' and his followers are enabled to recognise him as the one transformed by God. This gracious initiative is due entirely to God and to the sovereignty of his action. In the New Testament this is stressed continually by emphasising that it was *God* who raised Jesus (Jn 10:18 is the exception). We are further alerted to the initiative of God by the word chosen to speak about the appearances of Jesus who has been raised – *ophthe* –'he appeared.' (Note its repetition in 1 Cor 15:5-8.)

Ophthe is a word used in the Greek translation of the Old Testament especially in the context of speaking of God's revelation. As a passive form of the verb 'to see,' the stress is laid on the granting of the vision rather than the activity of the one who sees. God acts eschatologically by raising Jesus from the dead, and as the Risen One, through whom God is acting, he graciously reveals himself to disciples, who are furthermore enabled to respond in acknowledgment to this initiative of his. This is what is compressed into the word *ophthe*, the code word for the universal faith of the church, 'he appeared' (or made himself to be seen). Again, the stress is on identity-in-transformation; it is truly Jesus the crucified one who is raised from the dead and thereby radically transformed.

So they do not say, 'We have seen Jesus once again' but 'We have seen the *Lord*' (Lk 24:34; Jn 20:18, 25, 21:7) and 'They *worshipped* him' (Mt 28:17). We realise once again that 'words strain and crack and sometimes break under the burden,' that we, who 'have no words for hazels in October,' are literally at a loss for words. If we attempt to translate *ophthe* simply in our everyday sense of *seeing*, we will not at all be doing justice to its biblical meaning. At best, we distinguish between three dimensional seeing, insight, and visionary perception but none of these alone seems adequate. For the Scriptures alert us to the changed status of the one who makes himself be seen. We are told that it is difficult to recognise him, he comes and goes at will, then he vanishes, so he is not here to be observed neutrally as one object among others. Neither is it simply a matter of new insight. It is above all insight into a God-given revelation, not the subjective product of 'the overheated brain.' Nor is it a question of a visionary experience and perception. Language was available to speak about such visions and revelations and Paul uses it in 2 Cor 12:1ff, but the language used by Paul and the others in speaking of the Easter appearances is substantially different. They are telling their hearers about seeing Jesus *christologically*. St Thomas Aquinas expresses it thus: 'After his resurrection the disciples saw the living Christ, whom they knew to have died, with the eyes of faith.'[5]

If the everyday experience of 'seeing' does not measure up to the uniqueness of these revelatory encounters, we might begin to suspect that the categories of 'speaking' and 'hearing' may also be less than adequate. Many Scripture scholars[6] wonder whether the Risen One spoke 'words' as such or was 'heard' in the everyday sense of the word. They are not at all denying the reality of the communication between the risen Jesus and his followers – they are insisting on the profundity of this communication. But the ordinary sense of 'speaking' and 'hearing' seems inadequate to express the profound, life-transforming communication that is obviously in question here. They are grappling with an overwhelming, all-possessing, transforming experience that laid hold of the totality of their lives. Its meaning was communicated at a level literally too deep for words and yet was grasped by them at that profound pre-linguistic level. The experience of non-verbal communication in contemplation or between lovers ('We were together and said nothing all the day'[7]) may help to throw some light on this experience.

It seems permissible, then, to say that the words placed on the lips of the Risen Jesus in the Easter stories are later attempts by the community to give expression to what had at first been communicated to them at this most profound level. They are gradually verbalising their understanding of the significance of their primordial experience of the Risen One. Their lives have been transformed; they are called on to live differently and to communicate to others what God had done and was doing and would do for them through Jesus who is no longer held by death.

This was communicated as a mission to proclaim Jesus' death, resurrection, appearances, and enduring presence – to evangelise.

This commission is not something given alongside the experience of Easter but is its very heart, its inner meaning. Gradually, in the practice of their daily lives, they came to understand the universal implications of Easter and they can finally put it in the form of an explicit commission given by the risen Jesus: 'to make disciples of all nations' (Mt 28:19).

This articulation is not gratuitously added; it is the inner meaning of the appearances. When we look at it in this way we are helped to understand how we can have such a clear statement about a universal mission attributed to the risen Jesus (Mt 28:19), and yet the Council of Jerusalem hotly debates the question (Acts 11) and Peter does not appeal to this saying of the Lord in defence of what he is doing. Even more strangely Paul, who was certainly not among the eleven when they were supposed to have heard these words, is in fact obeying them, while some of those who were said to be there are ignoring them!

But already we have moved beyond the boundaries we set of looking only at the Easter kerygma and have encroached upon the Easter stories. We notice in these stories, by way of contrast with the kerygma, a growing stress on the corporeality of the Risen One and a tendency to elaborate words spoken by him. At this stage we cannot go into any more detail about these stories because they can really only be examined in the context of the gospels within which they are found and whose theologies they obviously reflect. However, by way of clarification, perhaps we should look briefly at the stories of the empty tomb and the three day tradition.

The Tomb Stories

Because of our desire to localise the eschatological, to use a model of resuscitation rather than resurrection, and because of definite pressures from apologetics, tradition, and artistic representation, we may be tempted to more or less identify resurrection and the empty tomb. The Scriptures offer no basis for such an identification. Indeed, there are so many difficulties and inconsistencies within the tomb stories themselves that no harmonisation of details is possible. We find discrepancies about the numbers of women who go to the grave, about their reasons for going (to anoint a corpse buried for three days!), about the number of angels, the reaction of the women afterward, etc. Walter

Kasper says, 'These and other differences which cannot be harmonised show that the events of Easter morning can no longer be reconstructed; indeed that a purely historical account is not what matters in the Easter stories.'[8] He sees Mk 16:1-8 as the oldest account, but on analysis (despite the fact that unlike other accounts 'only the kerygma of the angel is legendary'):

> It is clear that in its present form at any rate, it is in no way a historical account ... We are faced not with historical details but with stylistic devices intended to attract the attention and raise excitement in the minds of those listening. Everything is clearly constructed to lead very skilfully to the climax of the angel's words: 'He is risen, he is not here; see the place where they laid him' (16:6).[9]

Mark, he says, is clearly the editor of this account.

> The important point here is not primarily the emptiness of the tomb; it is rather the proclaiming of the resurrection, and the reference to the tomb is intended as the symbol of this faith in the resurrection. This ancient tradition is not an historical account of the discovery of the empty tomb, but evidence of faith. In terms of form criticism, this tradition can be most easily described as cultic; that is, it deals with a narrative intended as the basis for a cultic ceremony.[10]

In conclusion he says:

> It is of course impossible from an historical viewpoint to go any further than the statement that it is definitely a very ancient tradition, which must very probably be described as historical. To establish that there is an historical core to the empty tomb stories is not the same as providing proof of the resurrection as a fact. Historically it can only be put forward as probable that the tomb was found empty; how it became empty cannot be established historically. Of itself, the empty tomb is an ambiguous phenomenon. Different interpretations of it exist in the New Testament, of Mt 28:11-15; Jn 20:15. It only becomes clear and unambiguous through the proclamation, which has its source in the appearances of the risen Christ. For the faithful the empty tomb is not a proof but a sign.[11]

This linking of the empty tomb stories to the veneration of the tomb of Jesus has been taken up by many authors. To have such a practice 'at the place where they laid him' would have been very significant. Pilgrims would have been brought to this place where the corpse of Jesus was laid, this entry to the underworld, the mouth of the realm of death. There, in contrast to Jewish and Greek ideas about the 'richness' of the place of the dead, they are confronted with emptiness and they hear once again the God-given Easter message: 'He is risen.' In this liminal place between this world and the world of the dead they realise that the God of the living has invaded Sheol and conquered death, has raised Jesus and taken him beyond the final threshhold. Because this has happened he is alive in an absolute way, is present to them in a transforming way. So why should 'they seek the living among the dead' (Lk 24:5)?

The concern to establish the absolute identity between the crucified and Risen One is obvious here once again. God's new life has irradiated the place of death and the emptiness of this space is a negative token of the divine plenitude of the new creation. In this way those who did not directly experience the appearing of the Risen One would be given a rich liminal experience that could open up the significance of Easter for them in a new way.

So the tomb stories are important but, of itself, an empty tomb does not prove anything, least of all the resurrection of Jesus (Jn 20:8-9). In fact, these stories are emphatic that its emptiness at first led to confusion, fear, and dismay because it was open to many interpretations. If it were empty, it needed an explanation. The faith of disciples is faith in the raising of Jesus, not in an empty tomb.

Lastly, in these tomb stories the presence of women is a constant factor. Even more significantly, diverse traditions tell us that Jesus' first appearance was to Mary of Magdala. It seems that women disciples who, unlike his male disciples, followed him to his very death, were in fact the first to announce that Jesus was not held by death. They provide the element of continuity between death and the discovery of the empty tomb. Their conviction must have been very influential in shaping the early stages of the movement. The women's reports were at first disbelieved but later accepted when corroborated by Peter and the eleven. Their unique contribution tends to be down-played because the church's official witnesses to Jesus as the Risen One were Peter and the eleven (Mt 28:16-20; Lk 24:36-53; Jn 20:19-23;1 Cor 15:5). We have a very long way to go in acknowledging the role of women in the ministry of Jesus and the contribution they made to the post-Easter proclamation.[12]

The Three-Day Tradition

Once again, because of our desire to locate the eschatological we may tend to say: 'The resurrection took place on Easter Sunday morning' and go on to refer to the text 'and on the third day rise again.' (see Mk 8:31 and parallels). The 'third day' according to the Scriptures is not primarily about chronology but about theology and salvation. In the Bible 'the third day' is a way of speaking of divine vindication and fulfilment. It is the crucial time, the decisive turning point when God overcomes all distress and disaster (see Hosea 6:2-1). A Jewish tradition looked for the resurrection of the dead 'three days after the world's end' and Jesus himself seems to have used a 'third-day saying' about the consummation of his ministry (Lk 13:31-33) and about the Temple (Mk 14:58; Mt 26:61). So the references to Jesus being raised on 'the third day' are speaking primarily about the definitive action of God that inaugurates the new creation and marks the dawn of the new age. This theological third day tradition became linked to a chronological 'after three days' perhaps because of associating the tomb or appearances with the day 'after the Sabbath.' We again tend not to appreciate fully the references to 'the first day of the week' as speaking to us about the significance of the new week of the new creation and revert to understanding Sunday in terms of the Jewish Sabbath.

The Sequence [13]

Any attempt to retrace the sequence of the disciples' experiences between crucifixion and proclamation must be tentative and hypothetical because of the nature of the sources. Perhaps the disciples fled back to Galilee (before or after hearing the women's puzzling report about the tomb). Maybe they tried to pick up the threads of their former lives again. It is accepted that the first 'official' appearance of the crucified Jesus was to Simon, perhaps by the shore of the Sea of Galilee. Simon 'sees' Jesus as no longer held by death and obeys the new invitation, 'Follow me' (Jn 21:19). He takes the initiative and, in the name of Jesus who has been raised, gathers the eleven.

This foundational experience and his consequent primordial role among the disciples is what gains for Simon the new name of *Kephas*, Peter, Rock. He is the first male disciple to be converted to faith in Jesus as not held by death. It seems that at least some of the eleven had difficulty in accepting what Simon Peter said when he had 'turned again and strengthened the brethren' (Lk 22:31-33) and 'they doubted' (Mt 28:17). But together they experienced a confirmatory revelation of the crucified, risen Jesus. Everything that would be articulated later is contained in these revelatory experiences. They realise already what God had done for Jesus, that 'he had raised him,' as they later expressed it.

In a transforming experience, which they describe as a pouring forth of the spirit of the glorified Jesus, they realise that the future age has begun and they are galvanised into action. What all this means will gradually clarify itself (in the process of their conversion) as a commission to proclaim this as good news to Israel and to the whole world, to live together in communitas sustained by the Risen One; to reinterpret and celebrate all he had said and done and been among them, in the light of Easter, to baptise all people into his death and resurrection, and in the eucharist to praise God for his crucified and risen and soon-to-be consummated presence. Scholars say that when the New Testament speaks of Jesus as risen, glorified, self-revealing, ascended, spirit-giving, mission-inaugurating Lord, we should realise that these are complementary ways of speaking about the single mystery that he is. It is best to see the sequential spacing out of events, especially in Luke-Acts, as a vitally important attempt to accommodate the profound eschatological reality of this mystery, facet by facet, to our very limited, time-bound grasp of things.

11. RENAMING JESUS

The hint half guessed
The gift half understood
Is incarnation.
T. S. Eliot

After Easter the disciples profess that the new life they experience together is God's gracious gift to them, mediated through the crucified and risen Jesus. They had recognised this Jesus as alive in a new way and they now see who he truly is. Their turning to him after their abandonment of him must have involved an indescribably intense and poignant experience of forgiveness, of 'at-one-ment,' of salvation in the deepest sense. As Dodd puts it, 'The little flock ... was recreated by an act of forgiveness ... That was how the church was brought into existence and it could never forget that its foundation members were discredited men who owed their position solely to the magnanimity of their ill-used master.'[1]

They had failed him because of self-interest and cowardice. They had been unfaithful so they would have felt culpable and sinful, guilty and sick at heart. They had not returned his love at the time of crisis; they who had put their hand to the plough had looked back and turned back; they had refused the future. They had been inconsistent and the memory of Jesus' total consistency to the point of death stood in judgment on them. They could not rid themselves of this feeling; it was a self-inflicted wound that only Jesus could cure. But he was dead, so how could they ever be forgiven?

The overwhelming good news that they now tell is that Jesus took the initiative and was present to them to heal and make whole. He re-established them in the fellowship they had sundered but which, for his part, proved stronger than death. His presence makes clear to them that in life and death and glory he offers salvation and that offer cannot be rescinded by any force or power, not even by death. This offer is now experienced above all as gracious forgiveness after their disloyalty and they can once again 'follow him.' They may have thought of Jesus as finally dead, but now they realise that *they* were the ones who had passed into death but they have now been raised up to new reconciled life with him. *Abba* remained faithful to Jesus in his faithfulness and loved him into the fullness of new life by the strength of the same love with which he had always sustained him. He brought him through death to life. It is no wonder then that forgiveness and Easter are so closely linked (Jn 20:22-23; Lk 24:47; Acts 5:31,10:43, 26:23;1 Cor 15:17-18) and that disciples exercise a 'ministry of reconciliation' (2 Cor 5:18).

It also explains why their being together again (Lk 24:33; Acts 1:6, 2:1) is the place of forgiveness, 'being of one mind and heart' (Acts 1:14-15, 2:1, 44, 47). Jesus is raised and is bringing them through their manifold deaths to new life with him and with each other. It is hardly surprising then that resurrection and meal fellowship are so often associated in the New Testament and the disciples are described as 'those who ate and drank with him after his resurrection from the dead' (Acts 10:41). The joy of sharing in this eucharistic celebration of forgiveness, which points to the messianic banquet, is stressed in Acts 2:46 (see Lk 24).

The disciples did not immediately understand all the implications of the raising of Jesus, but what they did grasp of it immediately accounts for their literal re-creation as disciples of the Risen One. They believed that they had a disclosure of the mystery of God himself in their recognition of Jesus as raised by this God. In Jewish thought, the full self-communication of God could only take place at the end of all history.[2] Only then could history be an adequate medium for God's self-revelation. This would coincide with the resurrection of the dead and final salvation and judgment. Therefore if Jesus of Nazareth was 'raised from the dead,' it must mean that the end of history is experienced now, in anticipation. It also means that this is the time of the fullness of salvation, the ultimate decisive act of God, his final self-communication as kingly saviour of the world. So in the raising of Jesus they are dealing with God's self-communication, his revelation of his glory (Gal 1:15-16; 2 Cor 4:6).

Jesus' ministry and message had raised questions about his unity with God (or his opposition to God) but gave no conclusive answers to these questions. The disciples now understand that the raising of Jesus is the manifestation of the deity and glory of the God and Father of Jesus. Thereby Jesus' unity with God is eternally validated. God has shown that he has always been identified with Jesus who always united himself with God in life and death. 'You cannot think of God without Jesus or Jesus without God.'

Resurrection is not just a private isolated miracle to authenticate Jesus' claim nor a single act of God in the course of history. The raising of Jesus proclaims who God is and who Jesus is, and puts an end to history as disciples know it. This explains the eschatological urgency of their preaching.

It also throws light on the concern with and speculation about the *parousia* (final presence or arrival of the Risen One) in the early church. This preoccupation may seem strange to us but, for them, if that which should only occur at the end of all history. (resurrection) has already begun in the raising of Jesus, the consummation of the end must be at hand. If the risen Jesus can be described as 'the first fruits of those who have fallen asleep' (1 Cor 15:20), then only the final harvesting of collective resurrection remains to be achieved (see Mt 27:52-53). Only gradually will they learn to distinguish between his resurrection, the hope of a general resurrection, and his parousia. In the meantime they would have to live out of the power of the same spirit who raised Jesus from the dead and is now transforming their lives in anticipation of the end.

If God raised Jesus, he has shown himself to be the one true God who alone raises the dead. He is the faithful God of surprises who vindicates his righteousness and mercy as the Lord and giver of new life. If Jesus has been raised, then he is the one in whom humankind's hopes for fulfilment and the God of Israel's promises for salvation coincide. God's passionate concern for the future of the human race has been achieved, for Jesus has broken through to a future that fulfils all fundamental human hopes and dreams (see chap. 9). So the good news of the risen Jesus and the God who raised him can and must be proclaimed as salvation and judgment to all, and not only to Jews. Jesus had proclaimed that the reign of God was dawning and that God was beginning to fulfil the hopes of humankind.

The content of his preaching now becomes a reality in his own being raised from the dead. What had been proclaimed about God's transforming activity has been definitively fulfilled in his being raised. Now the disciples cannot simply repeat his message. To be faithful to the full implications of his proclamation, they will have to proclaim what has happened to him as a person. His preaching of the kingdom must now become a proclamation of Jesus himself as the crucified and Risen One because Jesus himself has been transformed.

The raising of Jesus sets God's seal on the message and ministry of Jesus as the medium through which his self-communication was taking place. It also points to definitive salvation and judgment and the final transformation of all things. Finally, it sees the present as crucial and decisive for the future. The full implications of all this will gradually unfold themselves in the process of the disciples' on-going conversion.

The Shape of this Proclamation

'There is salvation in no one else' (Acts 4:12). To try to uncover the different foundational layers of New Testament christology must be a diffident undertaking and be subject to revision and correction. Any attempt to examine how an explicit christology (discourse about how the totality of Jesus' life, death, and resurrection are related to God and to us) emerged after Easter necessarily involves us in a study of the growth of the New Testament. It is a complex and difficult undertaking. Above all, it means continuing to follow empathetically the path taken by these post-Easter disciples. We will try to be with them in their struggle to *rename* Jesus so that we may come to appreciate the absolute mystery of his person more deeply and thus be mystagogues for those who wish to become 'followers of the way.'

As we try to follow their approach, we see that they are searching for the most adequate language – witness and words – to express their faith-conviction about Jesus, the Crucified-Risen One. In that sense we can look on the New Testament as the final record of their struggle with images, symbols, metaphors, concepts, words from both the Old Testament and the hellenistic world to bring this mystery to expression. Through this the communitas itself is being structured and others are enabled to share in it. Their christology is concerned with the experience of salvation, with catechesis, with the way people live together because of what they believe.

This movement is constantly developing, so we find symbols and metaphors and words and titles are constantly being modified, re-handled, and given a new content. Therefore it is impossible to make a neat synthesis of what is developing and growing within these church groupings. In that sense it is simply not possible to talk about the christology of the New Testament – we must instead speak about the many *christologies* of the New Testament. In retrospect, we see that they are building up and narrating their own unique symbol-system whose foundation, centre, and inspiration is always Jesus of Nazareth who was raised by God. The extraordinary thing is that they went right to the heart of this mystery and succeeded in interpreting it in terms of the permanently powerful master symbols that lie at the heart of Christianity. Through their inspired struggle that mystery is mediated to us today and their interpretation remains permanently valid and normative.

We now begin to understand why it was so difficult to maintain the distinction between pre-Easter and post-Easter material, for the New Testament consists of a profound re-interpretation of Jesus' whole life in the intense light generated by their Easter experience. Every iota of it is christological. We tend, however, to see christological statements only when the signals are absolutely explicit and so the more subtle nuances are lost on us. We further realise that the distinction between Easter kerygma and Easter story, maintained in the last chapter, is highly artificial. The gospels are kerygma, Easter stories, from first to last. Indeed, we can also see that the attempt made there to deal with the Easter narratives was bound to be incomplete and inadequate. We cannot say what Easter means by concentrating on these narratives. What they can tell us is self-consciously incomplete. It is only by being sensitive to the pressure exerted on language, by trying to appreciate the transformation, the new being of disciples, by being attuned to the whole history of witness to Christ down to the present day, by cherishing the whole weight of Christian tradition that we can even *begin* to know what Easter means.

We are in touch with the process by which God's self-communication in Jesus is comprehended, translated into transmissible form, and communicated to others. It involves taking up, re-casting, re-forging the available forms so as to gain privileged insight into the newness of the mystery. This is the process by which the life, death, and resurrection of Jesus of Nazareth become the word of God that can be proclaimed and celebrated in ritual, word, and sacrament. If we could unravel something of this movement by which the Christian message was first put together, it should be of incalculable value to us in our living of discipleship, in our proclamation, in our catechesis. Such an undertaking must be tentative and hypothetical, but the very effort involved should be a source of new learning for us.

The Early Preaching

The early summary of their teaching and hopes already points in the direction of a parousia christology: 'to wait for his Son from heaven whom he raised from the dead, Jesus who delivers us from the wrath to come' (1 Thess 1:10; see 4:13-17). In this approach Jesus, who announced God's imminent reign, is seen as the eschatological prophet who, because of his goodness, is put to death as the antichrist by wicked, godless people. But God recognises this and overcomes their wickedness and raises him from the dead.

> Jesus of Nazareth, a man attested to you by God with mighty works and wonders and signs which God did through him in your midst as you yourselves know this Jesus ... you crucified and killed by the hands of lawless men. But God raised him up, having loosed the pangs of death, because it was not possible for him to be held by it (Acts 2:24-25).

The rejection of Jesus, his martyrdom at the hands of religious people, is sharply contrasted with God's validating acceptance of him. The human 'no' and the divine 'yes' are deeply opposed. The text, 'The stone which the builders rejected has become the head of the corner' (Ps 118:22 quoted in Acts 4:11) seems to have been important in this approach. We find the same no/yes contrast where it says, 'You denied the Holy and Righteous One and asked for a murderer to be granted to you and killed the Author of life, whom God raised from the dead' (Acts 3:14-15). The ambivalence of his ministry and especially his death has been definitively clarified by God's action in raising Jesus. He is vindicated as the eschatological prophet of salvation, who by being raised has absolute authority and is the very light of the world. He must be accepted as essential for salvation and his coming will be a judgement on all who do not accept him. So in this proclamation, Jesus is already exalted and will come as saviour and judge when the last days arrive (which have begun already). This will be his parousia. Thus the *maranatha* ('Our Lord, come') prayer (1 Cor 16:22; Rev 22:20) of their liturgy echoes this scheme of things which sees Jesus as the coming Lord of the future. Traces of it are also found in Phil 2:7-10 and Rom 10:5-10, 14:9ff. The interval between the present time and the parousia of Jesus, identified with the coming son of man, was envisaged as being very short (1 Thess 4:13-17). His coming is imminent and people must live accordingly. Jesus, who had called for *metanoia* , now, as Christ, issues the same call:

> Repent, therefore, and turn again, that your sins may be blotted out, that times of refreshing may come from the presence of the Lord, and that he may send the Christ appointed for you, Jesus, whom heaven must receive until the time for establishing all that God spoke by the mouth of his holy prophets from of old (Acts 3:19-21).

Early interpretations like these are found in several New Testament passages, though frequently combined with later and more developed christologies and soteriologies. We note that, as well as seeing Jesus primarily as the eschatological prophet who was put to death because of his ministry but vindicated by God, it also uses language drawn from the prophetic literature –'holy and righteous one,' 'author of life,' 'refreshing,' – to speak about the person and work of Jesus. These first attempts at renaming Jesus will not have long-lasting currency and will be replaced by more 'adequate' formulations.

We might be inclined to regard this simple approach, and the language used here, as theologically careless and prefer to see a stronger stress on his divinity. (The Acts of the Apostles must be disconcerting reading for anyone who thinks that the only valid categories for christology are those of Chalcedon). Perhaps this is the greatest value of searching the New Testament in this way. We are brought into contact with people who were utterly convinced that they were in touch with the very self-communication of God himself and who were struggling to give expression (inevitably inadequate) to that conviction. They were being true to their experience and the inadequacy of their language did not reduce them to silence nor to a simple repetition of what had been said before. Their search for language commensurate with the experience is itself constitutive of their understanding of it. We would stress that this language is not arbitrarily chosen. Easter has its own linguistic content built into it, so to speak, which determines what must be expressed. The disciples struggle is to find the language-witness and word that most accurately corresponds to this inner content.

One striking feature of these texts is that they do not as yet speak about any intrinsic salvific significance in the suffering and death of Jesus. The words and actions of his ministry mediated salvation, his parousia will bring definitive salvation, but his death was the death of a prophet brought about by the machinations of wicked people. So in one sense the no/yes prophetic scheme seems to enable them to 'cope' with his suffering and death – it was to be expected. But in another sense it simply sees the death of Jesus as a tragic mistake perpetrated by stiff-necked and lawless people against God's wishes. It does not at all face up to the awesome question of the meaning of the death of God's chosen one. We may hardly notice this because we constantly fit the cross and salvation neatly together in our thought and language. So even if a salvific interpretation of Jesus' death is lacking in a particular text, we simply supply it without thinking!

The first disciples could not do this. They had to struggle very hard to relate the death of Jesus to God's self, to discover saving significance in the cross. Indeed, some of the christological statements that we find in the New Testament do not seem to have been able to cope with the religious meaning, the theological problem of Jesus' death. If God were with Jesus always, if he vindicated him after death, why did he allow wicked people to carry their rejection of him to the point of death? Was it that God was with Jesus during his life but was absent from his death, intervening afterwards to reverse the worst that people could do by raising him from the dead? Or is the cross also to be related to the overall plan of God and to the very being of God? How are suffering and death related to what God has done for Jesus in his resurrection? What, if anything, is the inner meaning of the cross? There were no answers at hand to these questions for the disciples nor were they able adequately to express the redemptive significance of Jesus' death for some time.

The Problem

When disciples came to believe that God had raised Jesus from the dead, they were convinced that all the promises made to Israel were fulfilled in him. He was the source of their hope and salvation and they felt an irresistible urge to proclaim him as such to their fellow Jews. They would have wanted to say: 'Jesus is Messiah.' This was the power word, the rallying cry, that summed up the quintessence of the hopes for salvation of the covenanted people who looked forward to Yahweh's definitive reign. To speak about Messiah, to say someone is Messiah, is to speak about the one in whom is found the definitive action and presence of God. 'Messiah has come' was the most profound, total, and attractive message that could possibly be proclaimed to fellow Jews. To say 'Jesus is Messiah' was to say that in him is found the definitive presence and action of God.

Yet they could not preach such a message without further ado, for the majority of their hearers would say that it was flatly contradicted by the death of Jesus. Messiah does not die and certainly does not die the irreligious, inglorious death that Jesus died. A crucified Messiah was and remained the great 'stumbling block to Jews and folly to Gentiles' (1 Cor 1:23). Many of their contemporaries believed in resurrection but to be asked to believe in the resurrection of the crucified Jesus was an incredible and intolerable demand. It meant being asked to accept that God's final self-communication, his definitive righteousness, took the shape of a man rejected by due process of the Law and crucified as a state criminal. The nature of Jesus' death made faith in him difficult for all and impossible for many. Even disciples who believed in him found it difficult to formulate 'the word (or language of) the cross' (1 Cor 1:18) and answer the question why 'the Christ should suffer these things and enter into his glory' (Lk 24: 26). How can they move from saying what we have heard so far, that Jesus died because sinful people overcame him, to being able to say '*Christ* died for our sins' (1 Cor 15:3).[3]

A Common Framework

In trying to answer this question, perhaps we should try first of all to outline the common framework of what we find fleshed out in various New Testament christologies. It would provide a kind of grid to help us make our way through these complex developments.

Furthermore, it should put us in touch with some of the components of the creative tension that gave rise to christology and the growth of the New Testament under the guidance of the

Spirit leading them 'into all the truth' (Jn 16:13). The following components are found in all New Testament christologies:

A. *The present experience* of the crucified and risen Jesus who is bringing about the conversion of disciples by transforming their liminal lives in dedication to others and is encountered by them in prayer and liturgy.

B. *The grounding* of all attempts at an explicit christology now in the pre-Easter ministry of Jesus. It is the historical crucified Jesus of Nazareth who must always be preached as the Risen One.

C. *The sources* available for this undertaking include their entire Jewish heritage, especially strict ethical monotheism, prophetic and apocalyptic eschatology, Wisdom theology, and the culture, religious ideas, and language of the Hellenistic world. There is always a characteristic modification of this material bringing it into line with the uniqueness of the life, death, and resurrection of Jesus.

D. *The demands of proclamation* in the Palestinian, diaspora, and gentile milieux as they become his witnesses 'to the end of the earth' (Acts 1:8).

We cannot over-estimate the importance to the disciples of the foundational Easter experience nor the continuing transformed and transforming presence of the risen Jesus. The meaning of this was incarnated first of all in practical living in service to others rather than in a theological statement or in words only. They are living out of the presence of the risen Jesus and in this way his resurrection is constantly vindicated; it 'proves' its truth with an assurance that grows as the disciples surrender themselves to it. In service to others they experience and live out a love stronger than death, for he who was, and is, their master has himself mastered death. Here too the liturgy plays a vital role in shaping the communitas and its proclamation – *lex orandi, lex credendi*. Reflection on the significance of table fellowship with Jesus, especially his Last Supper and his offer there of renewed fellowship even in the face of death, must have had a powerful formative influence.

But they are not concerned only with the present and the future. No matter how preoccupied they may have been with the parousia or with celebrating the presence of the Risen One, they could never ignore the historical Jesus. Jesus of Nazareth is always the subject of their profession of faith. Every orthodox christology is grounded in the remembered ministry of Jesus. If ever their proclamation became detached from the historical Jesus (as is possible since Jesus is no longer physically present to them), then their proclamation would become an ideology or a mythology. It is evident from the New Testament that this could happen very quickly (see 1 Corinthians). To prevent this catastrophic misunderstanding, all orthodox statements of faith would have to be anchored in the historical Jesus. But different approaches would highlight different facets of that mystery, so differing christologies could exist side by side without being in conflict in any way.

Furthermore, they must interpret all this within the context of the religious background, ways of thinking, and world view of their contemporaries. It must be presented in an intelligible, cogent, and persuasive way to Palestinian Jews, Hellenistic Jews, and later to the gentiles. This involves them in catechesis in the deepest sense and we see them struggling with traditional concepts and symbols and language and re-handling them dramatically so that they can 'make disciples of all nations' (Mt 28:19). The care, the heart-searching, and the freedom with which they faced the massive problems of evangelisation and cultural adaptation in both the Jewish and Hellenistic worlds is fascinating. For them there is room for 'honest failure' in this process, for we see that they are never satisfied with what they have achieved and constantly search for more adequate expression of the mystery. They were, in fact, inviting people to join a symbol system, a new world religion, which was in the process of being worked out.

Can all this help us to understand how they discovered and brought to expression the theological and soteriological significance of the death of Jesus? His death was the direct consequence of the ministry in which he engaged. So sooner or later they must face up to its significance. They cannot continue to say that God was active through the ministry of Jesus, the eschatological prophet, pass over his death as a miscarriage of justice, and say that God begins to act again on behalf of Jesus after his death. If Jesus' ministry and resurrection are salvific, then logically they will have to raise the question of the significance of his death. They cannot destroy the unity of his person. It is the Jesus who was crucified *because* of what he said and did who was raised by God. So his death must have a part to play, somehow.

In trying to understand how they discovered the meaning of his death we will follow our grid in relation to three representative models: atonement, sacrifice, ransom/redemption.

The Model of Atonement

We have seen many aspects of their present experience (A) so far. Here we want to acknowledge once again that their being together, their experience of new life, is due entirely to the crucified and risen Jesus. They had been unfaithful so they felt the need to express their sinfulness, to be forgiven, to be offered a new beginning. Now that he is graciously present to them, they joyfully know that they are liberated from the crushing weight of the past, that they are reconciled, that they are at one again with Jesus, the crucified one. They experience in a most profound way the grace of at-one-ment, forgiveness, and reconciliation.

What they experience so powerfully now had also been mediated by Jesus when he was with them during the time of his ministry (B). In his presence they had felt at one with him, with each other, with God. Jesus himself had been absolutely dedicated to a ministry of reconciliation, to breaking down barriers, to enabling people to be one with God and with each other in mutual service. He engaged in a ministry of self-giving to *Abba* in service to the outcasts and he continued in this ministry right to the end, even when it was evident that death would follow. He was convinced that through it God could achieve a new covenant of reconciliation.

But were there any models or insights in the Scriptures (C) that would enable them to bring light to bear on the significance of brutal suffering and death for the chosen one of God?

For Jews, God speaks and reveals himself in Scripture, so if they wish to say that God was communicating himself even in the death of Jesus, they would have to show that this new interpretation of these events is 'according to the Scriptures.' Could they then discover some very strong Scriptural precedents for what they now wish to proclaim? As they searched the Scriptures (themes rather than texts), various images and models would have suggested themselves. In the passion history of Israel, prophets and mystics and priests had wrestled with the mystery of evil and suffering, especially the innocent and unrequited suffering of the righteous ones. We think of many of the psalms or the lamentations of Jeremiah, or Job, or the Servant (Is 53). The model of the atoning death of a martyr (2 Mc 7:37) had already been worked out in Israel's history. Also in Wisdom 2:12-20 and 4:20-5:7 we discover the language of the servant songs being used to interpret the life and suffering of a righteous person who is rejected by the godless but vindicated by God and now stands in judgment on his former oppressors. Furthermore, in certain strains of thought the prophet and the servant tended to be identified.

This wealth of insight was available to them and can now be applied to Jesus as the holy servant of God. Realising once again that in the passion history of the nation, and in the lives of its great figures, God's strength was revealed in weakness and suffering, they begin to interpret Jesus' death theologically. They could now declare emphatically that God was with Jesus, his servant, not only in life but also in death; that his death therefore is to be understood as a vicarious atonement for the 'sins of many.' God was not 'gainsaid' by anything that people did but was freely giving his son as a new covenant of unity. It was part of God's plan. He was acting even through the worst that people could do and had transformed an expression of hatred into an expression of love.

So the disciples could now proclaim that Jesus' death was not an accident or a tragic mistake. Those who killed Jesus did not frustrate the designs of God. The death of Jesus is the focus of the final communication of the crucified God himself. They insisted that Jesus did not die simply because he was rejected but he died 'for our sins' and on behalf of all, even those who rejected him. His scandalous death is salvific; his being overcome by hatred and sin is the moment when hatred and sin are overcome; death is the beginning of new transformed life; the silence and apparent absence of *Abba* is the moment of most profound communication; apparent forsakenness is the moment of supreme intimacy.

All this naturally had a profound effect (D) on the early oral proclamation and has left deep traces in the written accounts (see Acts 3:13-16, 4:27-30;1 Cor 15:3; Rom 4:25, 5:8; Mt 8:17,12:18-21). It has also clearly influenced the passion predictions, the Last Supper and passion narratives, the baptismal scene, etc. We notice too how frequently the phrase 'according to the Scriptures' occurs, e.g. 1 Cor 15:3ff. Throughout the sources we also find an emphasis on God-willed necessity: 'It had to be,' 'It was necessary' (Acts 2:23ff, 3:18, 24; Mk 8:31, 14:49; Lk 18:32-33, 24:26).

Finally, the disciples began to see and hear what they did not understand previously (Mk 9:32; Jn 14:26,16:12-13, 25). For the first time they really began to understand why Jesus so emphasised service, why he warned them to expect rejection and persecution, and why he urged them to pray that they would not fail in the time of testing. They also gained new insight into the lifestyle of Jesus, marked as it was by service, obedience, living for others, by poverty, insignificance, and powerlessness. Suffering and persecution are understood now as inevitable, given the lowly and hidden character of *Abba*'s kingdom.

The Model of Sacrifice

Having seen how the grid works, we should be able to apply it to other strands of the New Testament. For example, we could begin with the same present experience (A) but related now to table fellowship, forgiveness, and healing during the ministry of Jesus (B). This time, however, we turn for our sources to the ritual, cultic tradition of Israel, especially the institution of *sacrifice* (C). Sacrifice is a symbolic action that gives expression to a person's genuine attitude toward God.[4] Through the medium of visible realities, in symbolic gesture and interpretative word, the worshippers offer themselves to God in acknowledgment and thanksgiving and ask God for his blessing, mercy, and forgiveness. The essence of sacrifice in Judaism is not death but life. If an animal is killed this is incidental and preparatory to the real purpose of sacrifice. It is concerned with a sharing between the human and the divine, a union, or rather a communion, of mind and heart and life. The blood 'which is the life' (Deut 12:23) symbolises the deepest and most intimate relationship of life. We see how blood marks off the people for liberation and covenant (Ex 12:23-38, 24:5-9).

In Leviticus (16) we see the rites of the Day of Atonement when Israel atoned for failing to live up to the demands of the covenant. On that day the mercy seat of God, the place of his enthronement, was purified by blood and the people were re-dedicated to God after their defilement was removed. The language of sacrifice and atonement were later used to interpret the life and death of the servant of Yahweh. We are told that the suffering and death of the servant, contrary to all appearances, will be accepted as a sin-offering to purify the people and re-dedicate them to the covenant. The Maccabean martyrs understood their suffering and death as purifying Israel and atoning for her sins.

It is not surprising, then, that disciples, who lived within this cultic tradition, should draw on it to understand their own experiences of new life and communion emanating from the risen Jesus. In their own experience they now recognise the very fulfilment of what all sacrifices had tried to accomplish. It is not that Jesus has simply offered one other sacrifice in a continuing round of sacrifices. Rather, his whole life and death were characterised by an all-consuming dedication to the kingdom, a total self-giving to the Father and his people, founded in absolute communion with and dependence on *Abba*. They realise that what the Temple sacrifices tried to achieve – the perfect self-offering of the offerer and communion with God – has been accomplished for the *first time* in the life and death of Jesus.

They would also remember the confidences Jesus had shared with them about his own understanding of death. Death was the direct consequence of the self-sacrificing love of his ministry: 'Greater love has no man than this, that a man lay down his life for his friends' (Jn 15:13). Now they are able to see it as the moment when Jesus entered into definitive, eternal communion with *Abba* and shared fully the very life of God himself. His life and death are seen as the self-offering of the supreme worshipper of the Father and Easter is the Father's eternal acceptance of both offering and offerer. So they used material from the cultic tradition but modified it significantly. The life and death of Jesus both fulfill *and* surpass everything found in Temple sacrifice and traditional interpretations. This emphasis on the once-and-for-all character of Jesus' offering is found throughout the New Testament but the letter to the Hebrews, with its massive theology of suffering and death, places sustained stress on the uniqueness and superiority of Jesus' sacrifice.

We too must remember that the mystery of the crucified Risen One is so profound that no consideration of it, no category of religious acts, no model, however venerable or privileged, can exhaust its fullness. Every model and interpretation is limited and must not be absolutised or idolised. Above all, we must remember that we are dealing with the world of symbol and metaphor. As soon as the symbolic and metaphoric nature of this language was forgotten in the history of Christianity, tragic and grotesque misunderstandings of Jesus' death began to proliferate and we have inherited such misunderstandings of these metaphors.

In a dreadful travesty of Christianity, people were sometimes presented with a picture of some kind of vampire God, thirsty for blood-letting, who would only be placated by the blood of his own son. A text like Galatians 3:13, 'Christ redeemed us from the curse of the law, having become a curse for us' was taken as if God literally cursed Jesus. (In fact, the text refers to Deut 21:23.) Or, 'For our sake, he made him to be sin who knew no sin' (2 Cor 5:21) was likewise misunderstood. (Its reference is Jesus' death as *hattah*, sin-offering). Common to all these un-Christian misunderstandings was a literal interpretation of what was metaphoric and symbolic, together with a definition of sacrifice that equated it with death and saw it as being concerned with placating an angry God. This was never the case in the Old Testament and so such a misunderstanding was untrue, not only to Christianity but to the Old Testament tradition as well.

We must be very careful not to read into the New or Old Testament notions of sacrifice that do not belong to either. It is necessary to labour this point because these morbid misunderstandings have plagued the whole theology of salvation (soteriology), atonement, and eucharistic theology with disastrous consequences for Christian life.

(D) Finally, we look at the effects on proclamation. St Paul makes extensive but very careful use of the language of sacrifice (and many cognate ideas) to gain insight into the saving reconciling significance of Jesus' death. He speaks of Jesus as becoming the new purified mercy-seat of God (Rom 3:25, often inaccurately translated as 'expiation by his blood'), as the one through whom God's saving and forgiving presence is eternally accessible and available (see Heb 8-9). This theme is found in pre-Pauline hymns and in the Pauline and deutero-Pauline writings. Always the emphasis is on the initiative of God as a loving and merciful Father. God is not angry or remote. 'God shows his love for us in that while we were yet sinners Christ died for us' (Rom 5:8), or 'If God is for us who is against us? He who did not spare his own son, but gave him up for us all, will he not also give us all things with him?' (Rom 8:32).

The Johannine writings also use sacrificial language to meditate on the life, work, and the death of Jesus. He is the Lamb of God (1:29, 36) who, according to John's chronology of the passion, dies at the hour when the paschal lambs are being slaughtered at the Temple (see also 1 Cor 5:7). This theme runs through Revelation where Jesus is pictured as eternally expressing the supreme self-giving of his life, which is eternally accepted in communion by the Father. He is forever the Crucified-Risen One marked equally by both. Again in the Johannine writings, the stress is on the loving initiative of Jesus and the Father. 'The good shepherd lays down his life for his sheep' (Jn 10:11), 'For God is love. In this the love of God was made manifest among us, that God sent his only son into the world, so that we might live through him. In this is love, not that we loved God but that he loved us and sent his son to be the expiation for our sins' (1 Jn 4:8-10).

This theme obviously had a tremendous influence on the oral preaching and final written versions. It colours the whole presentation of the cost of discipleship (see Mark, esp 8:34-38), influences the accounts of the Last Supper and the passion narratives and indeed even the very structure of the gospels as we have them.

Ransom/Redemption

Another model that would have suggested itself to the disciples would have been that of ransom/redemption. These metaphors often have unfortunate associations for us today because literalised misunderstandings of them masqueraded as Christian interpretations and became part of our religious 'heritage.' Misrepresentations of, for example, St Anselm's satisfaction theory may have left us with an image of a begrudging, Shylock God, jealous for his divine honour, weighing scales in hand and ledger by his side, demanding the last ounce and the last drop, demanding even the death of his own son. This image of God, which is in opposition to the God of Judaism and Christianity, was further compounded by vague but persistent ideas about a ransom being paid to Satan in lieu of the rights he had won over humankind because of the sin of Adam.

Such grotesque misunderstandings of the Scriptures happened in the first place because people forgot that this is biblical language and that they are in the world of metaphor. Their literal understanding was a misunderstanding. These metaphors have their roots in the socio-economic world of buying and selling, of redeeming pledges and liberating slaves. But as metaphors they are used in religious contexts to speak of the liberation of what is bound (Ex 34:20; Num 18:15) or enslaved. In Israel if a man died, a relative was expected to care for his wife and children and if they were sold into slavery he was to redeem or ransom them even if it meant becoming a slave himself. He is said to be their *go'el* or redeemer. There is nothing mercenary about this. It is a loving act of unselfish dedication. This is then transferred analogically to Yahweh. 'I know that my redeemer lives' (Job 19:25) or 'Fear not, for I have redeemed you' (Is 43:1).

The metaphors of redemption and ransom are used especially to refer to God's action in liberating Israel from slavery in Egypt and Babylon and bringing them into the fullness of life. Their enslavement was a result of their sinfulness, so redemption from slavery involved liberation from the slavery of sin as well. When the Scriptures speak of God 'redeeming his people,' or when they use the cognate words of 'buying,' 'purchasing,' 'acquiring,' they use them as metaphors and they are not referring to a literal price paid to anyone. It is saying: 'Your situation is self-inflicted slavery; you are in futureless bondage to sin and death.' So salvation is a wonderful liberation from sin and death and an entry into transformed life. The 'price' is the crucifying price of the suffering love of God, which so identifies with his creatures that he passes over to their side to bring them over to his side.

All of this ties in perfectly with what the disciples experienced after Jesus' death and resurrection (A). They have been liberated from bondage and 'lostness' and sin into new, reconciled life. They had also experienced redemption during the time of Jesus' ministry (B). He had been their *go'el*. Now they bring the weight of this particular tradition (C) to bear on the life and death of Jesus. We find (D) the metaphor attributed to Jesus (Mk 10:45; Mt 20:28). It is found explicitly in 1 Tim 2:6: 'The man Christ Jesus who gave himself as a ransom for all' but it is also present by implication wherever the phrase 'on behalf of,' or its equivalent, occurs (1 Cor 15:3-5; Rom 4:25, 5:-8, 8:32; Eph 5:2; Mk 14:24; 1 Pet 2:21-24). In these references God is never hostile. It is we who have turned away and he draws us back, not through coercion or fear but by the leading strings of his loving initiative. Paul sums it up this way: 'If any one is in Christ he is a new creation ... All this is from God, who through Christ reconciled us to himself ... that is, God was in Christ reconciling the world to himself, not counting their trespasses against them, and entrusting to us a message of reconciliation' (2 Cor 5:17-21).

The Language of Titles

Having looked at these three models we now turn to examine three titles that played a decisive role in the proclamation of Jesus as the Risen One. (A title is a brief creedal formula summing up the faith of the community in densely compressed language.) We have seen some examples of how these disciples were working out 'the message or word or language of the cross' (1 Cor 1:18). They have moved from seeing it as a 'scandal' (stumbling block, v 23) to acknowledging the crucified one as 'the power of God and the wisdom of God' (v 24). They are preaching the crucified Jesus and maintaining that 'there is salvation in no one else' (Acts 4:12), which is the equivalent of preaching him as Messiah. We saw something of the impulse of the disciples to proclaim him as Messiah, but we also acknowledged the difficulties involved in such a proclamation. Now that they have gained new insight into his death, can they dare to preach him as a suffering Messiah to their fellow Jews and hope to convince them?

Messiah/Christ

We have already seen something of the history of this Christ title and its central place in the latter day hopes of Israel (pp 76-79). Basically the hopes associated with it took two forms, one linked to the Davidic dynasty, the other drawing its inspiration from the prophetic and Wisdom traditions. The former would restore the kingdom of David and free the people from foreign domination; the latter would be a wise but suffering Messiah. Yet while this latter conception of the Messiah did exist, most Jews, under pressure from historical developments, wanted the restoration of Israel as a kingdom independent of all foreigners. It would then be properly Jewish and faithful to the law. At the time of Jesus, three very strong groups, the Pharisees, the Sicarii, and the Zealots revived the royal or dynastic messianism but with very different emphases. Most of the people were probably not quite so chauvinistic and would have been affected by all kinds of influences, yet stirred by obscure feelings of expectancy and hope of a 'coming one.'

Jesus' own life and death were obviously not messianic in the Davidic-dynastic sense. Jesus was critical of current conceptions of Messiah and suffered because people wanted to cast him in that role. Yet ironically he was put to death on the charge of claiming to be Messiah. So if the disciples are going to speak about him as Messiah – and they must, otherwise they are not saying anything very significant about him to Jews – it could only be in terms derived from the prophetic and Wisdom traditions. Even then they would have to cope with great difficulties.

They seem to be pulled in two directions. First, they felt compelled to proclaim Jesus as Messiah but, second, they were aware of the difficulties associated with this title. True, the notion of a suffering Messiah did exist on the margins of their tradition and could be emphasised and they had succeeded in understanding his death as salvific. Jesus' life had been non-messianic, in the opinion of very many people, and he had been put to death as the anti-messiah. But the disciples wish to establish that, in fact, he was the true Messiah and press this claim even against those who were most immediately responsible for his death! They can succeed in this venture only if they are certain that the title was essential and right. It was, in their opinion, but even then it could be applied to him only when it was modified in such a way as to exclude the highly volatile, nationalistic overtones associated with it in the hopes of so many people. Everything used to gain insight into the mystery of the risen Jesus had to be modified. The process of modification in this instance is particularly fascinating and dramatic. A parochial and divisive title becomes the symbol of universal salvation. We will attempt to track this development by following our grid.

Their present situation (A) is best explained by saying that the salvation they now experience comes from Jesus who is reigning (2)[5] as Messiah and will return as Messiah (1). Jesus has been raised from the dead and this shows that God had been and is exercising his kingship, his reign, through him. He is therefore

Messiah. This harmonised with their own pre-Easter experience of Jesus (B) as the one announcing and inaugurating God's reign. Some had wondered even at that time if he might be God's Messiah. From all the sources (C) available to them, the selection of this title of Messiah was absolutely indispensable. It was *the* power word which could sum up the totality of the hopes of the nation for the coming of God's salvation. It alone magically caught the vibrant, pulsing expectations of the entire people. This quintessentially hopeful title would have to be preserved if they wished to proclaim the true significance of Jesus. Yet its content would have to be drastically revised to bring it into harmony with the concrete details of his life and death and present status.

The struggle here is analogous to what we saw in the case of the prophets as they retained the symbol of covenant while giving it a new content, but it is even more difficult. These disciples will have to draw on the full range of the tradition and yet radically modify it in order to accomplish their task. This struggle towards the re-definition of messiahship has left its traces within the Scriptures (D), but we cannot be overly schematic about the stages of its development.

Certain texts in Acts are of particular interest here. 'That he (the Lord) may send the Christ appointed for you, Jesus, whom heaven must receive until the time for establishing all that God spoke by the mouth of his holy prophets from of old' (3:20-21). 'He is the one ordained (predestined) by God to be judge of the living and the dead' (10:42). 'He has fixed a day on which he will judge the world in righteousness by a man whom he has already appointed, and of this he has given assurance to all men by raising him from the dead' (17:31).

In these passages Luke has preserved very ancient attempts to proclaim Jesus as Messiah which try to cope with his death as a contradiction of what so many Jews believed the Messiah to be. They are saying: It may be difficult to accept that he is Messiah, but he has been raised by God and installed as Messiah. He will return in glory to carry out the functions of God's Messiah and then he will be seen clearly as God's chosen one. The emphasis is on the future (1) without excluding the present (2). As yet, they do not seem to have theologised about the significance of the present status of Jesus but already they have greatly modified the content of this title. This is the *parousia christology* of the appointed Messiah.

As well as speaking about a parousia christology (1), the relevant texts modify the content of the Christ title firstly by presenting Jesus in his life and present activity as the kind of Messiah who could be harmonised with the *prophetic tradition*. The emphasis is on the present (2) and the past (3), while leaving room for the future, for they realise that Jesus is not only going to be revealed as Messiah at the parousia but that his life and ministry revealed who the *true* Messiah is and that in fact he suffered as Messiah on the cross.

Many of these texts use the prophetic vocabulary, but more particularly they draw on the traditional hopes for the coming of the eschatological prophet-like-Moses. 'The Lord your God will raise up for you a prophet like me from among you, from your brethren – him you shall heed' (Deut 18:15; see Ex 23:20-23; 1 Macc 14:41). Speculations about the coming of this prophet were rife at that time. Jesus had presented himself as the eschatological prophet and was rejected as a false prophet. (The taunts 'prophesy' during his torture point in this direction.) So now the disciples are saying that Jesus is the new prophet-like-Moses (Acts 3:22ff) leading the new Israel into the new promised land that has been opened up through his being raised from the dead. His prophetic ministry of bringing good news is understood as an anointing, a christening in the Spirit (Acts 10:38; Lk 4:18; 2 Cor 1:22). Obviously, the dynastic resonances in this title are being disavowed and the prophetic associations highlighted. This emphasis on prophetic messiahship not only influenced the proclamation but provided part of the thread on which to string together the beads of the gospel pericopes.

A second modification of the Messiah title is found in certain streams of tradition that present Jesus as a priestly Messiah, but the only extended treatment of this theme is found in the letter to the Hebrews.

Thirdly, the identification of the *Servant and Messiah* was a very important development and enabled them to take the suffering and death of Jesus into account by seeing him as a Messiah whose life and destiny will be like that of the servant. Only then, when they have re-read the Scriptures in the light of this insight, can they say that all the prophets had foretold that it was 'necessary that the Christ should suffer these things and enter into his glory' (Lk 24:26; see Acts 3:18). The passion history of Israel is being re-interpreted in the light of the suffering of Jesus.

Fourthly, *God's salvation* or simply *salvation* was another Messianic title in certain strains of Jewish thought. 'Salvation is from the Jews' (Jn 4:22). This 'spiritual' understanding of messiahship is now applied to Jesus (Lk 1:69, 2:30, 3:6). 'There is salvation in no one else' (Acts 4:12). Matthew has the text, 'You shall call his name Jesus, for he will save his people from their sins' (1:21). 'Yahweh is saviour' is his name; he is to be saviour. Again, this minimises the political associations of messiahship and relates it to salvation as forgiveness of sins.

Fifthly, we know that Son of David was another title equivalent to that of Messiah (2 Sam 7:12-13). It would have been easy to misunderstand this designation in a dynastic sense. But the way they handle it ensures that this will be avoided. In particular, it is made to refer to his ministry of healing, exorcisms, care for the sick and the suffering (Mt 12:23, Mk 10:47-48). Now reigning in glory he continues this same ministry through his disciples. 'His Son who was descended from David according to the flesh and designated Son of God in power according to the spirit of holiness by his resurrection from the dead' (Rom 1:3-4). And we also find that the dynastic overtones are further relativised by emphasising Jesus' superiority over David (Acts 2:25ff).

So thorough-going were these modifications, so successful was this renaming of Jesus, that at a very early stage (pre-Pauline), Messiah no longer referred to a function carried out for God by Jesus as the anointed one. It became a proper name that could be used interchangeably with his own name. It was now as powerful in giving insight into the mystery of the crucified Risen One as his own name was in identifying him during his lifetime. It fits him like a new skin. Jesus is Messiah, Messiah is Jesus. They evacuate the old nationalistic, political content of this title yet retain the word as a shell or mold with all its evocative power. Then they fill it with a new content determined solely by the concrete details of the life, ministry, death, and present role of Jesus.

Instead of the nationalistic hopes and expectations of Israel defining (as was the danger during his ministry) who Messiah is (Jn 7:26-27), it is now Jesus and *Jesus alone* who determines who the Christ is. So characteristic did this confession of faith become that in Antioch 'followers of the way,' the disciples, were for the first time called Christians (Acts 11:26). This title summed up and recapitulated all that was positive in Israel's history but they jettisoned its narrowly nationalistic content, thus leaving room for the radical newness of *'Jesus as the Christ'* (Acts 2:36, 8:5, 24:24). The *kenosis* (emptying) and fulfilling of Jesus Messiah himself is paralleled in the title.

Christ is only one new name given to Jesus (there are altogether 42 explicit titles in the New Testament) but this title has given us our name as Christians and has also given us a word for the entire struggle to rename Jesus, that is, christology. Christology is literally discourse about Jesus as the Christ but it is not confined to a study of the process by which Jesus came to be called by the Christ title. Rather, this process is seen as the paradigm for all attempts at renaming him or speaking about him then and now. So we must be attentive to their search for adequate language, their heart searching, their care to be true to the insights of faith. For the disciples it meant modifying and letting go of inherited and cherished ideas and relativising what had been looked on as sacred and immutable in order to proclaim the mystery in the best possible way to their contemporaries.

Jesus is Lord

When Messiah/Christ ceased to be a title, *Lord* took over its function of making the fullest possible statement about the mystery of Jesus Messiah. Insofar as it is possible to compress the faith of these disciples into a single phrase, 'Jesus is Lord' succeeded in doing so (Acts 2:36,11:17; Rom 10:9;1 Cor 12:3; Phil 2:11; Col 2:6; Acts 8:16, 11:20, 16:31, 19:5).

Once again, in trying to follow this development we will use our grid. The disciples now experience (A) a powerful presence of the crucified Risen One as they live out their daily lives in service to others. In acknowledging him who is the source of all they are and have –'he will live because of me' (Jn 6 57) – they allow themselves to be carried to new visions, new possibilities, new ventures they had never before believed possible. Jesus as risen is not absent but is present in a new way, exercising lordship by assuring himself to them. He is still challenging, still troubling, still calling them to 'come and see,' still comforting and forgiving them as he had done during his ministry(B).

So this title first of all found resonances in the pre-Easter ministry of Jesus. In their daily contact with him they had undoubtedly referred to him as *mar* (Aramaic) or *rabbi* (Hebrew) during his own lifetime. At first, this was probably simply a courtesy title like our 'sir.' But it was open to ever more profound understanding because, in their tradition, it was linked to a way of addressing a messenger from God 'on whom his name is set.' No doubt those disciples who grasped something of his powerful authority, the way he required obedience of them, impressed his stamp on their lives and yet enabled them to hope and to repent, would have filled this title with ever deepening content. However, if we want to discover the real source (C) of this title and the real content given to it after Easter, we will have to remember the text that says, 'My name is in him' (Ex 23:21). In the messenger who identifies with the cause of God, and carries out a ministry for him, is found something of the very nature of the one who sends him. So his name, Lord, can be given to the messenger and reaction to him is understood to be reaction to God.

In the Greek Bible, *Kyrios* (Lord) is used to translate the Hebrew, *Adonai*, the substitute word used for the sacred name of Yahweh. Whenever Greek-speaking Jews came to the unpronounceably sacred name, Yahweh, they said *Kyrios*. So such people, familiar with the Greek Bible, would associate *Kyrios*/Lord with the one God of Judaism. *Kyrios*/Lord is the name they would give to a messenger of God. When people with this background became followers of the way they gave 'the name,' *Kyrios*/Lord, to Jesus the messenger of God. So at an extremely early stage this title, with all possible overtones of divinity, was applied to Jesus as the Risen One. They have to use the 'name' of God to say who Jesus is. This is an astonishing development. In this transference the text 'The Lord says to my Lord: Sit at my right hand till I may make your enemies your footstool' (Ps 110:1) was very important. (Also Psalm 2 and Daniel 7:13-14.) The significance of this transfer of the name, used as the equivalent of the sacred name of the one God of Israel, to Jesus in their proclamation (D) needs no comment. It is transferred to someone who died as a state criminal and was rejected by the religious authorities.

For Jews this was an outlandishly brave step to take because it was the equivalent of attributing divine status to Jesus at the risk of being accused of blasphemy and being excommunicated. (They were in time driven out of Temple and synagogue.) Yet it was used as a worshipful acclamation, a doxology for Jesus, even prior to the conversion of Paul. (See Rom 10:9;1 Cor 12:3; Phil 2:11, and the Aramaic liturgical formula of 1 Cor 16:22, *Maranatha* –'Our Lord, Come.' *Mar* was the Aramaic substitute for *Adonai*. It is generally accepted by scholars that this is an eschatological prayer for his presence at the parousia. But disciples later realised that he who is called on to come and exercise his lordship and judgment now is already Lord and judge of the community.)

So in the beginning, as seems to have been the case with many of the titles, lordship was probably understood as that to which Jesus is predestined because of Easter (1). It is something he is now but which will be fully revealed in all its implications only at the end. He is Lord of the future (2). (It is a question of emphasis, not a matter of being exclusively present *or* future). This notion of lordship then epitomised all that was believed about Jesus now reigning with God. So they have to say that he did not simply become something new after Easter. The logic of Easter dictated that they recognise that he was always one with God and God always one with him. Thus, his lordship was manifested in his life and ministry (3) and even in his death. Furthermore, they now begin to see the fuller implications of their growing feeling during the ministry that it was right to call him Lord.

If they understood Jesus simply as future judge, future Son of Man, future Lord, future Messiah, they could not explain what Jesus was doing now in the interim period between Easter and the final inauguration of the kingdom at the end time. Nor could they explain their powerful experience of his presence to them in every moment of the day. But by using the concept of lordship they were able to say he has divine status, he is now exercising a saving, powerful, absolute lordship. 'For to this end Christ died and lived again, that he might be Lord both of the dead and of the living' (Rom 14:9; see Acts 2:36). They believed too that he was the only source of salvation (Acts 4:12; Rom 1:4).

If, however, they attribute titles such as Messiah and Lord to Jesus and transfer to him functions such as lordship and judgment and salvation, which previously belonged to God himself, then they must allow no part of the universe to be immune from his lordship, his lordly influence. Hence, the developing emphasis on the cosmic lordship of Jesus Christ. They are maintaining that he is the pre-existent creator, the constant sustainer, and the absolute end of all things. This preaching is found especially in the gentile mission for the Greek world already had many 'lords' (1 Cor 8:5) and therefore the missionaries had to emphasise the uniqueness of Jesus' lordship.

This theme is so all-pervasive in the Pauline corpus that we can do no more than note some of the references (1 Cor 15:24-28; Rom 14:7-11; Col 1:15-20; Phil 2:6-11; Eph 1:17-23, 4:4-10, 6:5-10; 1 Thess 4:13-18). Philippians sums it up thus:

> God has highly exalted him and bestowed on him the name which is above every name, that at the name of Jesus every one should bow, in heaven and on earth and under the earth, and every tongue confess that Jesus Christ is Lord, to the glory of God the Father (Phil 2:9-11).

The name of Jesus, however, is no longer simply Jesus. They cannot now refer to him in this unqualified way because he must be renamed, given the very name of God himself since he is his very presence and power. (To ignore this today may betray a certain fundamentalism in our approach.) It seems too that pious Jews simply used 'the name' as a substitute for saying God and Christians followed this custom but transfer it to Jesus. We find that 'name' occurs very frequently in the New Testament. In fact, Christians are characterised as 'all those who in every place call on the name of our Lord Jesus Christ' (1 Cor 1:2; see Acts 3:6, 3:16, 4:12, 9:15, 22:16; Rom 10:13). But not only do they transfer the name of God to Jesus but attributes and functions[6] that previously belonged to God alone are now predicated of him: 'The day of Yahweh' became the Day of Christ; God's tribunal becomes that of Christ; the 'I am' of God's self-revelation becomes the emphatic 'I am' of the Johannine Jesus. Furthermore, worship which had been reserved for Yahweh alone is extended to the Lord Jesus before whom 'every knee shall bow' (Phil 2:10). Prayer is addressed directly to Jesus (Acts 7:59) and Paul's stock greeting, 'The grace and peace of God our Father and the Lord Jesus Christ be with you,' places them on the same level of activity and being.

Son of God

Lastly, we look at the title, Son of God. This title was used widely in both the Jewish and gentile worlds. In Judaism it could refer to angels or heavenly beings, to Israel as a whole, to the king, or to someone chosen for a God-given task who obediently carried it through. Among Jews living in the Greek-speaking world, other notions of sonship had developed, especially in Wisdom/Sophia theology and speculation. This theology spanned the Jewish and gentile worlds and spoke of God and the world in language intelligible to both Jews and Greeks. It had interacted with the prophetic tradition and had expanded as prophecy faded out. This theology had a considerable influence on liturgy and it framed some of its profoundest teaching in the form of thanksgiving hymns. We are familiar with it from the Scriptures (Wisdom and Proverbs), but it is found in many other works as well.

Within Hellenistic Jewish speculation, the transcendent God is understood to be active through the mediation of his wisdom or his word or his power or his Spirit. The wisdom of God, through which he had created the world, is spoken of as God's daughter, Sophia; his *logos* or word or spiritual power is God's son from all eternity. In this tradition God's creative wisdom, word, spirit was understood to be identified with the Torah or law. It is this kind of theology that bridges the gap between the adapted biblical language we have seen emerge in New Testament christology and the rather different kind of language to which we now turn.

When disciples sought to express the ultimate implications of Jesus' resurrection (A and B) for Greek-speaking Jews, and in particular for gentile converts, they drew especially on the language and concepts of Wisdom theology as their source material (C). They wished to draw on what was best in both worlds to gain insight into the mystery of Jesus Christ and to express his definitive relationship with God. So it was natural to use Wisdom theology, for it had already established a bridge between these two cultures and worlds. But the disciples do not wish to engage in Wisdom speculation for its own sake. Their interest is always soteriological: How can we say that Jesus Christ is our saviour? Catechetical concerns and the pressures of evangelisation (D) play an important role here.

This christology was concerned with saying what Christ *was* and *is* as well as what he did or what God had done in him. Indeed it would be hard to think it otherwise. Had the church evinced no interest in the nature and being of him whose activity had called it to life, it would have achieved something of a record in the annals of human incuriosity.[7]

If these disciples wished to say who Christ was and is, in a way that was comprehensible to their contemporaries, they would have to do so in *their* thought categories. It would not be enough to repeat what they had already said and wait for it to be accepted. They had to reach out to people as they were and proclaim the ultimate significance of Easter to them in an intelligible way.

Given the catechetical demands of that situation, if they wished to proclaim that in Jesus God really communicated himself to humanity in a definitive way, it made good sense to say that he is God's *logos*, the incarnation of God's creative self-utterance, the pre-existent Son of God, who became flesh in Jesus Christ or that he is the embodiment of God's wisdom. If, for example, they speak of him as the Son of God, they do so because of the unique filial obedience to God which characterised Jesus' life and death. This is the specific content they give to this title. (If we give it a different content we must ask about its source.)

It is evident from the Pauline and Johannine writings that extensive and invaluable use was made of what had already been achieved in Wisdom theology. In particular, scholars[8] maintain that Wisdom hymns, or hymn fragments, have been worked into Phil 2:6-11; Col 1:12-20; John 1:1-5, 9-16; Rom 1:3-4; Heb 1:3. However, the golden rule for adaptation applies here as everywhere else.

No matter what they draw on or choose (which is already to reject others as unsuitable), they always modify, adapt, reject, always break it open to the new and the unprecedented. Whether it is a symbol, a title, a hymn, whether it is taken from prophetic, apocalyptic, or Wisdom literature, whether it was originally at home in Palestine, the diaspora, Greek philosophy or mythology, it is *always* brought into line with the historical reality of the ministry, death, and resurrection of Jesus of Nazareth. Irrespective of its original content or provenance, its content, its frame of reference now is always and only defined by the life and death of

Jesus of Nazareth. Whatever is borrowed is personalised, historicised in the light of the Jesus of history. But because the word or the form is retained, a very necessary bridge is built from the Jewish and gentile worlds into the mystery of 'Jesus ... who is called Christ' (Mt 1:16).

We see this verified in all the hymns mentioned above. Scholars point to the modifications that have been introduced to ensure that they are always anchored in history. The four passages that speak of 'sending the son' have been re-handled so that the focus is now on the lowliness, obedience, flesh, and death of this son. Many of the expressions used here, but especially 'the *logos* became flesh,' are without precedent in Wisdom theology and would remain unthinkable without the catalyst of Easter.

Christians were forced toward these radical re-interpretations of Wisdom theology, of the relationship between the human and the divine, because of their conviction about what had taken place in Jesus Messiah. We hear them speak of him in language that seems more concerned with his nature in itself rather than taking note simply of what he does – judging, ruling, saving. It is not enough to say Yahweh is God and, since Jesus carries out divine functions, he is to be given new titles.

The questions of who Jesus really is and how exactly he is related to the mystery of God were being asked and had to be answered. So in this theology he is spoken of as 'the image of the invisible God,' as being in 'the sphere of the divine,' that in him 'God dwelt bodily,' that 'God was in Christ reconciling the world to himself,' that he was 'the first born of all creation,' that he is 'the very being of God,' that 'he is the unique son of God,' that he is 'the effulgence,' 'the glory,' the 'form of God,' 'bears the very stamp of his nature,' 'upholding the universe by his word of power,' that he is the pre-existent one, the divine *logos*, cosmic Lord, resurrection of the dead.

The titles he receives and the divine status he is given through this language means that they are coming closer and closer to emphasising his unique relationship with God without diminishing his humanity.

But Jesus always maintained a distinction between himself and the Father, so Jesus is spoken of as distinct from God and yet as one with him in a way which does not destroy this distinction.

The question of his precise relationship to Yahweh now becomes more obvious and more pressing. The final answer given by the New Testament to this question might be summed up by saying that while it is very willing to give divine status to Jesus Christ, it is still very reluctant to call him God. This is quite understandable. Their question was: How were they going to be faithful to their present experience of the mystery of Jesus Christ, which mediated so many things previously understood as coming from Yahweh alone, and still believe in one God? Does faith in the divine status of Jesus involve acceptance of a second or secondary deity, or does it mean identifying him with his Father?

All they can do is be true to the fullness of their present experience, coming from the crucified and Risen One, without denying faith in one God. They naturally shy away from calling Jesus 'God' without qualification because *theos*, 'God,' was a title reserved for Yahweh and to call Jesus, a man they had known, 'God,' would to confuse him with Yahweh. They overcame this difficulty by reserving the title 'God' for the Father of Jesus Christ and in relation to him Jesus Christ is called 'Lord' (1 Cor 8:6). A further development took place in the father/son terminology from the general Old Testament sense, through 'son of the father' in a unique sense, to the late New Testament pairing, the Father, the Son. But eventually the New Testament not only proclaims Jesus as unique Son of God but actually calls him God, 'My Lord and my God,' at least once (Jn 20:28), and perhaps more frequently.[9]

12. TEACHING ALL NATIONS

By the drawing of this love
And the voice of this calling ...
T. S. Eliot

The disciples were convinced that if Jesus was not held by death, then it was due to an eschatological, saving act of God which, as his very self-communication, was the beginning of the end time. They had to begin to live the implications of this and try to communicate it to others. Their basic faith is an orthopraxis seeking ritual and theological expression. So they speak about it by using the language of resurrection and they expect the consummation of the kingdom, the collective resurrection of the dead and the final crisis to take place very soon, since in the raising of Jesus they have already begun. For them, the raising of Jesus is the fullness of salvation, the fulfilment of humanity's hopes, the final 'yes' of the promises of God. They expect that, at the parousia, Jesus will be carrying out the functions traditionally associated with the time of eschatological salvation. So they speak of him as 'appointed,' 'constituted,' 'predestined' to act as exalted, Son of Man, Judge, Messiah, Lord, Son of God and to be fully revealed as such at the parousia (1).

These various titles are all re-worked and re-modelled so as to refer to the Jesus of Nazareth whom they knew. All their attempts to say who he is are profoundly soteriological. (But in our assessment of these developments we should not try to play off christology against soteriology or future against the present or function against personal being. It is a question of emphasis, not opposition.) They further realise that these activities of the Risen One could not be confined to the future for they were even now experiencing the work of his Spirit, his reconciliation, his miracles in their life together. So they say that 'he became,' 'was made' (Acts 2:36) Messiah, Lord, Son of God at the moment of Easter and is exercising these functions among them now (2) to transform them into true disciples. The locus (focus) of salvation always involves an interpenetration of past, present, and future. A disciple is called out of the past to work toward a goal that is not yet achieved. They really learn to understand what took place at Easter through service carried out on behalf of the 'little ones' in the name of Jesus Christ, thereby allowing him to be truly Lord of their lives.

Of course, all this is grounded (B) in what they experienced during the days of the ministry. They now grasp its significance and realise more clearly that God had been acting through Jesus all along and not only since Easter. It is then vitally important to remember the words and actions of the historical Jesus, to build up a christology of the ministry (3) so that their discipleship now may be true to his discipleship of *Abba* then. Sayings and teachings of Jesus, descriptions of his activity clustering around individual master images in oral storytelling, form the core of the pericopes that are gathered together into the gospels. Here the master images, motifs, and language from the Old Testament (C) provided not only source material but also a core thread to link and pattern these gospel sources. The story of Jesus is being told as the retold story of Israel. His story is recognisable from the story of Israel but cannot be contained within it. The ancient core stories of Israel are retold so that the radically new story of God's activity in Jesus may be heard.

As the Scriptures are used to interpret and communicate the mystery of Jesus Messiah, the Scriptures themselves are constantly being re-interpreted christologically (1 Cor 10:1-11; Lk 24:44-46). The action of God in Jesus must be shown to be one with his action in creation and in the salvation of Israel. They succeeded in proclaiming (D) that the entire ministry and even the death of Jesus were the climax of God's constant involvement with humanity in the form of weakness. The cross reveals who God is and what the world both is and should be.

If Jesus acted in this way during his entire ministry, was he ever clearly manifested as Lord, Messiah, Son of God? Some christologies highlighted his transfiguration, others his baptism; Luke and Matthew tell us that he was Son of God from his conception (3). But whenever they proclaim these insights or say, for example, that Jesus is the eschatological prophet, the suffering Messiah, the coming Son of Man, they will have to authenticate these statements scripturally. Some scriptural images and traditional titles (servant and Messiah) spoke better of the ministry than of parousia; others were more suited to speak to his present glorified status rather than to underscore the hiddenness of the past.

At a very early stage other disciples, in contact with the gentile mission, began to use contemporary models and language and spoke of his unique sonship, his having the name of God, exercising absolute lordship, etc. They are proclaiming not only what he does but what his very mode of existence is and how it is related to the being of God. Increasingly they are being forced to re-interpret the doctrine of God himself. Not that this is the last stage in a logical process, because they have been re-interpreting the doctrine of God from the moment when they said 'God raised Jesus from the dead.' Jesus belongs to the very essence of God; you cannot be in touch with him without touching God.

Reviewing these christologies in this schematic way may give the impression that this was a neat logical development. We should not ignore the real difficulties that faced these disciples, nor filter out the differences and indeed divisions that existed among them. (Paul disabuses us of any such idealising tendencies.) In their struggle to rename Jesus, only a few names, even of the forty-two that remain in the New Testament, would have lasting currency. What was full of significance for a Jew might be an empty word for a gentile. Titles emerge, do service for a while, and are then subsumed into more powerful and lasting titles. Some titles seem full of promise but disappear; others run into difficulties almost from the beginning (see references to angels in: Gal 1:8, 3:19; Col 2:18). There are false starts, brilliant insights and new creations. Above all, the pluralism, pluriformity, and diversity are very striking and must be cherished. Yet, in this rich variety of orthodox christologies, there is a unity of faith and foundation.

However, false understandings of Jesus Messiah existed from the beginning. Orthodox titles could be retained but their old content restored, as in the case of the Ebionites. A model that gave a bridgehead into a new world could be used as a bridge back into the old world, while perniciously retaining its reference to Christianity! This is hardly surprising when we remember their difficulties in grappling with mystery and the strong grip of presuppositions on those who came to have faith in Jesus Christ – Pharisees, priests, Essenes, Zealots, Samaritans, Hellenistic Jews, Romans, and Greeks. All these had to be evangelised; they had to be catechised in language and in thought categories they could grasp. But the difficulties could not be ignored. They were being asked to accept that a state criminal was the saviour of the world, that a crucified man was the source of the Spirit and Lord of the universe. Who could accept such a scandalous message and, more pointedly, who would live out the implications of it in their own lives?

The Patristic and Conciliar Developments

We have been trying to see the New Testament christologies as the documentation of the struggle to come to grips with the theological and soteriological implications of the raising of Jesus. In this way we can begin to discern the unity of the New Testament, appreciate how it came into being, and realise that every atom of it is christological through and through. We have seen that their concern was with God's relationship to Jesus and through him to us, and with Jesus' relationship to God and to us. The theological aspect of this single concern climaxes in statements like 'My Lord and my God' an 20:28, 20:31;1 Jn 5:20; Col 1:19; 2 Cor 5:19). The soteriological aspect reaches its most profound expression in texts such as 'Jesus our Lord, who was put to death for our trespasses and raised for our justification' (Rom 4:24-25); 'I have been crucified with Christ, it is no longer I who live, but Christ who lives in me; and the life I now live in the flesh, I live by faith in the son of God who loved me and gave himself for me' (Gal 2:20). If they believe that God's definitive self-communication has taken place in the life, death, and resurrection of Jesus, they must begin to understand God in a radically new way: 'God is Christ-like and in him there is no unchristlikeness at all.'[1]

What was still lacking was some way of consistently bringing together traditional Jewish monotheism and the insight into God and his Christ which we have seen emerging. A specifically Christian doctrine of God was needed to cope with the questions: What can be said? What can not be said? What must be said about God in the light of the mystery of Jesus Christ? If 'God was in Christ reconciling the world to himself' (2 Cor 5:9), does this imply an absolute unity between them, or what kind of unity is in question? How are they to be faithful to the humanity of Jesus of Nazareth, their conviction about his divine status now, and yet believe in one God? We find these juxtaposed elements in the New Testament but they have not been brought together into a rounded doctrine of God and his Christ. That was still unfinished business when the last word of the New Testament had been written.

This is the awesome task that faces the post-New Testament disciples. They are still continuing the path of discipleship, still struggling to love the Lord their God 'with their whole hearts and souls and minds.' They did not lack the necessary toughness of mind to tackle the question of the intellectual consistency of their profession of faith, above all of their sacramental celebrations. How could they 'sing a hymn to Christ as to God,' proclaim him as the only source of salvation, baptise in the name of the Father, Son, and Spirit, and not face up to the ultimate question about unity and distinction in God that was inevitably raised by their clear-thinking contemporaries?

The faith they professed was based on a certain theology and found expression in terms of its choice of language. In the Greek and Roman world of this time, the adequacy, the consistency, the intelligibility of this language would be questioned. Much of what took place in the patristic and conciliar developments was the genuine and necessary advancement of what we have found in the New Testament. It is called for by the still latent depths of those christologies and despite the difference in language, patristic and conciliar christology is in core continuity with what we have seen so far. The church during these centuries is doing what always needs to be done: attempting to fathom something of this mystery and propose it to people of every age—both inside and outside the church—without diminishment, in their own language. They would have to attempt to clarify the full implications of the New Testament christology in all its plural unity. Like their New Testament predecessors,[2] they would have to say who Jesus Christ was and is in himself so as to proclaim credibly his unique significance and relevance for their contemporaries, believers and non-believers alike.

Although the history of the labyrinthine debates and the interminable wrangling over words may suggest otherwise, the developments during these centuries are inspired by profound pastoral concerns. How they spoke about Jesus Christ, how they related the life and death of Jesus of Nazareth to God and to human beings would be of crucial importance for the way in which people lived their lives as Christians. Indeed, the soteriological principle, 'What was not assumed was not healed,' was their basic guideline in distinguishing between orthodoxy and heresy. It was necessary to speak not only of God's capacity to communicate but of the capacity of humankind to respond. They would have to spell out the full implications of faith in Jesus Christ for our understanding of who God is and who human beings are (see *Gaudium et Spes*, 22).

In that culture and time they could no longer simply repeat what Scripture had said about the subject through whom salvation takes place. To do so would be to leave the Christian message open to misunderstanding and diminishment. They simply could not ignore the questions raised by the Scriptural statements themselves. They would have to re-interpret and re-express them using the resources available to them in the world of that time, without losing anything essential in the process.

In fact, we see them making brilliant use of contemporary ideas and language to communicate the mystery of Christ to people who had already reached a very sophisticated level of religious language and philosophical reflection. In this situation the full implications of the 'double assessment' of Jesus found in the Scriptures (Rom 1:3-5, 8:3; Phil 2:6-11; Gal 4:4; 2 Cor 5:21, 8:9; 1 Pet 3:8; 1 Tim 3:16; Jn 1:4) would have to be worked out. But they would have to be satisfied that these new categories, which they used in this process of evangelisation and catechesis, were adequate and consistent with the foundational revelation. Their endeavours are inevitably marked by a tension between tradition and newness, orthodoxy and heresy, insight and myopia, yet, in the midst of all, the Spirit is at work guiding the church toward the fullness of truth.

Still, there were heavy losses. The rich pluralism of the Scriptural approach, a pluralism which is essential if the mystery is to be adequately reflected, tended to be lost. One New Testament christology became dominant during these centuries: the *logos* (word) christology based on John's prologue. It seemed to be the one most capable of bridging the gap between the biblical and purely Greek cultures in order to establish a network of communication. Yet the choice of any single christology, with the consequent neglect of others, was bound to bring its own problems.

This *logos* christology (like all christologies) could remain orthodox only by re-immersing itself constantly in the concrete story of Jesus of Nazareth. Unfortunately, this was not always remembered and there was speculation about the *logos* which at times broke from its anchorage in history and floated toward the realm of abstract redemption. Indeed, at times it seems that people had forgotten about the historical origin and purpose of the *logos* concept in Wisdom theology and in the New Testament itself and began to speak of it as if it were an entity existing on its own. The lack of understanding of metaphor and story is painfully obvious during these centuries. Very serious damage was also done when bridge-concepts (like *logos*, itself) began to carry two-way traffic, not only forward but backward as well. They were made to jettison their newly acquired Christian content and reverted to pre-Christian type while still claiming to be Christian, thus drawing erstwhile disciples back into the pagan world of mystery religions. This is an exact and total reversal of the process we have discovered in the New Testament.

Finally, a constant temptation during these centuries (and always) was to 'dissolve the mystery of Christ' (1 Jn 4:3, Vulgate variant). Because he is the self-communication of God, Jesus Christ shares in the abiding and incomprehensible mystery of God. Yet people are constantly tempted to try to reduce it to manageable and eminently reasonable proportions. Good theology must always oppose this tendency, for it exists not to 'solve' problems but to prevent us from dissolving mystery so that we may be brought to kneel before it.

A Glance at History

We who have taken the creed of Nicea for granted cannot begin to imagine the difficulties of the task facing disciples in those pre-Nicean days. They had to forge a doctrine of God which was monotheistic, which was not purely Jewish but distinctively Christian, and which would be capable of communicating the mystery of this God and his Christ to a tough-minded Greek world. How were they to answer the questions: Can Jesus the Christ be confessed as divine without denying the oneness of God? Can they be said to share the same being and nature and yet be distinguishable? If you distinguish, how do you avoid polytheism?[3]

271

We can do no more than mention some of the approaches that failed to answer these questions satisfactorily and that tended to 'dissolve the mystery' during these centuries. They can be seen schematically as variations on the two basic error-types of docetism and subordinationism. If people started from the presuppositions of any dualistic philosophy (e.g. gnosticism), which was suspicious of the created world, they would be docetic in their approach. That is, they would maintain that Jesus Christ only 'appeared' to be human. He was really God in disguise, pretending to be man. God would not have entered into transforming contact with his creation, and humankind would be without any real hope of salvation. In reply, disciples insisted on the nearness, the compatibility of God and humankind, that in Jesus Christ God's self-revelation takes place in what we recognise as our own humanity.

Even if they begin with a well-intentioned concern for monotheism, they could end up subordinating Jesus to God. Their concept of the oneness of God might be such as to admit of no real distinction and Jesus Christ would be either a modality of the one God or some kind of secondary subordinate divine being. Or God's oneness might be preserved at the expense of declaring that Jesus was simply a remarkable human being adopted by God (a divine pretender) but who could not be confessed as 'true God of true God' (adoptionism).

All the possible positions and counter-positions work themselves out in the errors of arianism, appollinarianism, nestorianism, and monophysitism and in the answering councils of Nicea (325), Constantinople (381), Ephesus (431), and Chalcedon (451). Against Arius, but in terms conditioned by the language he had used, Nicea proclaimed the fullness of Jesus Christ's divinity: 'He is consubstantial with the Father.' He is the very self-communication of God and our doctrine of God must take account of this. It had answered one of the basic questions facing all christologies: How is Jesus Christ related to the being of God (divinity)? The church would now have to face up to the other two issues: (1) his relationship to us (humanity); (2) the mutual relationship of humanity and divinity in a single subject.

Given the creed of Nicea, the 'stone in the midst of all' (Yeats), future discussion of the mystery of Jesus Christ, these latter questions could now be posed in only one way. They would have to ask: How did the 'second *hypostasis* of the God-head, consubstantial ('of one being') with the Father, true God from true God,' become man? If he was the eternal Son of God, how could he be man? If he was really man, how could he be the eternal Son of God?

To hear the various answers to these questions we would need to follow the tortuous christological debates as these were fought out between the schools of Antioch and Alexandria (both of which worked with, though in very different ways, a *logos* christology). However, such an undertaking is not possible here. We simply note that the council of Constantinople defined the fullness of his humanity and Ephesus the oneness of his person.

Chalcedon in particular offered language with which to discuss the mystery of Christ to a church rent by disputes over terminology. It addressed itself to *one* basic question: How are we to speak about the relationship of humanity and divinity in Jesus Christ? In its regulation of language it brought together the best of the traditions of East and West and harmonised the approaches of the schools of Antioch and Alexandria. The formula of the council (see Appendix for text) gave the world an extraordinarily clear statement of what is involved in discourse about unity and distinction in Jesus Christ: 'Two natures united in one *prosopon* and one *hypostasis*.' It does not define these terms nor tell us how the union takes place. However it is saying: If you hold all these facets of the mystery together and use this terminology in speaking of them, then you will be proceeding into its infinite intelligibility.

But to do so, you must become skilled in using two languages, God-talk and human-talk, simultaneously. The opportunity to develop such a skill was not given in the changed historical circumstances that prevailed for many centuries after the council in both East and West. So the formula of Chalcedon, which should have initiated new developments in christology, was now repeated as if it were literally the first and the last word. We saw some of the consequences of this approach in Chapter 1.

In an essay[4] to mark the fifteen hundredth anniversary of Chalcedon (1951), Karl Rahner asked, 'Was Chalcedon an end or a beginning?' His reply was that it was both. In the thirty-five years or so that have passed since then, scholars have been trying to make a start on this new beginning that is so long overdue. They have been concerned to place Chalcedon in context, to study its immediate historical, cultural, and linguistic context and also to relocate it in the ultimate context of the Scriptures. Throughout this book we have in fact been drawing on the fruits of these researches. In that sense we 'have arrived where we started.' We too must now make a new beginning.

EPILOGUE

We are only undeafeted because
We have gone on trying.
T. S. Eliot

We have been reviewing the life, ministry, death, and resurrection of Jesus Christ from the vantage point of disciples. However, we did not run our mind's eye over the life and ministry of Jesus or over the New Testament or post-New Testament struggle to work out a witness and an interpretation in order to transplant the details of what is found there into a changed historical situation. We were looking for what must inspire and inform and criticise our discipleship now, as we struggle to be faithful to the meaning of Jesus Christ in the power of his Spirit. This is what is important. It is in this genuine struggle to listen to the word that gave birth to us, to be obedient to Christ who is present now, to participate in his struggle for justice and love through our praxis and praise, that we come to know who Christ is and begin to learn the way of discipleship.

There is no blueprint for all this, no way of saying beforehand what may be demanded, what form it must take, as if the conversion called for in following Jesus Christ were simply given once and for all. One thing is certain: No one can do this alone. We must work out new forms of living the gospel so that it may be translated into a consistent way of life *together*. Those who would be disciples of Jesus Christ must surely live together the alternative proposed by his good news, so that they may thus be companions to the poor, the oppressed, the crushed, the least, and the lost. The difference that Jesus Christ can make will only be known by those who attempt to live it. The signs of the times indicate that this is becoming a pressing need today.

Down through the centuries, at certain times groups within the church have succeeded in revitalising the way of discipleship. These liminal periods in history have been extraordinarily significant, creative, and challenging. They prevented Christians from becoming bound to the familiar, or being chained by the well-tried, or confirmed in comfortable routines. We seem to be living through such a liminal period now. The trauma, the fear,

275

the frustration, the sense of loss, that some people experience during liminal periods goes some way at least toward interpreting the polarisation that has been taking place recently in the church. But this liminal situation, this shift of consciousness is, as always, offering a fantastically challenging opportunity to the church. It asks that, in response to the present situation, we be together in a new way because of our commitment to the gospel of Jesus Christ. It seems to ask that a new of kind of communitas develop among us. Of course, we cannot say beforehand what concrete format this should take, nor what demands it will make on us. We will have to re-read the gospels constantly in the light of our situation, and our situation in the light of the gospels.

If we listen to the Latin American Church, it seems that this re-reading must be done, above all, out of a situation of solidarity with the poor, of becoming one with the oppressed for whom God and his Christ have made a preferential option. At all events, we will need to learn to be with others in radically new ways, for we will have to listen and respond with other hearts. The demands will be both liberating and crucifying if they truly come from the saving God and his crucified Christ. We hope what we have tried to do in the preceding chapters will help us in this life struggle. It is only part of our task, but it is vitally necessary and needs to be undertaken again and again. We need constantly to renew our contact with the message and ministry of Jesus if we wish to know the true relationship that God desires between all those who are sisters and brothers of his Son.

In a situation where the poor and the oppressed suffered more from their compatriots and co-religionists than from the Romans, that Son preached his good news and carried out his ministry. That situation, that oppression, those poor, dehumanised people determined his response in deed and word, in the name of the living God. If he is the one *Abba* of all, how can anyone be outside his reach? How can these, who claim to be his children, lord it over those who are equally his children? How can they build up their prestige and power and possessions at the expense of the dignity, humanity, the very daily bread of their own brothers and sisters?

He crosses over the thresholds, set in place by structures and institutions, and enters into solidarity with the 'poor and the sinners.' He does this in order to witness to the structural evil of what is blindly accepted as good and just in the name of politics or religion or 'common sense.' Jesus uses the power of parable to open eyes and minds and hearts to another vision of reality. He begins, not from above, but from below so that 'the last are first and the first are last.' Jesus breaks open systems that exclude and declares that disciples are to take the initiative and make themselves neighbour, sister, brother to those who are excluded or marginalised. People can be truly free only if they are together in a new way, serving the needs of the other. This is what he enfleshes in his own scandalous solidarity with outcasts and sinners. Thus he becomes the living parable of the kingdom of God. But for this he is rejected and is led to the place of final testing. Beyond the last threshold, 'outside the camp,' in the ultimate rite of passage, Jesus faces death itself. Yet even through death, sustained by the love of Abba, he calls disciples into renewed communitas with himself, based on forgiveness and atonement.

As they follow the way of discipleship as the imitation of the way of Jesus, they live at odds with the ways of the world of their time. They are taking very seriously the significance of the title, 'Second Adam,' which they have conferred on him, and are struggling to create a new humanity. When the reality of their liminal position is recognised, they are expelled from synagogue and Temple and persecuted by the empire. Faith in the lordship of the crucified Christ meant exile from all they had previously known, whether in Judaism or in the mighty Roman Empire. This is the cost of discipleship of a crucified and risen master – always.

In the cross/resurrection of Jesus Christ we touch the core of the mystery of our faith. It must, therefore, be the constant source, the burning focal point for the renewal of discipleship. We must insist on the absolute centrality of cross/resurrection in everything that is said and done in the name of Christianity. Without the cross and resurrection we have literally nothing to believe in as Christians. (Yet it is only recently that the centrality of resurrection in christology and in all theology is being once again maintained.)

The cross of Jesus is language (1 Cor 1:18), is parable and it provides us with a God-given reading of the human situation as it really is, a reading that unmasks as evil what parades as good. It reveals the heights and the depths of humanity, what we could be and our desperate need for salvation. It brings the all-pervasive but hidden power of evil and hatred and sin into the open. Precisely because it is hidden yet all-pervasive, it must be named if it is to be coped with. The cross symbolises this evil, articulates it, paradoxically in the dumb horror of death, and thereby exorcises its paralysing power. Evil, sin, and death are overcome by the power of resurrection which transforms an expression of hatred into an everlasting expression of love.

As parable, the word of the cross says twice over, 'That person is you.' The evil in your heart, your aggressive self-righteousness, your attempted self-sufficiency is what edges the Son of God out of the world and on to a cross. This is the extent of your alienation from God. If that were all it said, it would drive us to despair, but the same cross counter-poses a more powerful, positive, alternative reading of our lives. It reveals the mystery of consistent love, that it is possible to be for God and for the oppressed, even to the point of death. 'That person also is you.'

So the cross stands in searing judgment on the shallowness, the contradictions of our captive lives. We know that it need not be so, should not be so. For in the cross we see the manifestation of the weakness of love, the extent to which God is prepared to go in solidarity with humanity and, in the raising of the crucified, we glimpse the victory of the weakness and self-forgetfulness of love. He who was crucified as a criminal and as a blasphemer is loved by the Father into resurrected life. Human rejection and hatred can become the basis for God's new creation; he can mold it nearer to his heart's desire – Christ. Everything, no matter how profane or death-bound, can be transformed and everything, no matter how good or holy, stands in need of divine transformation. This renewal becomes the hope-full model for our world because it gives us the unshakable hope that a sin-threatened world can be transformed into a world of reconciliation, peace, and love, that we can 'christen our wild-worst best.' And this hope will not disappoint us, uttered as it is out of the suffering and death that mark our human existence. We can hope in life through death because our saviour has truly lived our life, endured our suffering, and been among the dead, but God did not allow him to be held by death.

The cross and resurrection reveal the utter graciousness of God to humankind and humankind's utterly hopeful dependence on God to vindicate the weakness of its life, even through death. So they reveal the true face of God as he is and the true face of humankind, both as it is and as it could be. Jesus Christ in life, ministry, death, resurrection has transformed the human condition into a condition of hope and salvation, a transformation which is epitomised by his addressing himself, and ultimately addressing us, to God as *Abba*, and enabling us to do likewise.

It is the Spirit of this Jesus that is given to disciples. This is 'a spirit of sonship, not a spirit of fear, which makes us cry "*Abba*"' (Rom 8:15). Disciples are challenged not only to believe this but to live it in the far country of their exile. We are to learn truly to say '*Abba*' to God by learning to say 'sister' and 'brother' to *all* God's children. In this way, we will be led out of self-imposed bondage and directed toward the newness of God's future and nudged into the infinite comprehensibility of his mystery.

The Instruction distinguishes between:

Stage 1 – His works and ... his Words.

Stage 2 – The Apostles proclaimed first and foremost the death and resurrection of the Lord, faithfully recounting his life and words and, as regards the manner of their preaching, taking into account the circumstances of their hearers. After Jesus had risen from the dead, the apostles, when handing on to their hearers the things which in actual fact the Lord had said and done, did so in the light of that fuller understanding which they enjoyed as a result of being schooled by the glorious things accomplished in Christ and of being illumined by the Spirit of truth. They made use ... of such various forms of speech as were adapted to their own purposes and to the mentality of their hearers ... These varied ways of speaking ... must be distinguished one from another and carefully appraised: catechesis, narratives, testimonies, hymns, doxologies, prayers.

Stage 3 – The Sacred Authors took this earliest body of instruction, which had been handed on orally at first and then in writing ... and set it down in the four gospels. They selected certain things out of the many which had been handed on ... especially those items which were adapted to the varied circumstances of the faithful as well as to the end which they themselves wished to attain; these they recounted in a manner consonant with these circumstances and with that end. [1]

In this rather lengthy extract from the Instruction we find a clear recognition of a developing christological evaluation from the ministry of Jesus to the pages of the gospel. The earthly Jesus is absolutely identified with the Christ proclaimed by the church but we can also detect a developing understanding of that relationship in the New Testament. This development takes place, the christology of the New Testament exists, precisely because of the desire to proclaim the universal significance of the historical Jesus of Nazareth.

Yet obviously Stage 3 is not the same as Stage 2 or Stage 1. This faces us with the challenge of moving through the gospels and through the post-Easter preaching of the disciples in order to come into contact with the ultimate origin of Christianity in the words and deeds of Jesus of Nazareth. But if the gospels are not 'on-the-spot' reports of what Jesus said and did, but the final edited version of a complex process of development, can we know anything with certainty about the historical Jesus of Nazareth? And if so how are we to arrive at it? How do we move back from Stage 3 to Stage 1? Can we show the correlation between Stage 1 and Stage 3? Once again, 'We have to raise the historical issue if we are to feel critically confident of our own Christian faith; otherwise theology will be blind and authoritarian.'[2]

The Instruction we have been quoting insists that this search for the historical foundation of Christianity is possible, legitimate, and necessary. It counsels us to 'make use of every means which will help ... to reach a deeper understanding of the character of the gospel testimony, of the religious life of the first churches, and of the significance and force of the apostolic tradition.' It also speaks of making skilful use of the new aids to exegesis. This means using the methodologies of source, form, and redaction criticism to uncover the development and growth of New Testament christology. In addition it will mean making judicious use of the criteria that have been evolved for establishing the authenticity of the sayings of the historical Jesus. We list four of these criteria here.[3]

1. *The criterion of the editing process.* Each gospel has its own theological viewpoint revealed in its choice of material and its way of ordering and presenting it.

Consequently whenever they hand on material not markedly in accord with their own theological view of things, we may take this to be a sign of deference in face of some revered tradition. It is then reasonable to suppose that we are dealing with traditional matter regarded by them as beyond challenge; matter which goes back, as they think, to Jesus.[4]

2. *The criterion of dissimilarity.* 'The earliest form of a saying we can reach may be regarded as authentic if it can be shown to be dissimilar to characteristic emphasis both of ancient Judaism and of the early church ...'[5] This criterion is useful in gaining insight into a 'critically guaranteed minimum' in the words and actions of

the historical Jesus. But since it does not acknowledge either Jesus' rootedness in Judaism or the necessary continuity between the church and Jesus, it leads to an excessive minimalism if rigorously pursued.

3. *The criterion of coherence.* 'Material from the earliest strata of the tradition may be accepted as authentic if it can be shown to cohere with material established as authentic by means of the criterion of dissimilarity.'[6] Or to put it differently: 'The parts illuminate the whole which itself renders the parts transparent.'[7] We might include here (it is sometimes proposed as a distinct criterion) the correlation between the death of Jesus and the offence caused by his words and deeds.

4. *The criterion of multiple attestation* (cross-section). 'A motif which can be detected in a multiplicity of strands of tradition ... and in various forms ... will have a high claim to authenticity, always provided that it is not characteristic of an activity, interest, or emphasis of the earliest church.'[8]

None of the criteria is foolproof, nor will they solve all our questions about authenticity. It would be a very serious mistake, indeed, to think that the mystery of Jesus Christ must be reduced to what is recoverable through the form-critical method and the application of these criteria! However, if taken together they enable us to establish and carry through 'a historical-critical' approach.[9]

Because of the introductory nature of this book, we have not constantly referred to these criteria nor debated the authenticity of individual gospel texts. Instead, we drew on the generally accepted findings of the historical-critical approach, which works with this methodology and these criteria, in order to bring us into contact with the life, the preaching, the actions of the historical Jesus. We hope that what is involved in this kind of approach has unfolded as the work progressed.

APPENDIX 2

The Definition of Chalcedon

Following then the holy fathers,
we all with one voice teach that it should be confessed
  that our Lord Jesus Christ is one and the same Son,
the same perfect in Godhead, the same perfect in manhood,
  truly God and truly man,
the same (consisting of) a rational soul and a body
  homoousios (consubstantial) with the Father as to his Godhead,
and the same *homoousios* with us as to his manhood;
  in all things like unto us, sin only excepted;
begotten of the Father before ages as to his Godhead,
  and in the last days, the same,
for us and for our salvation,
  of Mary the virgin, *theotokos* (mother of God) as to his
    manhood;
one and the same Christ, Son, Lord, only-begotten,
  made known in two natures (*physes*) (which exist)
without confusion, without change, without division, without
    separation;
  the difference of the natures having been in no wise taken
    away by reason of the union,
but rather the properties of each nature being preserved,
  and both concurring into one person (*prosopon*) and one
    hypostasis –
not parted or divided into two persons (*prosopa*),
  but one and the same Son and only-begotten, the divine *Logos*,
    the Lord Jesus Christ:
even as the prophets from of old have spoken concerning him,
  and as the Lord Jesus Christ himself has taught us,
and as the symbol of the fathers has delivered to us.

NOTES

INTRODUCTION

1. D. O'Grady, 'The Old Ways.'
2. See John Shea, *The Challenge of Jesus* (Chicago: Thomas More Press, 1975).

CHAPTER 1

1. See John F. O'Grady, *Models of Jesus* (New York: Doubleday, 1984) .
2. 'It is l) a christology 'from above,' which remains incarnation centred, 2) runs into philosophical problems, 3) mixes together historical, theological, and mythical language, 4) bypasses the ministry of Jesus, and 5) separates the person of Jesus Christ from his work, that is to say, separates christology from soteriology or the doctrine of salvation.' Gerald O'Collins, *What Are They Saying About Jesus?* (Ramsey, N.J.: Paulist Press, 1977), p. 1; see Dermot Lane, *The Reality of Jesus* (Dublin: Veritas, 1975) for summary of criticisms.
3. See Appendix 2 for full text.
4. Sermon 7 on the Nativity.
5. See Lane, *The Reality of Jesus*, 2 ff, for a brief survey.
6. See Appendix 1 for the relevant parts of this Instruction, its significance for our approach, and the criteria we will follow for establishing authenticity.
7. Edward Schillebeeckx, *Jesus: An Experiment in Christology* (London: Collins, 1979), 48 ff.

CHAPTER 2

1. See Joachim Jeremias, *New Testament Theology*, V 1 (London: SCM, 1972), 3 ff; C.H. Dodd, *The Founder of Christianity* (London: Fontana, 1971), 38 ff.
2. T.S. Eliot, *Burnt Norton* 1, 14 ff, *The Four Quartets*.
3. Rudolph Bultmann, *History of the Synoptic Tradition*, 2nd ed. (New York: Oxford Univ. Press, 1968), 115.
4. See Jeremias, *New Testament Theology*, V l; *The Prayers of Jesus* (London: SCM, 1973). See further Sally McFague, *Metaphorical Theology* (London: SCM, 1983), 36 ff, 61-68.
5. See especially John D. Crossan: *Parables: The Challenge of the Historical Jesus* (San Francisco: Harper & Row, 1973); *Semia* 1 and 2,1974; *The Dark Interval: Toward a Theology of Story* (Allen, Tex.: Argus, 1975); *The Cliffs of Fall: Paradox and Polyvalence in the Parables of Jesus* (New York: Seabury, 1980). See also Normal Perrin, *Jesus and the Language of the Kingdom: Symbol and Metaphor in New Testament Interpretation* (London: SCM, 1976) for a review of research on parables.
6. See especially the writings of Crossan but also Jeremias, *The Parables of Jesus* , and Perrin, *The New Testament: An Introduction*(London: SCM, 1974), 291 ff.

CHAPTER 3

1. For a more detailed study, see Sean Freyne, *The Wo~'d of the New Testament* (Dublin: Veritas, 1980).
2. Schillebeeckx, *Jesus*, 45 ff.
3. *New Testament Theology*, V 1, 49-61
4. *The Founder of Christianity*, 30, 122-23.
5. *Jesus*, 137-39.
6. *The Founder of Christianity*, 103.

CHAPTER 4

1. Rudolph Schnackenburg, *God's Rule and Kingdom* (Herder, 1963), 313.
2. Norman Perrin, *Rediscovering the Teaching of Jesus* (London: SCM, 1967), 55.
3. Wolfhart Pannenberg. *Theology of the Kingdom of God* (Philadelphia: Westminster Press, 1969), 55.
4. Pannenberg, *Theology*, 60
5. Perrin, *Rediscovering the Teaching of Jesus*, 56
6. Especially in *Jesus and the Language of the Kingdom*, and 'The Interpretation of a Biblical Symbol,' *Journal of Religion*, 1975, 348-70.
7. Bloomington, Ind.: Indiana Univ. Press, 1962, 92.
8. Boston: David R. Godine, 1971.
9. Patrick Kavanagh, *The Great Hunger* (Dublin: Cuala Press, 1971).
10. *Journal of Religion*, 1975, 354.
11. See Jeremias, *New Testament Theology*, V 1, 32-33.
12. Ludwig Wittgenstein quoted in Sam Keen, *To a Dancing God*, (London: Fontana, 1971).

CHAPTER 5

1. The frequent references to this kind of mentality in what follows is not an exercise in scapegoating; rather we concentrate on it precisely in order to see ourselves and our mentality reflected in it. Its links with a super ego religion and morality is suggestive. See J.W. Glaser, 'Conscience and Superego,' a key distinction, in *Conscience* by G.E. Nelson (ed.), Westminster, Md.: Newman Press, 1973).
2. *Ash Wednesday*, 5.
3. Patrick Kavanagh, *Having Confessed*.

CHAPTER 6

1. See Jeremias, *New Testament Theology*, V 1, 114 ff.
2. Kavanagh, 'If Ever You Go. . .'
3. T.S. Eliot, *Little Gidding V*, from *The Four Quartets*.
4. See Starobiuski in *Structural Analysis and Biblical Exegesis* (London: Pickwick Press, 1974).
5. Seamus Heaney, *Death of a Naturalist*.

CHAPTER 7

1. *The Ritual Process* (Pelican Books, 1974); *Dramas, Fields, and Metaphors: Symbolic Action in Human Society* (Ithaca, N.Y.: Cornell Univ. Press, 1974).

2. *Jesus*, 201
3. Julian of Norwich, *Showings*.
4. See Albert Nolan, *Jesus Before Christianity* (London: DLT, 1976) 54 ff.
5. See Schillebeeckx, *Jesus*, 233 ff.
6. Kavanagh, *Having Confessed*.
7. G. Bornkamm, *Jesus of Nazareth* (London: Hodder & Stoughton, 1960).

CHAPTER 8

1. Walter Kasper, *Jesus the Christ* (London: Burns Oates, 1976), 108
2. Jacques Guillet, in *International Catholic Review*, May/June, 1973, 148.
3. See Trocme, *Jesus and His Contemporaries* (London: SCM Press, 1973).
4. Schillebeeckx, *Jesus*, 224.
5. See Jeremias, *New Testament Theology* V 1, 278.
6. Jeremias, 287-88.
7. Schillebeeckx, *Jesus*, 209-11.
8. See Trocme, 75-77; Schillebeeckx, *Jesus*, 315-18; Nolan, 130-33.
9. I have found the material in Jurgen Moltmann's *The Crucified God* (London: SCM, 1976), 112-153 helpful in this meditation, although I would not agree with some of his conclusions.
10. Moltmann, *The Crucified God*, 127.
11. 'As it was, Jesus would not be slain in the temple nor after a synagogue ceremony. He died outside the proper place of religious people, away from the temple, all synagogues and other sacred zones where men venerated God's special presence. He suffered a secular death which was profane to the point of extreme degradation. For he died as a condemned criminal by public execution in a place appointed for such executions. A more unholy death could scarcely be imagined than when Jesus suffered outside the gate in a spot which—from a cultic point of view-counted as utterly profane.' Gerald O'Collins, *The Calvary Christ* (London: DLT), 19.
12. Eliot, *Gerontion*.
13. Mark (15:37) says with brutal simplicity, 'He uttered a loud cry, and breathed his last.'
14. Eliot, *The Waste Land V*.

CHAPTER 9

1. Bruce Vawter, *This Man Jesus* (London: Chapman, 1973), 60.
2. *The Crucified God*, 120-25.
3. *The Crucified God*, 125.
4. M. Kahler quoted in Moltmann, *The Crucified God*, 114.
5. See James Mackey in 'Grace,' *The Furrow*, June 1973 and in *Problems of Religious Faith* (Baltimore: Helicon Press, 1973).
6. Yeats, *When You Are Old*.
7. Paul Tillich, *Systematic Theology*, (Chicago: Univ. Press, 1967), 110-15.
8. See also Moltmann, *The Theology of Hope* (San Francisco: Harper & Row, 1976); John MacQuarrie, *Principles of Christian Theology* (New York: Scribner's and Sons, 1977); Karl Bratten, *The Future of God* (San Francisco: Harper & Row, 1969); Ernst Becker, *The Denial of Death* (New York: The Free Press, 1973); Paul Ricoeur, *The Symbolism of Evil* (Boston: Bea-

con Press, 1969); *Concilium*, November 1970; Pannenberg, *Basic Questions in Theology* I, II, III (London: SCM Press).

9. Dylan Thomas.

10. MacQuarrie, *Principles of Christian Theology*, 69

11. Shakespeare, *Macbeth*.

12 R. Alves, *A Theology of Hope* (Corpus Books, 1969).

13. Keen, *To a Dancing God*, 99.

14. Keen, *To a Dancing God*, passim.

15. Eliot.

16. Langdon Gilkey, *Reaping the Whirlwind: A Christian Interpretation of History* (New York: Seabury, 1977).

17. *The Symbolism of Evil*, 121.

18. *The Ontogeny of Ritualization in Man*, Philosophical Transactions of the Royal Society of London, 1966, 337-50.

19. Walter Zimmerli, *Man and His Hope in the Old Testament* (London: SCM Press, 1971).

20. W. Stephens, *The Man With the Blue Guitar*.

21. Hopkins, *The Wreck of the Deutschland*, 15.

22. See W.E. Nicklesburg, *Resurrection, Immortality and Eternal Life* (Cambridge, Mass.: Harvard Univ. Press, 1972).

23. Kavanagh, *Advent*.

CHAPTER 10

1. St. Augustine, Homily 26 4-6, on St John's Gospel.

2. The literature available on these narratives is immense as is evident from even the limited bibliography in this work. Here it is not possible either to examine the narratives in detail or to review even a representative cross-section of the relevant literature. I will simply try to draw together insights from various authors which should help the reader to approach the much more detailed and excellent expositions available. What follows is a kind of crude map of this area, which the reader must fill out and refine.

3. 'They saw again three men come out from the sepulchre, two of them sustaining the other, and a cross following them. The heads of the two reached to heaven, but the head of him whom they led by the hand outreached the heavens' (39-40).

4. *The Founder of Christianity*, 30.

5. *Summa Theologica*, III, 55, 2 ad 1.

6. See Raymond Brown, *The Virginal Conception and Bodily Resurrection of Jesus* (London: Chapman, 1973), 10 ff.

7. John Donne.

8. *Jesus the Christ*, (Ramsey, N.J.: Paulist, 1977),

9. *Jesus, the Christ*, 127.

10. *Jesus, the Christ*, 127.

11. *Jesus, the Christ*, 128.

12. Brown, *The Virginal Conception and Bodily Resurrection of Jesus*, 109-ff.

CHAPTER 11

1. *The Founder of Christianity*, 97.

2. For a summary of this thought, see Pannenberg, *Jesus, God and Man* and his *Revelation as History*.
3. In tracing this movement many scholars distinguish (1) a future or parousia christology, (to which we have referred above), (2) a present christology, (3) a christology of the ministry, (4) a pre-ministry christology. The present christology (2), with a strong emphasis on Easter, is associated especially with Acts 2:32-36; 5:30-31;13:26-41; Rom. 1:3-4; Phil. 2:5-11. Psalm 2 seems to have been influential on this 'two-stage' christology and the language speaks of 'making,' 'becoming,' 'being given.' The christology of the ministry (3) puts a special stress on the baptism of Jesus as declaring who he is and sees this unfolded in countless ways through his ministry. The pre-ministry christologies (4) speak (a) about the significance of his conception and birth as revealing his sonship and (b) pre-existence. These are helpful distinctions provided they are not pressed too sharply and that the impression is not given that they are stages that evolve neatly one after the other. Space does not permit us to pursue these categories. Instead, we will search for the 'common denominators' of christology. But we will of necessity refer to these categories frequently. The category in question will simply be referred to as (1), (2), (3), (4) in the text.
4. See Sean Freyne, 'Sacrifice for Sin,' in *The Furrow*, April 1974.
5. (1), (2), (3) refer to the categories mentioned in footnote 3 of this chapter.
6. See Wainwright, *The Trinity of the New Testament*, 89 ff.
7. Vawter, *This Man Jesus*, 141.
8. Vawter, 152 ff.
9. Raymond Brown, *Jesus, God & Man* (New York: Macmillan, 1967), 1 ff.

CHAPTER 12
1. M. Ramsey, *God, Christ and the World* (London: SCM Press, 1969).
2. A similar grid could be constructed for these patristic and conciliar development.
3. Aloys Grillmeir, *Christ in Christian Tradition* (Atlanta: John Knox Press, 1975) is the classic on this whole period. Excellent summaries are also found in many of the works listed in the bibliography.
4. *Theological Investigations*, vol. 1 (New York: Crossroad, 196]), 149-200.

APPENDIX I
1. For full text see *Catholic Biblical Quarterly*, July 1964, 305-12.
2. Schillebeeckx, *Jesus*, 86.
3. Authors name and number these criteria differently. See references in bibliography. Here we follow Perrin, *Rediscovering the Teaching of Jesus*, and Schillebeeckx, *Jesus*.
4. Schillebeeckx, *Jesus*, 91.
5. Perrin, *Rediscovering*, 39.
6. Perrin, *Rediscovering*, 43.
7. Schillebeeckx, *Jesus*, 96.
8. Perrin, *Rediscovering*, 46.
9. Schillebeeckx, *Jesus*, passim.

BIBLIOGRAPHY

Aldwinckle, R.F. *More Than Man: A Study in Christology*, Eerdmans,1976.
Anderson, C.C. *The Historical Jesus: A Continuing Quest*, Eerdmans, 1972.
Boff, Leonardo. *Jesus Christ Liberator*, SPCK, 1980.
Bonhoeffer, Dietrich. *The Cost of Discipleship*, SCM, 1963.
Bornkamm, Gunther. *Jesus of Nazareth*, Hodder & Stoughton, 1975.
Braaten, Carl E. *Christ and Counter-Christ*, Fortress, 1972.
Brown, Raymond E. *Jesus, God & Man*, Chapman, 1968.
_. *The Virginal Conception and Bodily Resurrection of Jesus*, Chapman, 1973.
Comblin, Jose. *Jesus of Nazareth: Meditations on His Humanity*, Gill & Macmillan, 1979.
Conzelmann, Hans. *Jesus*, Fortress, 1973.
Cook, Michael L. *The Jesus of Faith: A Study in Christology*, Paulist, 1981.
Crossan, John D. *In Parables: The Challenge of the Historical Jesus*, Harper & Row, 1973.
_. *Cliff of Fall: Paradox and Polyvalence in the Parables of Jesus*, Seabury, 1980.
_. *The Dark Interval: Toward a Theology of Story*, Argus, 1975.
Dodd, C.H. *The Founder of Christianity*, Fontana, 1971.
Dunn, James D. *Christology in the Making*, SCM, 1980.
_. *Jesus & the Spirit*, SCM, 1975.
Fiorenza, Elizabeth S. *In Memory of Her*, SCM, 1983.
Fitzmyer, Joseph, S.J. *What We Know About Jesus From the New Testament*, Paulist, 1982.
Freyne, Sean. *The World of the New Testament*, Veritas, 1980.
Fuller, Reginald H. *The Formation of the Resurrection Narratives*, SPCK, 1972.
_. *The Foundation of New Testament Christology*, Fontana, 1969.
_. and Pheme Perkins. *Who Is This Christ? Gospel Christology and Contemporary Faith*, Fortress, 1983.
Grillmeier, Aloys. *Christ in Christian Tradition*, Mowbray, 1975.
Gutierrez, Gustavo. *The Power of the Poor in History*, Orbis, 1983.
_. *A Theology of Liberation*, Orbis, 1973.
_. *We Drink From Our Own Wells*, Orbis, 1984.
Hengel, Martin. *The Son of God*, Fortress, 1976.
Jeremias, Joachim. *New Testament Theology*, Vol. 1. SCM, 1972.
_. *The Parables of Jesus*, SCM, 1963.
_. *The Prayers of Jesus*, SCM, 1967.
Kasper, Walter. *Jesus the Christ*, Burns Oates, 1976.
Keck, Leander E. *A Future for the Historical Jesus*, SCM, 1972.
Keen, Sam. *To a Dancing God*, Fontana, 1971.
Kung, Hans. *On Being a Christian*, Collins, 1977.
Lane, Dermot A. *The Reality of Jesus*, Veritas, 1975.
Linders B. & S.S. Smalley. *Christ & Spirit in the New Testament*, CUP, 1974.
McFague, Sally. *Metaphorical Theology: Models of God*, SCM, 1983.
_. *Models of God*, SCM, 1987.

Mackey, James P. *Jesus, the Man & the Myth*, SCM, 1979.
Miranda, Jose P. *Being & the Messiah*, Orbis, 1977.
Moltmann, Jurgen. *The Church in the Power of the Spirit*, SCM, 1977.
_. *The Crucified God*, SCM, 1974.
Moltmann, Wendel E. *The Women around Jesus*, SCM, 1982.
Nolan, Albert. *Jesus Before Christianity*, DLT, 1976.
O'Collins, Gerald. *Interpreting Jesus*, Chapman, 1983.
_. *The Calvary Christ*, SCM, 1977.
_. *The Easter Jesus*, DLT, 1973.
_. *What Are They Saying About Jesus?* Paulist, 1977.
O'Grady, John F. *Models of Jesus*, Doubleday, 1981.
Pannenberg, Wolfhart. *Jesus: God and Man*, SCM, 1968.
Perkins, Pheme. *Reading the New Testament*, Chapman, 1988.
Perrin, Norman. *Jesus and the Language of the Kingdom*, SCM, 1976.
_. *The New Testament: An Introduction*, SCM, 1974.
_. *Rediscovering the Teachings of Jesus*, SCM, 1967.
Power, David N. *Unsearchable Riches*, Pueblo, 1984.
Rahner, Karl. *Theological Investigations*, Vs. 1, 3, 4, 5, 9, 11, 13. DLT, 1961-75.
Rahner, Karl and Wilhelm Thussing. *A New Christology*, Seabury, 1980.
Richard, Lucien J. *A Kenotic Christology*, Univ. Press of America, 1982.
Robinson, J.A.T. *The Human Face of God*, SCM, 1973.
Ruether, Rosemary R. *To Change the World*, Crossroad, 1981.
Schillebeeckx, Edward. *Christ, The Christian Experience in the Modern World*, SCM, 1980.
_. *The Church With a Human Face*, Crossroads, 1985.
_. *Jesus: An Experiment in Christology*, Collins, 1979.
_. *Interim Report on the Books Jesus and Christ*, Seabury, 1982.
Schmaus, Michael. *God and His Christ*, Sheed & Ward, 1971.
Schoonenberg, Piet. *The Christ*, Sheed & Ward, 1972.
Schweizer, Edward. *Jesus*, SCM, 1971.
Segundo, Juan Luis. *The Historical Jesus of the Synoptics*, Sheed & Ward, 1985.
_. *The Humanist Christology of Paul*, Sheed & Ward, 1986.
Shea, John. *An Experience Named Spirit*. Thomas More Press, 1983.
Sloyan, Gerard S. *Jesus in Focus*, Twenty-Third Publications, 1983.
_. *The Jesus Tradition*, Twenty-Third Publications, 1986.
Sobrino, Jon. *Christology at the Crossroads*, SCM, 1971.
_. *The True Church and the Poor*, Orbis, 1984.
Sykes, S. W. and J.B. Clayton. *Christ, Faith and History*, OUP, 1972.
Thompson, William. *The Jesus Debate*, Paulist, 1985.
Turner, Victor. *The Ritual Process: Structure and Anti-Structure*, Cornell Univ. Press, 1977.
Van Beeck, Frans J. *Christ Proclaimed: Christology as Rhetoric*. Paulist, 1979.
Vawter, Bruce. *This Man Jesus*, Chapman, 1973.
Young, F. *From Nicea to Chalcedon*, Fortress, 1983.
Zimmerli, Walter. *Man and His Hope in the Old Testament*, OUP, 1971.